MW00906034

...FOR DUMMIES ™

References for the Rest of Us

COMPUTER BOOK SERIES FROM IDG

Are you intimidated and confused by computers? Do you find that traditional manuals are overloaded with technical details you'll never use? Do your friends and family always call you to fix simple problems on their PCs? Then the *"...For Dummies"*™ computer book series from IDG is for you.

"...For Dummies" books are written for those frustrated computer users who know they aren't really dumb but find that PC hardware, software, and indeed the unique vocabulary of computing make them feel helpless. *"...For Dummies"* books use a lighthearted approach, a down-to-earth style, and even cartoons and humorous icons to diffuse computer novices' fears and build their confidence. Lighthearted but not lightweight, these books are a perfect survival guide for anyone forced to use a computer.

> *"I liked my copy so much I told friends; now they bought copies."*
>
> **Irene C., Orwell, Ohio**

> *"Quick, concise, nontechnical, and humorous."*
>
> **Jay A., Elburn, IL**

> *"Thanks, I needed this book. Now I can sleep at night."*
>
> **Robin F., British Columbia, Canada**

Already, hundreds of thousands of satisfied readers agree. They have made *"...For Dummies"* books the #1 introductory-level computer book series and have written asking for more. So if you're looking for the most fun and easy way to learn about computers, look to *"...For Dummies"* books to give you a helping hand.

IDG BOOKS

WORD 6 FOR DOS FOR DUMMIES™

Victor Williams

Mar. 20/97

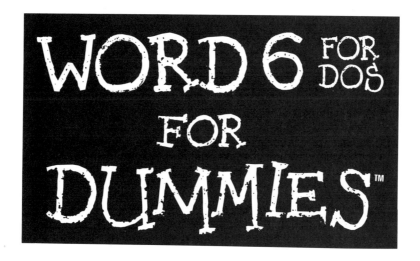

WORD 6 FOR DOS FOR DUMMIES™

by Beth Slick

Foreword by Larry Gelbart, Writer/Producer of M*A*S*H

"My First Computer Lesson" by Carol Burnett

IDG BOOKS

IDG Books Worldwide, Inc.
An International Data Group Company

San Mateo, California ✦ Indianapolis, Indiana ✦ Boston, Massachusetts

Word 6 For DOS For Dummies

Published by
IDG Books Worldwide, Inc.
An International Data Group Company
155 Bovet Road, Suite 310
San Mateo, CA 94402

Library of Congress Catalog Card No.: 93-78253

ISBN 1-56884-000-4

Printed in the United States of America

10 9 8 7 6 5 4 3 2 1

Distributed in the United States by IDG Books Worldwide, Inc.

Distributed in Canada by Macmillan of Canada, a Division of Canada Publishing Corporation; by Woodslane Pty. Ltd. in Australia and New Zealand; and by Computer Bookshops in the U.K. and Ireland.

For information on translations and availability in other countries, contact Marc Jeffrey Mikulich, Foreign Rights Manager, at IDG Books Worldwide. Fax: 415-358-1260.

For sales inquiries and special prices for bulk quantities, write to the address above or call IDG Books Worldwide at 415-312-0650.

Acknowledgments

I would like to thank John Kilcullen and David Solomon at IDG Books for being smart enough to have a sense of humor. I also want to thank Janna Custer (and Megg Bonar) and Mary Bednarek, who manage to keep theirs in the middle of a whirlwind.

Special thanks to my editor, Greg Robertson, for not letting me make a colon out of myself. Also thanks to tech editor Linda Slovick for keeping me on the straight and narrow, to proofreader Sandy Grieshop, and to the production staff — Cindy Phipps, Drew Moore, Mary Briedenbach, Beth Baker, and the folks at University Graphics — who sure made this book look great.

Thank you to Donna Ichinose at Microsoft Corporation, who kept answering my questions and sending me new disks as Word 6 evolved. And a tip of the hat to Steve Gerber for letting us use his BBS as this book evolved.

I also, of course, appreciate the generosity of Larry Gelbart and Carol Burnett for their contributions to this book — not to mention the countless hours of humor they have brought to my life.

Finally, Michael Cahlin, for getting me into this game in the first place and for not turning off his fax machine in the second place. And Steven Laff for handing me Microsoft Word Version 2 and saying, "Hey, take a look at this. I think you'll like it."

About IDG Books Worldwide

Welcome to the world of IDG Books Worldwide.

IDG Books Worldwide, Inc., is a division of International Data Group (IDG), the world's largest publisher of computer-related information and the leading global provider of information services on information technology. IDG publishes over 190 computer publications in 61 countries. Thirty million people read one or more IDG publications each month.

If you use personal computers, IDG Books is committed to publishing quality books that meet your needs. We rely on our extensive network of publications, including such leading periodicals as *Macworld*, *InfoWorld*, *PC World*, *Computerworld*, *Publish*, *Network World*, and *SunWorld*, to help us make informed and timely decisions in creating useful computer books that meet your needs.

Every IDG book strives to bring extra value and skill-building instruction to the reader. Our books are written by experts, with the backing of IDG periodicals, and with careful thought devoted to issues such as audience, interior design, use of icons, and illustrations. Our editorial staff is a careful mix of high-tech journalists and experienced book people. Our close contact with the makers of computer products helps ensure accuracy and thorough coverage. Our heavy use of personal computers at every step in production means we can deliver books in the most timely manner.

We are delivering books of high quality at competitive prices on topics customers want. At IDG, we believe in quality, and we have been delivering quality for over 25 years. You'll find no better book on a subject than an IDG book.

John Kilcullen
President and C.E.O.
IDG Books Worldwide, Inc.

IDG Books Worldwide, Inc. is a division of International Data Group. The officers are Patrick J. McGovern, Founder and Board Chairman; Walter Boyd, President; Robert A. Farmer, Vice Chairman. International Data Group's publications include: **ARGENTINA's** Computerworld Argentina, InfoWorld Argentina; **ASIA's** Computerworld Hong Kong, PC World Hong Kong, Computerworld Southeast Asia, PC World Singapore, Computerworld Malaysia, PC World Malaysia; **AUSTRALIA's** Computerworld Australia, Australian PC World, Australian Macworld, Network World, Reseller, IDG Sources; **AUSTRIA's** Computerwelt Oesterreich, PC Test; **BRAZIL's** Computerworld, Mundo IBM, Mundo Unix, PC World, Publish; **BULGARIA's** Computerworld Bulgaria, Ediworld, PC World Bulgaria; **CANADA's** Direct Access, Graduate Computerworld, InfoCanada, Network World Canada; **CHILE's** Computerworld, Informatica; **COLUMBIA's** Computerworld Columbia; **CZECH REPUBLIC's** Computerworld Elektronika, PC World; **DENMARK's** CAD/CAM WORLD, Communications World, Computerworld Danmark, Computerworld Focus, Computerworld Uddannelse, Lotus World, Macintosh Produktkatalog, Macworld Danmark, PC World Danmark, PC World Produktguide, Windows World; **EQUADOR's** PC World Ecuador; **EGYPT's** Computerworld Middle East, PC World Middle East; **FINLAND's** MikroPC, Tietoviikko, Tietoverkko; **FRANCE's** Distributique, GOLDEN MAC, InfoPC, Languages & Systems, Le Guide du Monde Informatique, Le Monde Informatique, Telecoms & Reseaux; **GERMANY's** Computerwoche, Computerwoche Focus, Computerwoche Extra, Computerwoche Karriere, edv aspekte, Information Management, Macwelt, Netzwelt, PC Welt, PC Woche, Publish, Unit; **HUNGARY's** Alaplap, Computerworld SZT, PC World, ; **INDIA's** Computers & Communications; **ISRAEL's** Computerworld Israel, PC World Israel; **ITALY's** Computerworld Italia, Lotus Magazine, Macworld Italia, Networking Italia, PC World Italia; **JAPAN's** Computerworld Japan, Macworld Japan, SunWorld Japan; **KENYA's** East African Computer News; **KOREA's** Computerworld Korea, Macworld Korea, PC World Korea; **MEXICO's** Compu Edicion, Compu Manufactura, Computacion/Punto de Venta, Computerworld Mexico, MacWorld, Mundo Unix, PC World, Windows; **THE NETHERLANDS'** Computer! Totaal, LAN Magazine, MacWorld Magazine; **NEW ZEALAND's** Computer Listings, Computerworld New Zealand, New Zealand PC World; **NIGERIA's** PC World Africa; **NORWAY's** Computerworld Norge, C/World, Lotusworld Norge, Macworld Norge, Networld, PC World Ekspress, PC World Norge, PC World's Product Guide, Publish World, Student Data, Unix World, Windowsworld, IDG Direct Response; **PANAMA's** PC World Panama; **PERU's** Computerworld Peru, PC World; **PEOPLES REPUBLIC OF CHINA's** China Computerworld, PC World China, Electronics International, China Network World; **IDG HIGH TECH BEIJING's** New Product World; **IDG SHENZHEN's** Computer News Digest; **PHILLIPPINES'** Computerworld, PC World; **POLAND's** Computerworld Poland, PC World/Komputer; **PORTUGAL's** MacIn; **RUSSIA's** Computerworld-Moscow, Mir-PC, Sety; **SLOVENIA's** Monitor Magazine; **SOUTH AFRICA's** Computing S.A.; **SPAIN's** Amiga World, Computerworld Espana, Communicaciones World, Macworld Espana, NeXTWORLD, PC World Espana, Publish, Sunworld; **SWEDEN's** Attack, ComputerSweden, Corporate Computing, Lokala Natverk/LAN, Lotus World, MAC&PC, Macworld, Mikrodatorn, PC World, Publishing & Design (CAP), Datalngenjoren, Maxi Data, Windows World; **SWITZERLAND's** Computerworld Schweiz, Macworld Schweiz, PC & Workstation; **TAIWAN's** Computerworld Taiwan, Global Computer Express, PC World Taiwan; **THAILAND's** Thai Computerworld; **TURKEY's** Computerworld Monitor, Macworld Turkiye, PC World Turkiye; **UNITED KINGDOM's** Lotus Magazine, Macworld, Sunworld; **UNITED STATES'** AmigaWorld, Cable in the Classroom, CD Review, CIO, Computerworld, Desktop Video World, DOS Resource Guide, Electronic News, Federal Computer Week, Federal Integrator, GamePro, inCider/A+, IDG Books, InfoWorld, InfoWorld Direct, Laser Event, Macworld, Multimedia World, Network World, NeXTWORLD, PC Games, PC World, PC Letter, Publish, Sumeria, SunWorld, SWATPro, Video Event, Video Toaster World; **VENEZUELA's** Computerworld Venezuela, MicroComputerworld Venezuela; **VIETNAM's** PC World Vietnam

 The text in this book is printed on recycled paper.

About the Author

When my mother read the "About the Author" page in my last book for IDG (*The Official XTree MS-DOS, Windows, and Hard Disk Management Companion*, 3rd Edition), she remarked, "Oh, they said such nice things about you!" I looked at my trusting parental unit and sighed. I decided to tell her the truth. "Mom, I wrote that stuff myself." I explained to her that these "About the Author" pages are usually written by the authors about themselves — using the third person to make it sound journalistic and official.

So, not wanting to mislead my — or anyone else's — mother, I thought this time I'd introduce myself and my credentials in the first person.

I'll start out with a true confession. Unlike a lot of other computer writers, I don't have a degree in computer-anything or engineering, and I couldn't care less about programming. My entree into computers came in 1982, from the retail end of things, when I suddenly found myself managing a computer store. It was there that I first encountered Microsoft Word for DOS — Version 2.

Over the next seven years, I taught Word — in its various incarnations — to businesspeople, writers, accountants, film studios, lawyers, professors, students, famous people (like Carol Burnett, Gene Roddenberry, and John Lithgow, to casually drop a few names), and even psychiatrists. Probably a thousand people all told — not to mention daily support phone calls. You can imagine that I've had a lot of experience explaining Microsoft Word for DOS to people.

The other reason I'm qualified to write this book is that I use Microsoft Word myself. Every day. I write screenplays, teleplays (including two episodes of *Star Trek: The Next Generation*), press releases, articles, and even books (like this one, for instance), using Microsoft Word. Though it might be natural to assume that anyone who writes a book about a program actually uses the software on a daily basis, it doesn't always work out that way. I'm certainly not saying that those writers don't provide fabulously helpful expertise on the programs they cover — I'm just saying that the perspective from the trenches is a little different.

Enough about me, already. Now I understand the other reason why they put these pages in the third person: It's embarrassing to talk about yourself for so long!

Editor's note ...

Beth Slick lives in Venice, California, with her cat and fax machines.

Credits

Publisher
David W. Solomon

Managing Editor
Mary Bednarek

Acquisitions Editor
Janna Custer

Project Editor
Gregory R. Robertson

Technical Reviewer
Linda Slovick

Editorial Assistant
Patricia R. Reynolds

Production Manager
Beth J. Baker

Production Coordinator
Cindy L. Phipps

Production
Mary Breidenbach
Drew Moore

Proofreader
Sandy Grieshop

Indexer
Anne Leach

Production
University Graphics, Palo Alto, California

university Graphics

Contents at a Glance

Cartoons at a Glance

By Rich Tennant

page 133

page 45

page 277

page 7

page 245

page 244

page 44

page 145

Table of Contents

Foreword

· ·

I don't want to brag, but when it comes to being a computer dummy, I don't have to take my dunce cap off to anyone.

Loath as I am to admit this, and if anyone quotes me, I'll deny I ever wrote it, but for a long time, I was a total idiot, a macromoron on the subject of computers. Had you asked me years ago what IBM stood for, I would have replied it was probably some sort of medical term used by proctologists. A baud rate, I suspected, was a price list in a brothel, and microchips were things used by tiny gamblers.

I like to think I came by my ignorance honestly. When I started writing professionally in 1944, I took the word "writing" literally. My tools were pencils and paper. I enjoyed the feeling, the almost mesmerizing ritual of watching my hand act as an extension of my head, delighted in the sensation of watching the soft, dark lead move across the bright yellow pad, as it took dictation from my brain. I worked this way until well into 1988, eschewing the typewriter (which is much harder to do than eschewing a pencil), when my son, Gary, an early devotee of the computer, began trying to talk me into buying one.

My first impression of computers came from photographs that showed the simplest kinds to be room-sized, with dozens of men in white coats working on one. Anyone who suggested laptops in those days might have been taken away by a different set of men in white coats. True dummy that I was, I was unaware that I wouldn't have to build a wing onto my house to accommodate what Gary was suggesting.

Turning me on to computers, dragging me into the twentieth century, was the second great favor he did me. The first was to start earning his own living. The third, and greatest favor by far, was when he introduced me to Beth Slick.

At this point, I should warn you that this foreword is about to become a love letter, for when Ms. Slick agreed to become my computer/tutor/mavis (feminine maven), my professional life changed completely.

My productivity increased tenfold. I believe the quality of the work vastly improved. Working with this new tool, seeing my words appear before me on a screen, my words took on a *visual* quality I had never known before. Wordplay became an automatic by-product. The sooner I can see a word, the sooner I can play with it. I was tempted to throw my hands away. My *head* had become an extension of my head.

And all because Ms. Slick took the Ms. Tery out of computers for me. With her quick mind, her sharp wit, and her inexhaustible patience with reformed dummies, she can make the technological miracle I so blithely control seem like a cyberwalk in the park.

If she had taught me how to fly the Concorde instead of how to use Microsoft Word, I have absolutely no doubt that I would have become a pilot in a matter of days (or a pilote in a matter of jours, for that matter).

One final word about the remarkable Ms. Slick. My own, not Microsoft's, magical though they are. If I ever lost her, I would type, save, and print a rather pathetic suicide note, then lay my head down on my keyboard, and press Ctrl, Alt, Del.

Larry Gelbart
Beverly Hills, California

My First Computer Lesson

"I'm terrified," I croaked.

"There's no need to be," was the calm, irritating reply.

"I've never done this before."

"Remember, you are not alone." (Spare me the platitudes.)

"Maybe some other time..." I was *pleading* now.

"You have to bite the bullet sometime."

"I need another glass of water."

"That'll be your sixth one in five minutes."

"Excuse me, I think I have to go to the powder room."

"It's all that water."

"Do I hear the telephone?"

"No."

"Oh, my God, my ears are ringing... I'd better call the doctor right away."

She had had enough. "Sit down," she ordered. I did. She picked up the evil-looking prongs and plugged them into the socket. I inadvertently jumped. There was no going back. The horrifying thing was staring at me blankly. My heart was pounding in my eardrums and for the first time in my life, I thought fondly of my dentist.

I had given up. "All right, I'm ready for whatever is ahead."

"Good for you," she smiled. "Now here's the On button..."

An hour later, I was like a kid in a candy store. (How's that for a platitude?)

That was 1985. My computer and I are best friends now.

Thanks to Beth Slick.

Carol Burnett
Los Angeles, California

Introduction

· ·

*T*his book is dedicated to all the normal people who successfully navigate the immense complexities of daily life, yet feel as though they've entered the Twilight Zone whenever they're in front of a computer.

If you've ever been so dumbfounded by what your computer has just done that you half-expect Rod Serling to step out of the shadows to introduce *your* strange story to the viewing audience, then this book is for you.

Word 6 For DOS For Dummies, unlike Microsoft's official, insomnia-busting manual, doesn't exhaust you by reporting every single, solitary little twist and turn to Microsoft Word's massive command structure. In fact, *Word 6 For DOS For Dummies* proudly thumbs its nose at the boring details and esoteric commands. Instead, the book jumps straight to the important, real-world, problem-solving how-tos — the basic steps that enable you to turn out a decent letter or an impressively formatted report. With the right answers under your belt, you may even discover that computers actually *can* make your job easier!

Yeah, right.

Anyway, before you start learning how to whip Word into shape, I want to tell you more about this book and how it works. And how you can work it.

About This Book

Unlike most books, *Word 6 For DOS For Dummies* is designed so that you don't have to read the whole thing. Honest! Not only are the chapters created to stand on their own — you don't have to read Chapters 1-8 to understand Chapter 9 — each *section* within the chapters is also a self-contained unit. In other words, by using the Table of Contents or the Index, you can quickly find step-by-step relief for your painful headaches. If, for example, formatting makes you crazy, go straight to Chapter 7.

If you *do* start flipping through the book sequentially, the keen observers among you will notice that the farther and farther you delve into the book, the more and more bizarre the topics become. You may find that you never look at the last third of the book — except for the cartoons, of course. And that's okay. Really. If you ever *do* need help making labels or macros, the info will be there waiting for you.

However, be *sure* that you don't skip the last part, "The Part of Tens." This last part alone may be worth the price of admission.

What You See Is What You Do

When you look up a topic, you get an explanation of what's going on and a set of instructions for dealing with these goings-ons. Typically, you are told to type a specific sequence of keystrokes, like this:

Press Alt+**File** ⇨ **S**ave

Translated, this means that you are to press and hold down the Alt key while pressing F. After you've done that and released those keys, press S. Don't type the plus sign (+) or any other punctuation. Nor do you type the word *File*. Just press the letter that is boldfaced (in this case, **F** and **S**). Alternatively, if you're using a mouse, you can click File and then select Save. It's the same command either way.

Speaking of mice, now's as good a time as any to make sure that we have our vocabulary in synch: *Left-click* means to quickly press and release the left mouse ear (button). *Right-click* means to do the same thing to the right button. *Double-clicking* means to click twice — really, really fast.

As we go through the steps to accomplish a particular task, Microsoft Word asks questions or offers guidance. When I want to show you Word's message from beyond, it'll look like this:

```
Are you sure you want to do this?
```

Finally, throughout the book, you'll see plenty of pictures of my computer screen to help you compare what's happening on your computer with what's *supposed* to happen on your computer. If you're not seeing the same thing as what's in the figures, you may have missed a beat somewhere. Back up and start again.

What to Skip Over

Yes, there's even *more* you can skip over.

Frankly, there are some topics that I just can't resist giving more detail on. When I do elaborate on a point, it is boxed in so that you can recognize it for what it is. If you need more help, you'll find the detail beneficial. If things are working out for you, you can disregard the text.

Occasionally, you'll bump into sections labeled "Technical Stuff." These segments provide the author with an opportunity to dazzle everyone with a blast of high-tech computer jargon. If you do decide to read this Technical Stuff, do so with caution. Getting caught reading too many of them may endanger your status as a beginner. If you read *all* of them, you'll have taken those first fatal steps on the pathway toward becoming a … *nerd*! So watch it.

Your Current Skill Level

Let's see whether you match this profile: You have a computer with some version of Word installed on it. You've created and printed at least one document. And, finally, you have a nagging suspicion that there are some things about Word that you just don't get.

Does this sound like you? If it does, then you'll be happy to know that you're 100% qualified to use this book.

And by the way, if you're still desperately clinging to Version 5 of Word — trying to decide whether 'tis nobler to suffer the slings and arrows of upgrading — you're welcome here, too. Granted, the folks at Microsoft behaved very poorly by introducing Version 5.5 with *all new commands* (augh!). But the cold, hard fact is that they did it. It's done. Now it's time to move on. Face reality. We'll help you with a special appendix and notes along the way addressed to you Version 5 users. Now, let go of your anger and embrace Version 6! Do I hear an "amen?" Okay!

What You'll Learn

This book contains five major parts, arranged in a logical order (or so it seemed when I started out), from "easy" to "more difficult." At the end, of course, are the incredibly interesting appendixes.

Part I: How Word Thinks

Word 6 has its own *laws of nature*, a foundation of rules, a logic — a twisted logic, perhaps, but a logic nonetheless — that governs how everything works. When you understand that logic, Grasshopper, Word becomes less mysterious. Things don't seem so out of control, and you're able to handle problems with more confidence. In essence, Part I covers the basic mechanics of Word — the Zen of Word — for those interested in *why* Word behaves as it does.

Part II: How to Out-Think Word

Here's some good news: If you're familiar with 30 percent of Word's features, you can accomplish 99 percent of everything you want to do, word processing-wise. Part II cuts through the you-know-what and provides the actual steps, tips, and techniques to wrestle Word 6 to the ground.

Part III: Life in the Fast Lane

Are you an animal? Here's your chance to prove it. Part III goes after those Word features you always thought you should learn about, but were afraid to tackle. After all, bitter experience has taught you one thing: Experimentation leads to problems. Be honest now, do you wish you knew about style sheets? Do you secretly want to trick your computer with macros? So you get locked in a subelectronic dilemma at the thought of sharing files with a Mac? Have no fear, gentle reader, we're here to help.

Part IV: Part of Tens

If you like lists, you'll love these: Ten Most Important Commands, Ten Ways to Get out of Trouble, Ten Ways to Avoid Trouble in the First Place, Ten Ways to..., well, you get the idea. Only Guinness has more lists!

Part V: Appendixes

If you're metamorphosing from Version 5 to Version 6, this is where you need to start — there's an appendix in Part V with your name written on it. Other odds and ends stuck in this "junk drawer" section include favorite mouse and keyboard command lists and a product resource guide (in case you have any spare change burning a hole in your pocket).

Icons Used in This Book

Following is a list of the icons used in this book. They help point you to, well, important and unimportant points!

Tech alert! Tech alert! Read this material only if you're interested in all the nitty-gritty details.

This icon is the flag for the ultra-cool stuff: shortcuts, hints, special tips, and so on.

This icon is your mother reminding you, in that special loving tone of hers, not to forget something important. Even though you never listened to *her*, please listen to *me*.

This icon is your father talking. If you don't watch your step, you could be heading for trouble. Big time.

For users of Version 5 (or earlier) — this icon indicates a helpful hint or observation especially for you.

For users of Version 5.5, this icon flags a feature or change that's new to Version 6 — in case all you want to do is flip through the book and study the new Version 6 features.

If a cool mouse trick is applicable, you'll see this icon and a bit of text sharing the cool trick.

Where to Go from Here

And now, a word from our sponsor.

After you've had a chance to put this book to use, I hope you'll find the time to fill out the Registration/Response page in the back of the book (photocopy it if you don't like the idea of ripping out the page) and mail it to us. Because *Word 6 For DOS For Dummies* is for you, your comments are vital. Although we're not popping for the postage, what else could you do with 29 cents that would do so much good? If you want to contact me directly, you can do so through IDG Books Worldwide (or, if you use a modem, via CompuServe at 72366,1310).

Now, back to our regularly scheduled program.

Do you remember that scene in the movie *Network*, where the crazy newsman urges everyone to open their windows, stick their heads outside, and shout, "I'm not going to take it anymore!"? Well, now I'm going to urge you to do the same thing.

I want you to stand up, scan the Table of Contents, and find a topic that's always made your life miserable — some aspect of Word that has consistently made you nuts. Now, open up this book to that page and shout, "I'm not going to take it anymore!" — and get out of the Twilight Zone once and for all.

Part I
How Word Thinks

In this part . . .

*I*f we drop a rock, does it not fall? If the sun rises, does it not also set? If one is in the shower, does not UPS arrive? These familiar laws of nature help to make order out of our chaotic world. When things in our environment behave in a predictable pattern, we can anticipate the outcome of our actions. Microsoft Word also behaves according to a preset pattern, believe it or not. In Part I, we shall meditate on the underlying forces that govern how Word works and experience the Zen of Word.

However, if you've got a project that was due yesterday, you may want to pass on the meditation scenario for the moment and scoot on over to Part II for the quick answers.

Chapter 1
Making Sense of the Screen

*T*here's no doubt that Word's screen may be daunting when you first get into it — okay, so looking at the screen makes you feel as though you're the stewardess in one of those airplane disaster movies who's suddenly given the job of flying a 747.

The first step, then, is to take a tour of the instrument panel, learn some terminology, and flick a few switches on and off to get the feel of things.

Just keep in mind, as we proceed, that the stewardesses in those movies always successfully land the plane.

Getting into Word

Because there are a billion ways to set up a computer, there are two billion ways to get into Word. Some of you have custom menu systems of one kind or another. Some of you just turn on the computer and get Word automatically. However, just in case you have problems starting Word, here's the bare-bones way of going about it. Use these instructions *only* if you don't already know how to get the program going.

1. Turn on Mr. Computer.

2. When everything finally settles down and you see a C : \ > on the screen, type **CD\WORD** and press Enter.

3. Finally, type **WORD** and press Enter.

   After a few seconds, you see the Word opening screen, shown in Figure 1-1, signifying that you now actually have to do some work.

✔ If you already know the name of the file you want to edit, type **WORD** *YOURFILE* — using your own file name instead of *YOURFILE* — and before you can say "where's my coffee," the Word screen *and* your file appear. Wow.

✔ Not only that, but even if all you know is that you want to go back to the file you worked on during the previous session, you can type **WORD/L**, and Word puts you right smack-dab in the last file you were working on — in the very spot where the cursor was sitting when you last saved the file and exited Word.

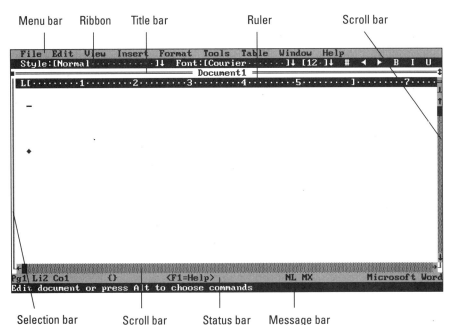

Menu bar   Ribbon   Title bar   Ruler   Scroll bar

Selection bar   Scroll bar   Status bar   Message bar

Figure 1-1: Word's opening screen, with all the bells and whistles.

Making Friends with the Screen

First of all, if you absolutely *hate* the way the screen looks in Figure 1-1, don't fret. You can turn off, or on, any of the screen elements. In fact, you can have a simple, clean screen (see Figure 1-2).

Figure 1-2: Word's opening screen, with nary a bell nor a whistle to be seen.

Okay, we've established that you can "have it your way" and order up your screen like a hamburger. Now, let's settle down and discuss what all these swell options can do for you.

Mamboing with the Menu Bar

The menu bar, the top line on the screen in Figure 1-1, is where you issue commands to Word that have nothing to do with entering or moving text. Such commands include printing, saving, formatting, and all the other intriguing activities that will take the rest of this book to explain.

To discontinue entering text and jump up to that menu bar, all you have to do is press the Alt key. The menu bar lights up like Vegas — and reveals *accelerator keys* (see Figure 1-3)!

Active menu bar

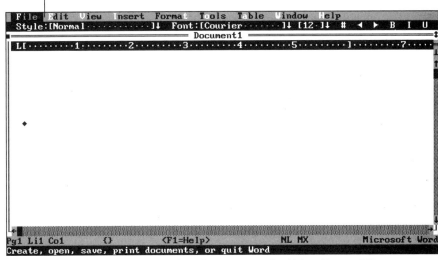

Figure 1-3: The menu bar becomes active when you press the Alt key. Hey, you'd become active, too, if *your* Alt key was pressed!

If knowing that you alone are responsible for remembering to press Alt to activate the menu bar is too much pressure, here are a couple of helpful hints. First, remember that the menu bar is on the top of the screen, at the highest *Alt*itude. Another way to remember is just to look at the bottom of your screen. While you are editing, as shown in Figure 1-1, Word always reminds you:

```
Edit document or press Alt to choose commands
```

The accelerator keys are the one-letter shortcuts to a particular command. For example, if you press V after activating the menu bar, you jump straight to the View menu. Guess where pressing O lands you — right in the Tools menu.

After you've accelerated yourself to a particular command, Word reveals the associated *pull-down menu* (see Figure 1-4).

If your coordination was off and you chose the wrong menu, *no problemo*. Just press the right- or left-arrow key to move from one menu name to another to another — this is the mambo part.

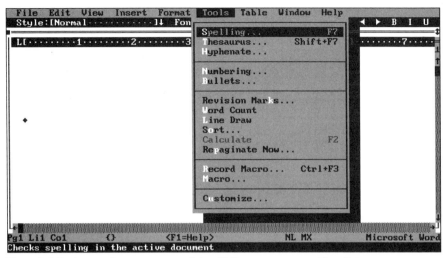

Figure 1-4: Each menu item comes complete with its very own gee-whiz pull-down menu. Batteries not included.

If you get all the way to the end of the menu bar, pressing the right-arrow mysteriously takes you back to the File menu. This feature is called *wrap around.* Try it. It's fun for the whole family!

- ✔ After the menu bar is active, function keys don't function. So, if your function keys are beeping instead of functioning, it may be because your menu bar is turned on. Press Esc to get out of the menu bar.

- ✔ If all else fails, then just do the Hokey Pokey and turn yourself around, 'cause that's what it's all about!

Word 5 used the Esc key to get to the menu. Word 6 uses the Alt key. Be honest now, isn't the Alt key more conveniently located on the keyboard? And besides, you've got two — count 'em — two Alts at your disposal and only one measly Esc! After you're in the menu, you're still pressing one-letter commands, just like what you're used to.

Revealing the Pull-Down Menus

After you have dropped the drawers on one of these menus, you see all sorts of commands (see Figure 1-5). Each of those commands has its *own* — you guessed it — accelerator key! Again, press the boldfaced letter to activate the command. Could there be a pattern developing here?

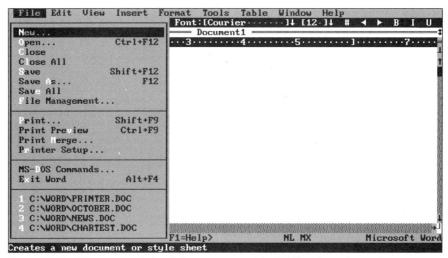

Figure 1-5: The File menu, unchained! Just press one of the boldfaced accelerator keys to activate a command.

✔ Again, if you prefer, use the up- and down-arrow keys to highlight a function and then press Enter to activate it.

✔ The pull-down menus also have a wrap-around function — this time from top to bottom.

But wait, there's more! It slices, it dices! Believe it or not, all symbols and dots *inside* the pull-down menus mean something.

Shortcut keys: Shortcut keys are the function keys that appear to the right of a command name. Using a shortcut key lets you cut through the red tape — bypass the menu entirely — and just carry out the function (a radical concept). For example, you can press Shift+F9 to print the current document instead of using Alt+File ⇨ **P**rint.

Now, if you'd rather give up your Christmas bonus than memorize a bunch of shortcut keys, relax. As long as you can print, nobody cares which key you pressed or what mouse you dragged to do it. If you use certain functions a lot, you may find yourself memorizing the shortcuts by osmosis.

Ellipsis: No, ellipsis isn't some ancient Greek guy. It's fancy English for three dots (...). Which is also fancy English for "more." What it all boils down to is that when you activate a command that has three dots following it, you're going to get some heat from Word in the form of a *dialog box* (explained in nauseating detail shortly) — which you must fill out before Word can perform the task you have in mind.

On/Off Indicator: On some of the pull-down menus, you see a dot to the left of a menu item (see Figure 1-6). The dot indicates that the item is turned on. No dot, it's off. On or off, just like a light switch.

Dimmed Items: When I'm talking about dimmed items, I'm not alluding to how you feel before your first cup of coffee. Dimmed items are commands in the pull-down menus whose lettering is not as "bright" or dark as the other words in the menu. In Figure 1-6, for example, Footnotes/Annotations is a shade lighter and is even missing a boldfaced accelerator key! The truth is, Word automatically dims an item — not to save on electricity — but because that command is not relevant in the current reality.

See, I told you this would be Zen.

In the Footnotes/Annotations case, because no footnotes or annotations are in the document, you don't need a command to view them. If you did, you could.

Sometimes, finding an item dimmed can serve as a helpful reminder. For example, you can't use Tools/Calculate unless you first highlight something to calculate. If you see the command item dimmed, it serves as mute testimony that you forgot to highlight.

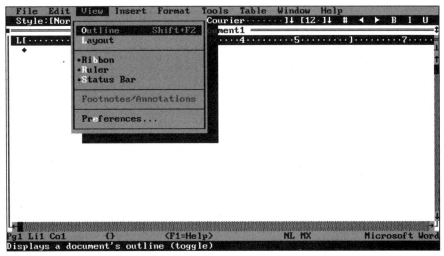

Figure 1-6: The View menu shows that the Ribbon, Ruler, and status bar are turned on. Pressing B at this point turns *off* the Ribbon.

Dialoguing with Boxes

When you choose a menu item with an ellipsis (...), a dialog box pops up over your screen, as in the case of the Search dialog box shown in Figure 1-7. Sometimes, the dialog box shows you a bunch of preset options and you can just agree with everything. Sometimes, though, you have put some effort into it. After all, in Figure 1-7, Word can't know what word you want to search for — you have to fill in that information.

To move from one item to another in a dialog box, press Tab. If you overshoot, press Shift+Tab to move backwards. It may sound outrageous, but Shift+Tab does, indeed, send you backwards in a dialog box. Look at your Tab key; you see arrows pointing right and left. Forward and backward. It really works. After you get to an item, pressing the spacebar turns the item on or off.

Using Tab and the spacebar in the dialog box may be confusing at first. Just remember this: Pressing Tab, if you are typing a document, moves the cursor forward in a big way. Pressing the spacebar moves the cursor in a small way. Moving from item to item in a dialog box is a big move — Tab. Moving within the item is a small move — spacebar.

Check boxes   Text box   Option buttons

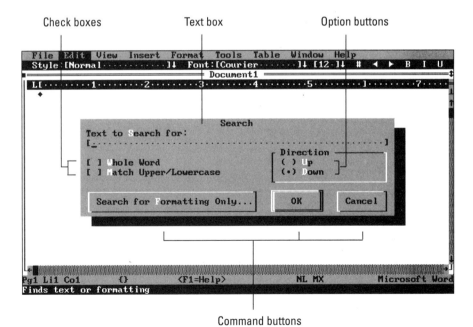

Command buttons

Figure 1-7: A dialog box — where you can tell Word exactly what to do and where to go. Well, let me put it another way...

Like menus, dialog boxes also have accelerator keys. There's one catch — you have to stick an Alt in front of the boldfaced key. So, in the Search dialog box, to get to **W**hole Word, you press Alt+W.

As with the pull-down menus, each symbol and shape inside the dialog box has a special way of behaving.

Text Box: This is where you type what you want (what to search for, what file to get, and so forth). Use Backspace to erase, and use the left- and right-arrow keys to move around.

List Box: This is a box that contains a bunch of items — like font names or whatever — to choose from. Highlight your choice.

Text Box/List Box: A hybrid combo box. You can type your choice or choose from a drop-down list. You know you're in a list box when you see a down-arrow ($\downarrow$) next to a text box. The list drops down when you're in that box and you press Alt+down arrow. (Or click the $\downarrow$ with the mouse.) Highlight your favorite item and press Tab to move to another part of the dialog box.

Check Box: Check boxes are square. You can have as many or as few of them checked as you want. In the infamous Search dialog box from Figure 1-7, you can check off **W**hole Word, or **M**atch Upper/Lowercase, or both of them, or neither of them. By the way, don't worry about what **W**hole Word or **M**atch Upper/Lowercase means right now — we're just talking about how square check boxes work. But, if your curiosity cannot be denied, go to Chapter 4 and read all about searching.

Option Box: An option box is round. Only in computers is a box round. An option box is where you are allowed to choose only one item. You cannot choose fewer or more than one item. The idea here is: Choose one item. In the Search dialog box, the options are **U**p or **D**own. The way it's usually set is **D**own. You can change it to **U**p. But you can't do both at the same time.

Command Buttons: A command button carries out some sort of action that takes you out of the current dialog box. There are *usually* at least two command buttons in every dialog box: OK and Cancel. OK means to carry out the command. Cancel means to forget it — put things back the way they were.

If you take a look at the Search dialog box, in addition to OK and Cancel, there's a third command button: Search for **F**ormatting Only.

Let's see if you're awake.

I'm going to ask you two questions about the Search for Formatting Only command button. Using what we've just covered, you should do fine. Ready?

First, if you are in this Search dialog box, what keystrokes do you use to jump straight to the Search for Formatting Only command button? Hum the Jeopardy theme to yourself while you write down your answer.

All set?

The answer is: Alt+F. Use Alt (because we're talking about a dialog box) and the boldfaced accelerator key.

Let's move to the bonus round, where anything can happen and usually does. Now, contestants, what do the three dots after Only mean?

Ready?

The three dots mean "more" — choosing the Search for Formatting Only command button takes you to another dialog box! Unbelievable.

And now, Don Pardo with the prizes!

When choosing an item from a list box, press the first letter of the item you want to select, and you are popped straight to the first item that begins with that letter. Press the letter again, and you move to the next item beginning with that letter, and so on. This works with any item in a list box — file names, font names, page range, and so on. Save yourself some keystrokes. It doesn't cost anything to try.

- ✔ Dialog boxes also have wrap around. If you press Tab on the last item in the box, you'll find yourself back at the beginning. Far out.

- ✔ As always, pressing Esc gets you out. Esc closes down the dialog box and returns things to the status quo. Pressing Esc is the same as choosing Cancel.

- ✔ Press Enter *only* when you have finished choosing all items. Pressing Enter is the same as choosing OK. You can press Enter no matter where you are in a dialog box.

- ✔ Do not press Enter to select an item in a list box unless that's the last parameter you want to choose in the entire dialog box. Pressing Enter means you're all finished with everything — not just all finished with this list box. After you've highlighted your list box selection, press Tab to move to the next item.

To eliminate or to restore the menu bar, press Alt+View ⇨ Preferences ⇨ Alt+**M**enu and press Enter. Turning off the menu bar doesn't mean you can't *use* menu commands any more. It just means that the menu bar is not visible as you work, so you get one more line of space for your prose. If the menu bar is turned off, pressing Alt causes it to appear until you press Enter or Esc.

Turning off the menu bar is like Esc Options, Show Menu: No.

Missing Menus Mystery

Not all menu bar items and pull-down selections are available at all times. Like the idea of items being *dimmed* when not applicable, whole menu items are completely — but temporarily — removed if they are not currently needed (see Figure 1-8). This is not a big deal. It can be a surprise if you're not expecting it, but now you've been warned. Getting into a file restores your menu bar.

Rocking with the Ribbon

The Ribbon duplicates commands found elsewhere in the regular menus. If you use these commands a lot, you'll love the Ribbon. If you don't, you won't.

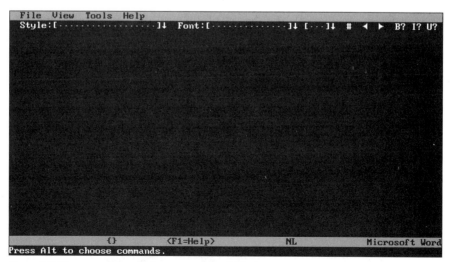

Figure 1-8: The case of the missing menus solved. No document, no need for most menus. After all, only the Dalai Lama can format nothing.

Okay, take a look at the Ribbon for just a second (see Figure 1-9). Notice that the Ribbon is composed primarily of three text-and-list boxes — just like the ones in the dialog boxes. Looks like things are starting to come together here.

The Style, Font, and the box with a number in it (called the Points box, which has nothing to do with a score box or a penalty box — *points* is a typesetting term that — wait a minute, all that stuff is covered in Chapter 7) are accessible by pressing Ctrl+S (for Style), Ctrl+F (for Font), and Ctrl+P (for Points). After the text box is highlighted, your basic Alt+down-arrow maneuver drops down the current choices. Press Tab to move to the next box — press Enter when you're finished.

Access the Ribbon with Ctrl — not Alt — commands. With some commands starting with Ctrl and some with Alt — how do you remember which is which? Here's how: If it's in the menu bar, it's Alt. If it's not in the menu bar, it's Ctrl. Alt+F is the File menu. Ctrl+F is the Font text box in the Ribbon. It makes sense. In a way. Just go with it, okay?

The last six symbols on the Ribbon work especially well with the mouse. For example, clicking the B on the Ribbon boldfaces your text. Click B again, and the text becomes unboldfaced. Another on and off switch. The I stands for Italic. The U means Underline.

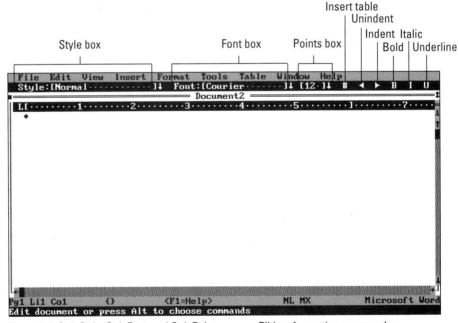

Figure 1-9: Ctrl+Style, Ctrl+Font, and Ctrl+Points access Ribbon formatting commands.

Clicking the right-facing triangle (▶) indents your text. Keep clicking it, and the text keeps moving in. I'm confident you can figure out what the left-facing triangle (◀) does. (If you can't, then try them both and you'll see.)

Finally, the pound sign (#) is a fabulous shortcut for creating a Table. More about this in Chapter 12.

To eliminate or to restore the Ribbon, press Alt+**View** ⇨ Ri**bb**on. Even if you don't have the Ribbon turned on, you still can use the Ribbon commands if you happen to know what they are. When you press Ctrl+F (or Ctrl+S or Ctrl+P), the Ribbon pops up. After you've completed your business and pressed Enter or Esc, the Ribbon disappears from view.

You can turn the Ribbon on or off by pointing to the symbol on the right-hand side, as shown in Figure 1-10, and pressing the right mouse button.

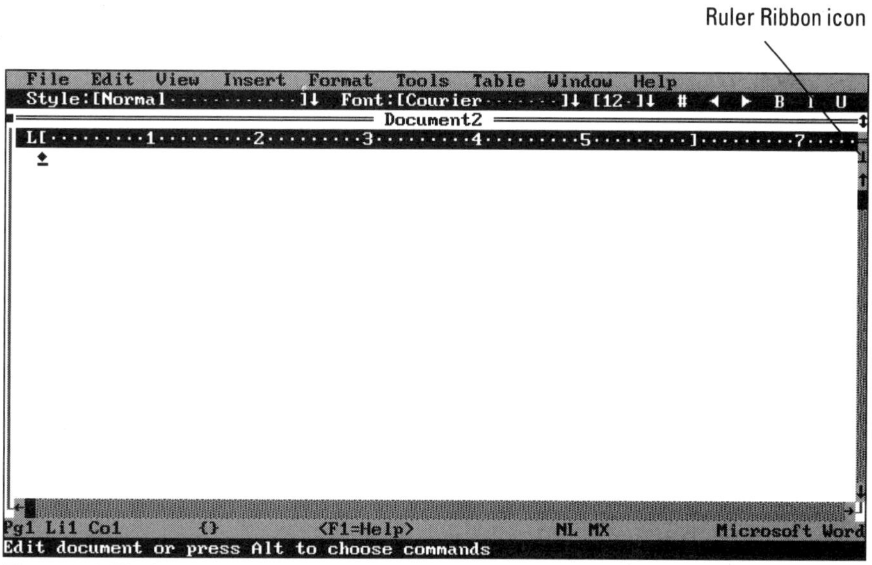

Ruler Ribbon icon

File   Edit   View   Insert   Format   Tools   Table   Window   Help
Style:[Normal···········]↕ Font:[Courier·······]↕ [12·]↕ # ◀ ▶ B I U
═══════════════════════════ Document2 ═══════════════════════════
L[···········1·········2·········3·········4·········5·········]·········7····

Pg1 Li1 Col   {}   <F1=Help>   NL MX   Microsoft Word
Edit document or press Alt to choose commands

Figure 1-10: The Ruler/Ribbon mouse icon. Click the left mouse button to turn the Ruler on or off. Click the right mouse button to turn the Ribbon on or off.

Rolling with the Ruler

Chapter 7 discusses the Ruler in more detail, but basically, its purpose is to display the left and right paragraph settings and tabs. It also provides a shortcut for adding and deleting tabs.

To eliminate or to restore the Ruler, press Alt+**View** ⇨ **R**uler. You also can make the Ruler pop up by pressing Ctrl+Shift+F10. After you press Enter or Esc, it goes away again.

You can turn the Ruler on or off by pointing to the symbol on the right-hand side and pressing the left mouse button (see Figure 1-10).

Bellying Up to the Bars

Do you ever watch one of those financial channels where the stock market prices march by at the bottom of the TV? Well, Word offers this sort of continually updated data at the bottom of your computer screen. Unlike your TV, you can turn the data off, if you want. See Figure 1-11 for the big picture.

Title Bar: This is where the name of your document appears. If you haven't named the document yet, it says `Document1` (whoa, real clever, Microsoft) until you've saved the file. After you save the file, your file name is up in lights.

Status Bar: A status bar is not where Donald Trump used to go for cocktails. Rather, it's that next-to-the-last line on your computer screen — and it's jam-packed with great data (see Figure 1-12).

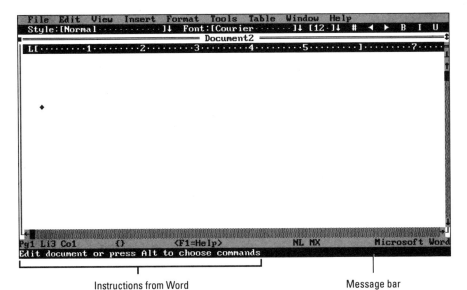

Instructions from Word   Message bar

Figure 1-11: An on-going parade of information, right in front of your face.

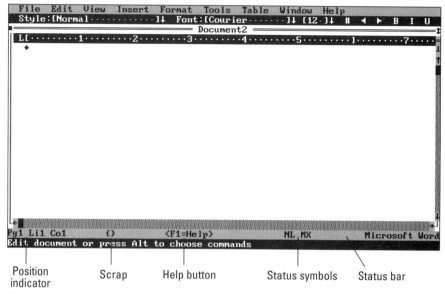

Figure 1-12: The status bar.

There's a homing device connected to your cursor. Word continually monitors the cursor's location and reports it to you via the *position indicator*. If the Page and Column location information is not enough detail, you can also find out which line it's on by pressing Alt+**View** ⇨ **Preferences** ⇨ Alt+Show Line **Num**bers and then Enter.

Next comes the *Scrap*. The very last thing you deleted by pressing Shift+Del (be it a word, a paragraph, or 30 pages) is held in stasis for you between the two squiggly brackets — { }. Anything in the Scrap can be inserted into a document by pressing Shift+Ins. More about this in Chapter 4.

In the middle of the screen is the *Help reminder*. Basically, the message here is simple. Press F1 — you get *context-sensitive* help. "Context-sensitive" means that when you ask for help, Word pops up relevant help. For example, if you were in the Save **As** dialog box, pressing F1 nets you a helpful box explaining all the ins and outs of Save **As** and where to find more info in the manual. Or, if you are in Print, you get help on printing. Now, if only your mate were so sensitive. More about Help in Chapter 15.

The *status symbols*, those two-letter goodies to the left of Microsoft Word — pardon me for a moment here, but why in the heck does Microsoft think we need the words Microsoft Word on the screen? We're going to forget what program we're using or something? I don't get it.

Anyway, where was I? Oh, yeah. The two-letter goodies to the left of you-know-what can help out when unexpected things start happening on your screen. Table 1-1 shows you a *few* of the status symbols — mostly just the ones you see when you're in trouble — what they mean, and how to get out of them.

Table 1-1		Status Symbols	
Code	*English*	*What Is Happening*	*How To Stop It*
CL	Caps Lock	Everything is coming out uppercase	Press Caps Lock
EX	Extend	Cursor grows in size instead of moving	Press Esc
OT	Overtype	New letters erase old letters underneath, Backspace doesn't work	Press Ins
LY	Layout	Screen flashes, text spreads out	Press Alt+**V**iew ➪ **L**ayout
SL	Scroll Lock	Left-arrow doesn't work	Press Scroll Lock
MX	Maximize window	This is okay	
NL	Num Lock on	No problem	

If you want, you can nuke the status bar by pressing Alt+View ➪ **S**tatus Bar — and Enter — though I highly recommend that you keep it.

Message Bar: The message bar, now appearing at the bottom of screens everywhere, is your secret pipeline of hints, suggestions, and gentle reminders. It's the first place you look when things go wrong. Unless you are a total Word Terminator, you won't want to turn it off. If you do, press Alt+View ➪ **P**references ➪ Alt+**M**essage Bar.

Sushi Bar: Oops, wrong list.

Cursor-ing the Darkness

There are two other items on the basic Word screen worth mentioning (see Figure 1-13).

Cursor   Endmark

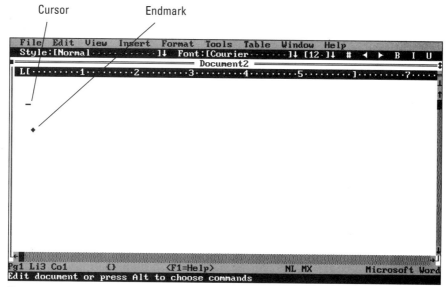

Figure 1-13: Your friends, the cursor and the endmark.

The *cursor*, which is not you screaming at the computer when things go wrong, is the little underline that tells you where the next thing you type will appear. If you have a mouse, you also have a mouse pointer — which shows you where the cursor will move to when you click the mouse.

Another much-maligned item is the *endmark* — the little diamond (♦) that lets you know you've reached the end of the file. The strategy with the endmark is to leave it alone. You can't delete it, and it doesn't hurt anything. It's just there — gently telling you that you have reached the end of your document's reality.

Maybe yours, too.

Chapter 2
Toiling with Text

* *

In This Chapter

▶ Exposing text's secret life
▶ Defining nonprinting symbols
▶ Using nonprinting symbols
▶ Highlighting text
▶ Typing etiquette

* *

*T*he whole point of an airplane is to — no, it isn't to make money, smart aleck — especially these days — the whole point of an airplane is to service passengers. Sure, you knew that. And *text* is the passenger on our Word 6 airplane.

How's that for stretching an analogy?

Anyway, the point is that it's wise to understand how Word looks at your text. It's good to have a grasp of what's going on behind the scenes. After all, although you certainly realize that you're not using a typewriter, you may not realize how many typewriter-reality assumptions are still rattling around inside your head.

Exposing Text's Secret Life

How *does* a word processing program look at text? What is Word's secret text life? Inquiring minds want to know. Our photographer took a "before" picture of Word's normal display (see Figure 2-1).

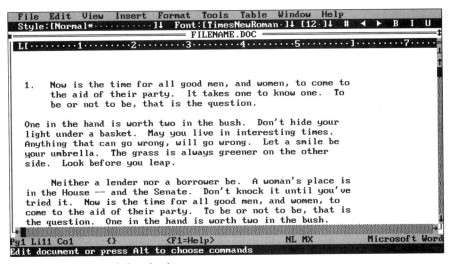

Figure 2-1: Normal text, in happier times.

However, after following Word for weeks, our intrepid photographer finally caught Word in the act, with its *nonprinting symbols* on full display (see Figure 2-2).

Nonprinting symbols in Word 6 perform exactly as they did in Word 5.

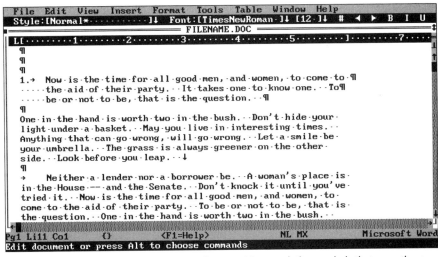

Figure 2-2: Inquiring minds finally get to see the parasitic nonprinting symbols that secretly swarm around text, doing unprintable things.

Defining nonprinting symbols

The dots between words, the arrows, and so on — all the funny-looking things that *aren't* in Figure 2-1 but show up in Figure 2-2 — are called *nonprinting symbols*.

The idea of a nonprinting symbol isn't nearly as hard to understand as it is to pronounce. In fact, you use one nonprinting symbol all the time — the page break symbol.

That's right. That horizontal line of periods that stretches across the screen, telling you when you've reached the end of the page — it's a nonprinting symbol. The periods symbolize the end of the page, but the periods don't appear on the printed page. It's a symbol. It doesn't print. What more could you ask of a nonprinting symbol?

Hang onto your hats, folks, because there is a whole battery of nonprinting symbols that are normally *invisible*.

Yeah, I know. Just hang in there with me.

An example of an invisible nonprinting symbol is our friend the space. Normally, there is no actual visible "space character." Unless you count E.T.

Spaces *are* visible to Word, though. The dots between words in Figure 2-2 are how Word sees spaces. Other exciting nonprinting keystrokes visible to Word are Tabs and Enters, which are symbolized by the → and the ¶, respectively.

To make those invisible nonprinting symbols visible, as in Figure 2-2, just press Alt+View ⇨ Preferences ⇨ Show All. After you are in Show All mode, you can see what Word sees — the underlying skeleton of the document. Think of Show All mode as x-ray vision for your document.

Turning *off* nonprinting symbols requires a bit more dexterity. You start out by pressing Alt+View ⇨ Preferences, but then you have to go to each option one at a time (by pressing Tab, using the mouse, or pressing the boldfaced key) to uncheck the box.

Word's point of view about text is a whole lot different from yours or mine. Humans regard letters of the alphabet as important and spaces as nothing. Word places no such value judgment on all the electronic impulses that arrive through the keyboard. Everything must be interpreted, tracked, acted upon, and preserved with equal weight. After all, without spaces, words would collide.

Nonprinting symbols at work

Other than being able to impress coworkers of the opposite sex with all the hidden symbols lurking in the background of your document, why would anyone give a flying fig about invisible symbols? Let 'em stay invisible, right?

Wrong.

Nonprinting symbols simplify text formatting

Look at Figure 2-2 and you can instantly detect that the first line was indented with a Tab, but the second line was indented with spaces. This kind of analytical skill may save your life when we get to Chapter 7.

Nonprinting symbols are keepers of the format

When text is formatted — centered, for example — Word stores the centering instructions *in the paragraph symbol*. Don't ask me why, but that's where it goes. You may want to think of the paragraph symbol as the genetic code for the preceding paragraph.

Now here's the key concept: If you delete the paragraph symbol (¶) — you *also delete the formatting of the paragraph.*

Say what?

You heard correctly. The genetic instructions — the formatting commands — for the paragraph are kept in its paragraph symbol. Remove the symbol, and you remove the paragraph's formatting. Formatting includes Tabs, line spacing, indents, and whatnot. Delete the paragraph symbol, and all that formatting goes away — and the paragraph adopts the formatting of the following paragraph.

If you've ever had the experience of seeing a paragraph suddenly lose its shape, you now know it's not for lack of exercise — it was because you deleted the hidden, nonprinting paragraph symbol at the end the paragraph.

This also applies to the Section symbol — the line of colons that holds the formatting for the page (margins, numbers of columns, and so on).

Anytime your formatting goes south on you, immediately press Alt+Backspace — Edit Undo. It just may set you right.

Nonprinting symbols can be cloned

The other key secret about the paragraph symbol is that if you press Enter when the cursor is on the paragraph symbol, *the current formatting will be replicated* for the next paragraph.

Have you ever centered a paragraph, pressed Enter, and wondered why Word kept on centering? That's because you pressed Enter on a paragraph symbol that had the centering gene, so the cloned paragraph was also a centered paragraph. Sounds like we're talking about a mad scientist's laboratory, doesn't it?

Don't forget — press Enter at the end of the paragraph to create a new paragraph with the same formatting. If, instead, you press the down-arrow key, you will not have cloned the formatting from the preceding paragraph and it will seem as though the formatting has mysteriously disappeared. In reality, you have left it behind. No problem. Just go back up and this time press Enter.

Nonprinting symbols are always there

Even though you may choose to keep them invisible, the nonprinting symbols are still there, like the invisible man — guarding formatting and waiting to be cloned.

You might as well relax and decide that nonprinting symbols are your friends. Hopefully, you don't have too many other invisible friends. We wouldn't want to make them jealous.

Hidden text

Can you imagine the programmer going to the boss with this winning idea — "Hey, I've got an idea for a great feature — it lets you type text that not only won't print out, but you also can make it invisible on the screen." Clearly, this idea has "merit bonus" written all over it.

The only reason I'm mentioning hidden text — which you'll probably never use — is so that you won't confuse it with nonprinting symbols.

Hidden text consists of words or characters you type and you hide. Word manages nonprinting symbols. Hidden text is needed when you enter special codes to create an index or table of contents for your document — you need the codes to create the index, but you don't want the codes to print out and mess up your document.

One way ordinary humans can use hidden text is to jot down follow-up notes, phone numbers, and reminders — formatted as hidden text — at the bottom of the letter you're sending. That way, when you call up the file, all your information is there — but it won't print. Hidden text is also good for writing yourself notes, like "double-check figures with Stan before sending this letter." As I said before, however, mostly you can ignore it.

Highlighting Text

Highlighting is another key activity when you are dealing with text. Think of highlighting as the airline passenger turning on the flight attendant button. After the passenger comes to the attention of the flight attendant, the attendant is more than willing to do his or her part (see Figure 2-3).

You can't format text without first highlighting the text to be formatted. You can't cut and paste without highlighting text first. If you want to apply numbering to a series of paragraphs, the first step is to highlight the paragraphs concerned. No matter what you want to do, it seems like the first step is to highlight. After highlighting a sentence, for example, you can delete it, underline it, check its spelling, or whatever. That sentence is totally at your mercy.

Because Word wants you to spend so much time highlighting, the folks at Microsoft stayed late one night to come up with lots and lots of function-key commands to cover every conceivable highlighting desire with elegance and grace. We care naught for elegance and grace here. We prefer to learn one function key that'll brutishly get the job done in almost every situation.

If anyone really cares, a list of the most helpful keyboard commands and mouse commands are listed in Appendixes C and D. Knock yourself out.

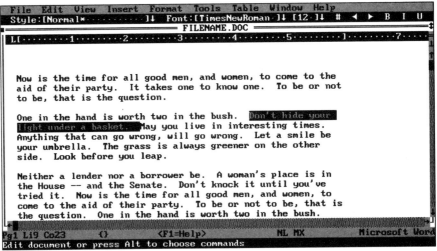

Figure 2-3: Here is a sentence that has been highlighted. Highlighting is the first step in almost any command involving text.

Highlighting with F8

F8 is very cool. Table 2-1 shows how this one key can take care of all your high-lighting needs. Just keep hammering away on F8 until you get what you want. If you get carried away and highlight too much, start pounding away on Shift+F8 to make the highlight get smaller and smaller and smaller.

Table 2-1	Mastering F8
Press	*To Highlight*
F8+arrow keys	From point of cursor in any direction
F8 two times	Current word
F8 three times	Sentence
F8 four times	Paragraph
F8 five times	Document
Shift+F8	Decrease highlight incrementally
Esc	Turn off F8 (Extend) mode

Press F8 twice and any character (like a period or a letter of the alphabet or whatever), and Word highlights from the current cursor position to the first occurrence of the character. So, pressing F8 F8 + . (period) highlights to the end of the sentence. You can press another character, and the highlight expands farther. Continue until you've got everything covered.

When you're working with F8, Word turns on the EX status symbol in the status bar to let you know you're in F8, or Extend, mode. It's called Extend mode be-cause the cursor keeps getting bigger and bigger, like a monster in a 50s B movie, as it mercilessly engulfs words and sentences.

Pressing Esc turns off Extend mode.

After Extend mode is turned off, pressing any arrow key instantly restores the cursor's girlish figure.

Highlighting with a Shift

If F8 seems too techy for you, another way to highlight makes use of your already finely tuned cursor-moving talents. By adding Shift to arrow keys, PgUp and PgDn, Home, and End, you can highlight as you move.

Pressing Shift+right arrow and Shift+left arrow highlights one character at a time. Pressing Shift+up arrow or Shift+down arrow grabs a line at a time, and Shift+PgUp and Shift+PgDn cover a page at a time. Oh, and don't miss out on Shift+Home and Shift+End to highlight from the cursor to the beginning or end of the line. This is probably the first time being "shifty" is a positive thing.

Word lets you mix and match highlighting commands. You may start highlighting using one technique, but that doesn't preclude you from using others. For example, if you highlight with cursor keys, you can still start pressing F8. Or vice versa. Press F8 three times to highlight a sentence and then use the cursor keys to continue to expand the highlight. Experiment. Be bold. It costs nothing to try.

F8 is the new Extend key (formerly F6). As Table 2-1 shows, however, it does a lot more than the old F6 did. Ctrl+Shift+left arrow and Ctrl+Shift+right arrow are equivalent to Word 5's F7 and F8 keys, respectively. Ctrl+Shift+up arrow and Ctrl+Shift+down arrow are equivalent to Word 5's F9 and F10 keys, respectively. Shift+left arrow and Shift+right arrow still highlight one character at a time.

In addition to your normal mouse pointing and dragging, you can highlight the current line of text by pointing to the space between the left window border and the beginning of text (in graphics mode, when you're "there," the mouse arrow will point to the right instead of to the left; in text mode with a color monitor, the mouse rectangle changes color) and clicking the left mouse button (left-click). Highlight the whole paragraph with a right-click (click the right mouse button). You can even highlight the whole document by clicking both mouse ears.

Typing Etiquette

There are certain no-nos about entering text in a word processor. Most of the "bad" stuff is done in the name of formatting — getting text to look a certain way on-screen by manhandling it with spaces and Tabs. Spaces and Tabs, we now know, Word carefully records and certainly will blackmail you with later if you issue a formatting command.

The right way to format text is covered in Chapter 7. And as is always the case, the right way is much, much easier than the wrong way. The only problem is, bad habits can be difficult to overcome. Maybe a week at the Betty Ford Clinic can handle your addiction to spaces.

```
File  Edit  View  Insert  Format  Tools  Table  Window  Help
Style:[Normal*··········]↓   Font:[TimesNewRoman·]↓ [12·]↓   #  ◄  ►  B  I  U
═══════════════════════════ FILENAME.DOC ═══════════════════════════
L[·········1·········2·········3·········4·········5·······]·····7····
¶
¶
→       →       →       →       ·····APHORISMS·¶
¶
·····Now·is·the·time·for·all·good·men,·and·women,·to·come·to¶
¶
the·aid·of·their·party.···It·takes·one·to·know·one.···To·be·or¶
¶
not·to·be,·that·is·the·question.··¶
¶
·····→       →       One·in·the·hand·is·worth·two·in·the·bush.··¶
→      →       Don't·hide·your·light·under·a·basket.··¶
·→      →       →       May·you·live·in·interesting·times.··¶
¶
1.→    Anything·that·can·go·wrong,·will·go·wrong.··Let·a·smile·
→      be·your·umbrella.··The·grass·is·always·greener·on·the·→
→      other·side.··Look·before·you·leap.··↓
¶
Pg1 Li17 Co6      {}         <F1=Help>           NL MX        Microsoft Word
Edit document or press Alt to choose commands
```

Figure 2-4: Examples of very bad behavior when typing text.

Here are some of the most common wrong ways, as illustrated in Figure 2-4.

Ignoring text etiquette causes nothing but headaches when it comes time to make changes.

✔ Don't press Enter at the end of every line — use Enter only at the end of a paragraph.

✔ Don't press Enter to double space lines in a paragraph — press Enter twice only when you want a blank line between two paragraphs.

✔ Press the space bar to separate words in a sentence only. Don't use spaces to indent a paragraph, separate columns of text, or go from a numbered item to the following text (such as "1.").

✔ Don't press Tab to make a paragraph line up under a number.

✔ Don't press Tab or Enter to indent the paragraph from the left and the right.

✔ Unless you know what you're doing, don't create a file that's longer than 100 pages.

Although there are always exceptions to the preceding rules — in computers, there are always exceptions — in general, it is a good idea to practice safe text. Your efforts will be repaid in ease of formatting, fewer incidences of disaster, and a reduced amount of printout panic.

Chapter 3
Wild, Wild Windows

*N*ow that we've examined the Word 6 cockpit and have our passengers entered properly, we'll try some flying and maneuvering. And, some good news, this is the last use of the airplane analogies.

Doing Windows

A *window*, by any other name, is still just the place where a document appears on-screen. Word's opening screen could be referred to as an empty window.

And, regardless of the weather, you can have as many as nine windows, each with its own file, open at the same time.

If the concept of nine open files is a little weird to imagine, try thinking of it as holding a bunch of playing cards in your hand. Each card represents a file. Opening another file is like drawing another card from the deck and adding it to your hand. In this case, Word even holds the cards for you.

After more than one file or document is in play, you can flip through the documents one at a time, or arrange the windows as shown in Figures 3-1 and 3-2.

Active window

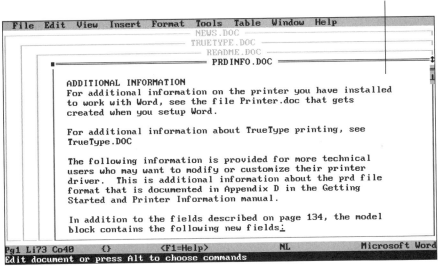

```
 File   Edit   View   Insert   Format   Tools   Table   Window   Help
                                    NEWS.DOC
                                 TRUETYPE.DOC
                                   README.DOC
                         ======== PRDINFO.DOC ========

 ADDITIONAL INFORMATION
 For additional information on the printer you have installed
 to work with Word, see the file Printer.doc that gets
 created when you setup Word.

 For additional information about TrueType printing, see
 TrueType.DOC

 The following information is provided for more technical
 users who may want to modify or customize their printer
 driver.  This is additional information about the prd file
 format that is documented in Appendix D in the Getting
 Started and Printer Information manual.

 In addition to the fields described on page 134, the model
 block contains the following new fields:

Pg1 Li73 Co40        {}            <F1=Help>              NL            Microsoft Word
Edit document or press Alt to choose commands
```

Figure 3-1: An example of four open files in *cascading* — overlapping — windows.

Active window

```
 File   Edit   View   Insert   Format   Tools   Table   Window   Help
                        ======== NEWS.DOC ========
 cells.  Initially, the cells are all equal in size and cover
 the distance between the margins.  The size of the columns
 can then be adjusted to one's personal preference.  Don't
 worry if you do not know how many rows or columns that you
 will need.  Additional rows and columns can be added or
 deleted from the table as needed.

                        ======== PRDINFO.DOC ========
 The following information is provided for more technical
 users who may want to modify or customize their printer
 driver.  This is additional information about the prd file
 format that is documented in Appendix D in the Getting
 Started and Printer Information manual.

        ====== README.DOC ======                    ====== TRUETYPE.DOC ======
 . More Information on Tables              If you did not install TrueType font
 . More Information on editing symbol      Word, run Setup again and choose the
 . More Information on Numbering           version of 6.0" option. If you want
 . Spelling Dictionaries Available         for both previewing and printing doc
 . Additional Outline Information          printer driver. Then, when prompted,

P1 S2 L8 C1        {}            <F1=Help>              NL            Microsoft Word
Edit document or press Alt to choose commands
```

Figure 3-2: An example of four open files, in a *tile* configuration — think of the placement of tiles on your kitchen floor — so that a little bit of every file is visible.

At this point, someone usually chimes in with "Gee, that's nice, but why in the world would I want to access more than one document at a time?" At least, that's the cleaned-up version of the question.

There are lots of reasons to have more than one file open:

1. Mainly, when you want to copy text from one file to another.

2. When you want to compare one version of a document to another.

3. When notes are in one file and the final document is in another.

4. When the overall document is composed of several smaller files and you need access to all the material.

5. When you need to be able to view footnotes while writing the main document.

6. When you want to impress everyone around you with a complicated-looking computer screen.

Anyway, you get the idea. Using several files at a time can be very convenient.

The only thing to remember about operating with a bunch of open windows is that at any given moment, only one of them is considered *active*. And, it follows, the others are considered *inactive*. Basically, this means that you can edit only one file at a time. Which is no limitation, because who in the devil can edit more than one file at a time? Right? I mean, if you can edit two files at the same time, I'd be very interested in meeting you. In fact, if you're a single male, I'll marry you.

The active window in Figure 3-2 is the one containing the file NEWS.DOC. You can tell it's active because the title bar is darker than the others. Usually, as in Figure 3-1, the active window is simply the one on top. It's the one you can see.

In Version 5, every time a new file is transfer/loaded, the file already on-screen is automatically closed in favor of the new one. As you may have figured out by now, that's not how it works in Version 6. Now, when you load (or open) a new file, the current file remains and the new one is merely added to the stack of other previously open files. Sort of like when you used to split a window and had a different file in each window. The two windows functioned independently. Think of both those windows as taking up the full screen. Then pretend there are nine of them. If you want an old file to go away, you have to close the window yourself (**Window/Close**).

Storming Windows

Managing windows mostly means opening and closing windows — not a big thing. If you've got more than one window going, then it's a good idea to expand your skill base to the extent that you know how to move from one open window to another. Finally, if you are easily amused, you'll be thrilled to move windows around on the screen with your arrow keys or mouse.

Opening windows

The basic way to open a window is to press Alt+File ⇨ **O**pen. You'll get Figure 3-3, which shows the Open dialog box. Sounds like the meeting place for an encounter group, doesn't it?

After you're there, you can use any of your new-found dialog boxing skills to choose the file you want to get into. For example, you can do any one of the following:

- ✔ In the text box, type the name of the file to be opened (you don't have to type the **.DOC**) and press Enter.

- ✔ Press Alt+Files to jump down to the list box of file names, highlight the victim file, and then press Enter.

- ✔ Double-click the name of the file you want to open.

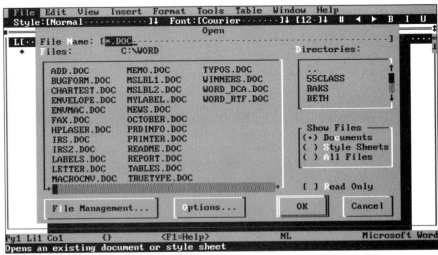

Figure 3-3: The Open dialog box lets you see and select which file you want to work with.

Although Microsoft has generously provided an elegant Alt+File ⇨ New command that you're supposed to use when you're starting a new file from scratch — versus "opening" an existing file — you can just type the proposed name of the new file in the Open dialog box, and Word obligingly creates the new file, after you confirm that that's what you had in mind.

Appearing at the bottom of the File menu is a handy shortcut — the names of the last four files you opened are listed, as shown in Figure 3-4, each with a bold number next to it. All you have to do is press Alt+File ⇨ bold number, and Word grabs that file for you.

If you accidentally open the same document twice, the document title bar says:

————————— FILENAME.DOC:2 —————————

When you issue the Close command, if Word asks whether you want to save changes, the changes you will be saving (or not) are the changes made to *both* the first and second windows of the document.

Closing windows

After you've finished with a document, you should close it and put it away. In addition to the fact that it's just plain tidy to do so, remember that each file is a drain on the system. A bunch of unneeded open files can slow down the computer. Also, if the power goes out or a meteor hits, all of the open files could be lost.

Figure 3-4: Press Alt+File ⇨ **1** to open OCTOBER.DOC.

After you have saved a file (more about saving in Chapter 5) by pressing Alt+**F**ile ➪ **S**ave, you can close the file by pressing Alt+**F**ile ➪ **C**lose.

The shortcut function key for closing one window is Ctrl+F4. We all know that memorizing function keys is "out" for the 90s, but Ctrl+F4 also closes a window in Microsoft Windows and, like, if you use Microsoft Windows, you may find it a useful habit to get into.

Don't confuse closing a window with exiting Word. They are not the same. When you press Alt+**F**ile ➪ **E**xit Word, you have finished working with Word. When you close a window, you have finished working with a particular file. You can be running Word and have no open files at all — the ultimate Word Zen moment.

Moving between windows

To jump from one window to another is very simple. All you need to do is press one of the following:

- ✔ Ctrl+F6. Pressing Ctrl+F6 moves you, one window at a time, forward through the stack of open windows. Use this method when you have only two or three windows open, or if there's something that you like about pressing Ctrl+F6. (In case you overshoot, Shift+Ctrl+F6 cycles you backwards through the windows.)

- ✔ Alt+**W**indow ➪ *number*. The Window menu shows the currently open documents, with a number to the left of each of the file names. By pressing Alt+**W**indow ➪ *number*, you can jump directly to any of the current documents. This is the fastest way if you're screamin' from window to window like a crazed animal.

If you have more than one window visible on-screen, clicking any window makes that window active.

Changing the size and location of windows

All your window-changing commands are listed in the Alt+**W**indow menu (see Figure 3-5). After you know where the commands are hiding, they're pretty self-explanatory. Alt+**W**indow ➪ **A**rrange All gives you something like Figure 3-2. Notice that when windows get small, it's the view that gets small — the text doesn't shrink. Alt+**W**indow ➪ Ma**x**imize restores a shrunken window to the full screen size so that you can work with it more easily.

When more than one window is open, Word normally handles how those files are placed on the screen. If you don't happen to like Word's window auto arrangement, try Alt+**W**indow ➪ **M**ove and Alt+**W**indow ➪ **S**ize and regroup to taste.

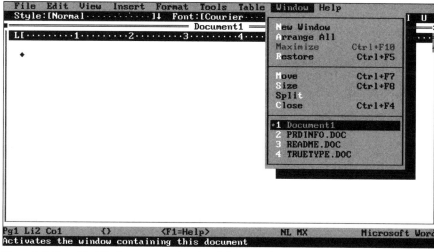

Figure 3-5: From Alt+Window, you can bend and shape a window into any size you want.

The mouse and the window

Sounds like the name of a fable, doesn't it?

The moral of this fable is to always remember that in Word, along with most well-bred mouse-aware software, the title bar and scroll bars contain areas and icons sensitive to the click of a mouse.

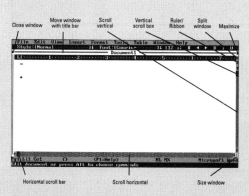

Figure 3-6: A mouse can close, move, scroll, split, and do darn near anything you want with only a flick of its ears.

This is in addition to the Ruler/Ribbon icon discussed in Chapter 1 and the basic vertical and horizontal scroll bars (if you've got them turned on). Did you know that a single click to the Close Window icon, for example, neatly closes the current window (see Figure 3-6)?

The title bar is also the window's "handle." Grab it with the mouse and drag the window to a new locale on the screen if that will make things easier.

By dragging the lower right window border, you can make the window smaller or larger. After you've resized the window, clicking the minimize/maximize icon flips back and forth between the normal window and the customized window.

The split window icon lets you divide a window into two panes so that two parts of the same document are visible. Drag the icon down to where you want to divide the screen and let go. Double-click the split window icon when you want to stop splitting.

The 5th Wave — By Rich Tennant

"GATHER AROUND, KIDS. YOUR MOTHER'S WINDOWING!"

Part II
How to Out-Think Word

In this part . . .

*I*f Part I was the blueprint of Word 6, then Part II is the nuts and bolts. And I *don't* mean that I drive you nuts and everyone bolts from the room. The chapters are presented in roughly the same order one might go through when constructing a document — from editing to backing up. In short, sports fans, in Part II, you experience the thrill of opening and the agony of delete. And now, Microsoft Word, up close and personal.

Chapter 4
Putting Text in Its Place

. . . .

In This Chapter

▶ Setting up

▶ Controlling the cursor

▶ Searching

▶ Replacing

▶ Cutting and pasting

▶ Dragging and dropping

▶ Editing etiquette

. . . .

I remember the first time I ever used a word processor, way back in the old days — ten years ago. Typing that first document was easy. I felt excited, confident; some might say, "cocky." Then my perfectly typed, perfectly printed page was handed back to me with changes — and I was plunged into the editing nightmare!

Editing that document was like battling Medusa — every time I chopped off one problem, nine sprang up in its place. Text came together and flew apart as though it had a mind of its own — things moved off the screen — and worse. The clock inexorably moved toward five o'clock. Things got tense.

I finally gave up and desperately started a new file, typing the whole thing over from scratch.

I swore I'd never go hungry again!

No, wait, wrong story.

The point is, editing is supposed to be the civilized process of making sure that the right words are in the right order — not a barbaric contest of wills between you and the computer. With a few basic rules under your belt, you'll be able to tame the beast.

Getting Ready

What happens when I press the Del key on my computer may not be the same thing that happens when you press the Del key on your computer. This isn't because my computer is different from yours. It's evidence of the fact that Word lets you customize the program and your copy of Word may be set up differently from mine.

Things are enough of a challenge without adding out-of-synch commands to the list. So, what *are* my settings? To find out, send five dollars to — no, just kidding — press Alt+View ➪ Preferences ➪ Customize, to compare your settings with mine (see Figure 4-1).

The following three Settings *must* be turned on for the keystroke commands in this chapter to work on your computer:

1. Use **INS** for Overtype Key

2. **D**rag-and-Drop Text Editing

3. Typing **R**eplaces Selection

At this point, you aren't expected to know what these settings mean or do. Just look to see whether the boxes are checked. If they're already checked, great. If they aren't already checked, you should make note of which ones *aren't* checked so that you can put them back that way later, if you want. Then check (turn on) the ones that need to be checked (see Figure 4-1).

These are the default settings. They also most closely match how Windows works.

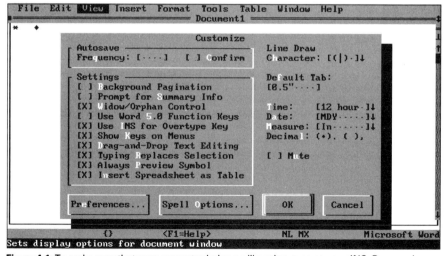

Figure 4-1: To make sure that your computer behaves like mine, turn on your INS, Drag-and-Drop, and Replaces settings.

Controlling the Cursor — Are We There Yet?

The cursor has two very important jobs: To indicate where the next thing you type will appear and to serve as the beginning point for highlighting. So, whether the job is typing or highlighting, the first step is to put the cursor where the action is.

Two minutes after sitting down in front of a computer, anyone is expert at moving the cursor around one baby space at a time.

But did you know that by adding Ctrl to the up- and down-arrow keys, you can move up or down a *paragraph* at a time? And there's more! Ctrl+right arrow or left arrow moves the cursor a *word* forward or backward, respectively. Table 4-1 lists the commands to warp the cursor all over the document.

Table 4-1	Cursor Commands
Press	*Move to*
Home	The beginning of the line
End	The end of the line
Ctrl+Home	The beginning of the document
Ctrl+End	The end of the document
Ctrl+PgUp	The top of the current screen
Ctrl+PgDn	The bottom of the current screen
Ctrl+up arrow	The preceding paragraph
Ctrl+down arrow	The next paragraph
Ctrl+left arrow	The preceding word
Ctrl+right arrow	The next word

Searching

When it's time to change a particular passage in your document, which would you prefer to do: Scroll, scroll, scroll your cursor, looking through the text, or sip a cup of coffee while your computer finds it for you?

To find something in the current document, follow these steps:

1. Press Alt+**E**dit ⇨ **S**earch. The Search dialog box appears on-screen (see Figure 4-2).

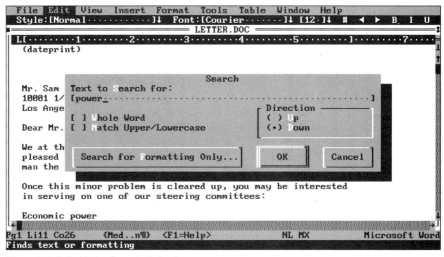

Figure 4-2: Behold, the Search dialog box.

2. Type the word you want to find.

   The idea here is to search for something unique. Don't search for *and*, for example. If the word you're searching for occurs throughout the document, type the search word plus the word next to it. In other words, if you were searching for *Jane*, you might type *Jane run* to move to that particular instance of *Jane*. You also can type punctuation, spaces, or anything else that makes your search word unique.

3. Press Enter.

   After finding the search text, Word highlights it for you. After the text is highlighted, you can delete it or press F8 and continue the highlighting — or do anything else you normally can do with highlighted text.

You can use the Search command to highlight a large area of text. Press F8 (to turn on the Extend mode) and then issue the Search command. Word highlights all the text between the F8 starting point and the found text.

  ✔ If Word finds your text, but it's not the location you had in mind, press Shift+F4 to repeat the search. Keep pressing Shift+F4 until Word gets it right and lands on the spot you want.

  ✔ If Word cannot find your search text, it beeps and a dialog box pops up to let you know.

  ✔ If you get a "can't find it" message, make sure that the search text was typed *exactly* as it appears in the document.

✔ If you highlight text in the file before you begin the search, Word conducts the search only within the highlighted area. Remove the highlight and try again (press Shift+F4).

✔ Word normally searches from the cursor downward. If the search has been fruitless by the time it gets to the end of the document, Word offers to go to the top and continue the search.

✔ You can determine which direction Word searches by pressing Alt+Up or Alt+**D**own when in the Search dialog box.

✔ Be careful about how you enter the search text. If you search for the word *let*, for example, and do not have the **W**hole Word option selected, Word stops on words such as *"Let*ters," "plate*let*s," and any other word with *let* in it.

✔ If you search for the man's name *Ray*, choosing **M**atch Upper/Lowercase ensures that Word bypasses "*ray*s of sunshine" and "stin*gray*."

There may be times when you'd like to search through many documents to find the one document containing a particular word or phrase. You can do that with Alt+**File** ➪ **File** Management ➪ **Search** ➪ **Text** (described in Chapter 13).

Replacing

I remember my first global search and replace. Granted, it's kind of pathetic to be nostalgic about computer functions, but that's my life. Anyway, I was working on a story and I decided to change a character's name from Gina to Peg. I waited while the machine clicked away, searching for "Gina" and replacing with "Peg," doing all the work for me — I was in the computer age! For weeks afterward, however, I kept running into bizarre words such as "imaPegtion" and "oriPegl" (previously ima*gina*tion and ori*gina*l).

I learned two lessons that day: Save before you do a search and replace (so it can be undone) and always **C**onfirm Changes. Oh, but I'm getting ahead of myself.

To replace, then, follow these steps:

1. Press Alt+**File** ➪ **S**ave.

   Technically, this isn't part of the replace process. However, by saving first, you have a fall-back position in case something, uh, interesting happens with your replace commands.

2. Press Alt+**Edit** ➪ Replace (see Figure 4-3).

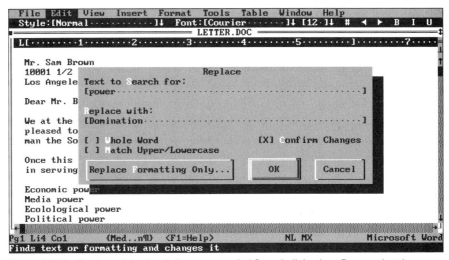

Figure 4-3: The Replace dialog box is just an extended Search dialog box. Be sure that the Confirm Changes option is checked before you press Enter.

3. Type the word you want to replace.

4. Press Tab (or Alt+**R**eplace with).

5. Type the new word.

6. Make sure that the **C**onfirm Changes box is checked.

   Confirming changes means that each and every time Word thinks it has found a word to replace, it has to get permission from a human being — specifically you — before actually doing the replacing. Think of Confirm Changes as the "Mother, may I?" box.

7. Press Enter.

8. Go through the document with Word, confirming — or not — the changes, as illustrated in Figure 4-4.

   ✔ To undo the entire Search and Replace session, press Alt+Backspace. If it's too late to perform an undo, and if you have not saved since the search-and-replace session (and made no major changes to the document), press Alt+**F**ile ⇨ **C**lose and say **N**o to saving changes.

You can also search and replace formatting (such as change all the centered paragraphs to justified paragraphs). See Chapter 7 for an explanation of this procedure.

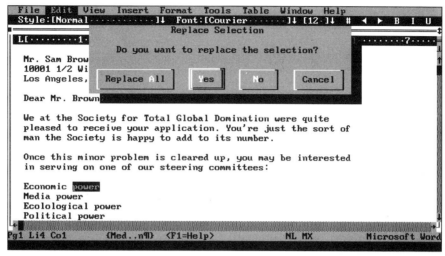

Figure 4-4: The Replace Selection confirmation box. Sounds vaguely religious, doesn't it?

Cutting and Pasting

Ever since Dr. Frankenstein, people have been working on ways to perfect cut and paste. The steps for cutting and pasting are to cut first and then — well, paste. You can also cut and not paste if you just want to annihilate something. It could happen.

The first step in cutting and pasting is to highlight the text you want to lop off. To review the basic highlighting moves, jump back to Table 2-1 in Chapter 2. Otherwise, find the appropriate how-to instructions that follow — or hop to Table 4-2 for instant gratification.

Table 4-2	Cut and Paste
To	*Highlight Text and*
Cut forever	Press Del
Cut for paste	Press Shift+Del
Copy for paste	Press Ctrl+Ins
Paste	Move cursor to new locale and press Shift+Ins

Cutting for good

1. Highlight the text you want to cut.

2. Press Del.

> ✔ Text that has been cut with the Del key cannot be retrieved with the Paste command. Press Del when you want something gone forever, never to darken your doorstep. Remember: Delete = Dead.
>
> ✔ You can undo (press Alt+Backspace) a cut with the Del key only if it was the last command. Otherwise, the text is hasta la bye bye.

Cutting and pasting

1. Highlight the text you want to cut and paste.

2. Press Shift+Del.

   Notice that this time there's a Shift in front of the Del. Shift+Del puts the text in the Scrap (visible in the squiggly brackets in the status bar). Whatever is in the Scrap can be brought back to life like something in a Stephen King novel: "It Came from the Scrap: The Tale of the Un-Deleted." The bottom line here is: Shift+Del = Save Delete.

3. Move the cursor to where you want the text to appear.

   If, during your travels to the new text location, you notice some other text you want to delete, you may do so as long as you cut it with the Del key and not Shift+Del.

4. Press Shift+Ins.

Copying for pasting

Sometimes you want to have your cake and eat it too. In point of fact, we all want to have our cake, eat it, and not gain any weight — but that's another story.

In this case, we're talking about the magical key combination that puts highlighted text in the Scrap, *without* deleting it from the document.

1. Highlight the text you want to copy and paste.

2. Press Ctrl+Ins.

   This puts a copy of the highlighted text in the Scrap.

3. Move the cursor to where you want the text to appear.

4. Press Shift+Ins.

You can Shift+Ins repeatedly, if you want many copies of whatever's in the Scrap. Why would you want many copies? Well, suppose that you had drawn a line of hyphens across the screen as the first step in creating some sort of a form. If you cut and paste and paste and paste and paste the line of hyphens, you pretty quickly will have enough lines for your form.

Cutting and pasting between two documents

This sounds like a complicated, advanced feature, but actually cutting and pasting between two documents is almost *exactly* the same as cutting and pasting within one document. The only difference is when you travel to the location where the text is to be inserted.

1. Highlight the text you want to cut and paste.

2. Press Shift+Del.

3. Press Alt+**File** ⇨ **O**pen to open the file where you want to paste the text.

   Alternatively, you can use any of the techniques described in Chapter 3 to move between currently open windows and so on.

4. Go to the place in the file where you want to deposit the text.

5. Press Shift+Ins.

   ✔ The Scrap is common to all documents. There is only one Scrap. No matter what file you're in, whatever is in the Scrap can be retrieved with Shift+Ins.

   ✔ If a paragraph — or more — is highlighted and you want the paragraph to keep its formatting when it's pasted, be sure that the highlight covers the *hidden paragraph symbol* at the end of each paragraph, which is where the formatting instructions are kept (see Figure 4-5).

   ✔ Press Alt+Backspace to undo the paste if you make a boo boo.

If you're pining for the way Word 5 deleted and inserted, you can make Word 6 bring back the good old days by pressing Alt+**View** ⇨ **Preferences** ⇨ **Customize**. Just make sure that the Use **INS** for Overtype Key box is unchecked. Then press Enter. From that point forward: Del deletes to the Scrap, Ins inserts from the Scrap, and Shift+Del deletes without disturbing the contents of the Scrap — just like in Version 5.

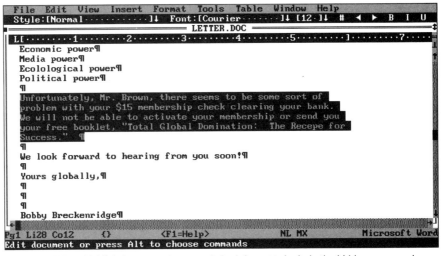

File Edit View Insert Format Tools Table Window Help
Style:[Normal···········]↓ Font:[Courier·······]↓ [12·]↓ # ◄ ► B I U
═══════════════════════ LETTER.DOC ═══════════════
L[····1·········2·········3·········4·········5·······]··········7····
    Economic power¶
    Media power¶
    Ecological power¶
    Political power¶
    ¶
    Unfortunately, Mr. Brown, there seems to be some sort of
    problem with your $15 membership check clearing your bank.
    We will not be able to activate your membership or send you
    your free booklet, "Total Global Domination: The Recepe for
    Success." ¶
    ¶
    We look forward to hearing from you soon!¶
    ¶
    Yours globally,¶
    ¶
    ¶
    ¶
    Bobby Breckenridge¶
Pg1 Li28 Co12   {}   <F1=Help>   NL MX   Microsoft Word
Edit document or press Alt to choose commands

Figure 4-5: When highlighting text to be moved, don't forget to include the hidden paragraph symbol, or the text will lose its formatting when you paste it.

Cut and paste big time

Sometimes you may be consumed with the burning desire to pour the entire contents of one file into the current file. You can save yourself a lot of cut-and-paste steps by using the Insert command instead.

1. Place the cursor where you want the inserted text to appear.

2. Press Alt+Insert ⇨ File.

3. Type the full name of the file you want to insert.

Be sure to include the **.DOC** at the end of the file name. If you don't include **DOC**, Word says the file doesn't exist.

4. Press Enter.

There are many uses for Alt+Insert ⇨ File. For example, if part of your job is to create contracts or reports that have certain sections that repeat from contract to contract, you can keep those standard sections (called *boilerplate text*) in their own separate files. Then, when it comes time to build your report or contract, you can insert the stock paragraphs into the document as needed.

Dragging and Dropping

"Dragging and Dropping" sounds like the first symptoms of some awful disease — or what to do in the case of nuclear attack. But it is actually a Windows command brought over to DOS. And it is wonderful. The only bad news about Drag and Drop is that it works only with a mouse.

With Drag and Drop, you can move highlighted text by pointing with the mouse. After you've used it a few times, you'll wonder how you ever got along without it. Follow these steps:

1. Highlight the text (with the mouse or the keyboard) you want to move.

2. Point to any place inside the highlight and press — and do not release — the left mouse ear.

   When you press the left mouse ear while in the highlighted text, a square appears next to the mouse pointer and a small underline near the tip of the mouse cursor begins flashing. (If your mouse cursor normally looks like a rectangle, it'll just start flashing like crazy.)

3. Move the mouse to the text's new home.

   Position the *flashing underline* where you want the text to appear.

4. Release the left mouse ear.

   The text appears instantly!

   ✔ If you didn't hit the bull's-eye, press Alt+Backspace to undo it and try again.

   ✔ If you want to drag a copy of the highlighted text, use Ctrl+left mouse ear in Step 2.

Editing Etiquette

Eventually, you'll want to add some smooth moves to your editing techniques. Following are some good places to start.

Deleting surgically

Just like surgical bombing, be precise when you highlight material to be deleted. If, for example, you want to remove *Monday* and type in *Tuesday* — just delete the *Mon* in *Monday* — you'll need the *day* for *Tuesday*. Why retype what's already there? Besides, if you save enough keystrokes, you'll get a free decoder ring!

Moving backward with the cursor

Don't use Backspace to move backward unless you need to wipe out everything in your path. Instead, use the peaceful, gentle arrow keys to get to the word you need to delete or correct. And remember, pressing Ctrl+left arrow and Ctrl+right arrow leapfrogs a whole word at a time. After making corrections, press End to zoom back to the end of the line, where you can continue typing.

Wrapping with the cursor

Here's a neat trick — with the cursor at the beginning of a line, left arrow moves the cursor to the end of the *preceding* line. Try it. It's another one of those moves that you may not think of because you were brainwashed in typewriter thinking.

Joining and separating paragraphs

As you're revising your document, you may want to meld or separate two paragraphs. As discussed in Chapter 2, it's the presence of the paragraph symbol (that is, where you pressed Enter) that separates two paragraphs. It's the lack of the paragraph symbol that brings them back together — not years of counseling. However, you don't have to understand how it works as long as you can follow these instructions:

Breaking one paragraph into two

1. Put the cursor on the first letter of the word that will be the first word in the new paragraph.
2. Press Enter twice.

Merging two paragraphs

1. Put the cursor at the very end of the first paragraph.
2. Press Del until the first letter of the second paragraph sits under the cursor.

Making extra space at the top

Suppose that you want to add text (like a title) to the top of a document you have typed. The logical — and correct — first move is to get the cursor to the top of the document. However, no matter what you do, you can't move higher than the current top of the document. How the devil do you get the cursor above that text?

As it turns out, the question is really, "How do you get the current text *lower*?" The answer is to press Enter a few times to shove the current text down. That'll create the space at the top.

Using Overtype

There are two ways you can tell that Overtype is turned on: Your text and formatting starts disappearing as you type, and the status bar says OT. In general, it's safer to leave this feature turned off. If it has been turned on, turn it off by pressing Ins (the OT goes away).

Generally, Overtype gets turned on accidentally during a cut-and-paste procedure when, instead of pressing Shift+Ins, you accidentally press just Ins. You see, when Overtype is off, pressing Ins turns Overtype on. And, when Overtype is on, pressing Ins turns it off. Ins is, basically, the light switch of Overtype.

Typing Replaces Selection

Using this feature saves you an extra keystroke every time you want to delete text. It can be very handy, or it can make you crazy. You decide.

Here's the way it works.

1. Highlight the text you want to delete.

2. Start typing replacement text.

   The moment you start typing, the highlighted text is deleted and the new stuff appears in its place.

This is a feature that is so completely nontypewriter that you'll have to try it a few times before deciding whether it's for you.

> ✔ Typing **R**eplaces Selection can get you into serious voodoo if you forget you have highlighted text and blithely start typing away. For example, if you've highlighted some text for formatting and then start typing, you'll nuke the highlighted text. An immediate Alt+Backspace could save the day. However, if you find yourself in a panic every few minutes because of disappearing text, you'll want to turn off this feature.

To turn off Typing **R**eplaces Selection, follow these steps:

1. Press Alt+**V**iew ➪ **P**references ➪ **C**ustomize.

2. In the Customize dialog box, make sure that Typing **R**eplaces Selection is not checked.

3. Press Enter.

Changing upper- and lowercase

Did you know that Word can instantly change the capitalization status of a word? If you want to capitalize a word, you don't have to retype!

1. Highlight the word (or words) to be transformed.

2. Press Shift+F3.

    Shift+F3 is a *rotary key*. It toggles your text from all lowercase, to all upper-case, to initial cap (first letter capitalized). Keep pressing Shift+F3 until you get what you want.

Saving often

Okay, saving isn't an editing technique, per se. But what's the point of editing and refining if you're not saving often? Aw, c'mon, press Shift+F12 (or Alt+**File** ⇨ **S**ave) every now and then. You don't want to end up on America's Most Wanted — another tragic case of a person pushed over the edge by failure-to-save syndrome!

Chapter 5

Saving — The Road to Salvation

*R*emember that old adage (I guess there's no such thing as a "new adage"): "You can never be too rich, too thin, or save a file too often?"

Well, the greed decade is over (or so they say) and we now know that you *can* get too thin — so the only aspect of that old adage to stand the test of time is the bit about the importance of saving often.

I have never heard of someone having a disaster because of saving too often. On the other hand, I'm creating a soap opera based on the pain and tragedy of those who didn't save often enough.

Saving is critical because what's on the screen exists only as long as electricity is reaching the computer. If there is an interruption in the flow of power — poof! — your work has begun its journey to Alpha Centauri.

How often, exactly, should you save? Probably every two or three minutes. The real question is, How much do you want to lose? Two minutes of work? Ten minutes? An hour? What's the work worth to you? Or to your boss? Or to your lifestyle? After you've got that figured out, let your conscience be your guide.

Making Sure That There's Room for More

Whenever you save a file, you have assumed that there's room on the hard disk for what you're saving. Mostly, that assumption is valid. Eventually, however, it may not be. The space on a hard disk is finite and, if you're extremely productive, you may actually push the envelope on space. Get in the habit of double-checking every now and then (once a month) to make sure that your disk space isn't getting tight. Here's how:

1. Press Alt+File ⇨ MS-DOS Commands.

2. Type **dir** in the MS-DOS Commands dialog box and then press Enter.

3. After the scrolling stuff comes to a rest, look *above* where it says:

```
Press a key to resume Word
```

A line of text indicates how many "bytes free" you have.

✓ If the number is greater than one million (1000000), you're okay. However, if last month you had ten million bytes free and this month you have two million free, don't think you're safe because you're still above the one million mark. Think of the hard disk as a gas tank: Last week you had ten gallons of gas. During the week, you used eight. You now have two gallons of gas left. Do you think those two gallons will last you another week? Probably not.

✓ If the number is less than one million, it's time to do some serious housekeeping. If you're the one responsible for the care and feeding of your computer, see the section "Getting Rid of Unneeded Files" in Chapter 13. If it's not your responsibility, let your computer person deal with it while you have a cup of coffee.

4. Oh, yeah, be sure to press a key to return to the normal Word screen.

Saving One Measly Document

Actually, saving the active document is very simple. In fact, there's only one step:

1. Press Alt+File ⇨ **S**ave.

That's it. You don't even have to press Enter.

After you enter the Save command, the message bar tells you that Word is saving your file:

```
Saving C:\WORD\YOURFILE.DOC
```

You can't do any work on your document until Word is finished saving. You'll know it's finished when you see something like:

```
C:\WORD\YOURFILE.DOC 3542 characters
```

You're free to go back to work when the word Saving no longer appears in the message bar and, as a no-cost, fun bonus, Word has tossed in some tantalizing info about how many letters and numbers are in your document. Party.

Naturally, because saving is so important, Microsoft decided to assign an impossible-to-reach shortcut key combination: Shift+F12. The best approach, if you want to use this so-called shortcut to save, is to hold down the Shift key with your left hand and press F12 with the right.

Version 6's **File/Save** command is equal to Version 5's Transfer/Save command.

Saving all documents

If you're the type of animal who works with lots of files at the same time, Word provides a super way to save *everything* that hasn't been saved, faster than a speeding bullet and in a single bound.

1. Press Alt+File ➪ Sav**e** All.

The message bar keeps you posted as Word goes through all the unsaved documents (including things we haven't even talked about yet, like style sheets, macros, and glossaries), grimly saving them all, regardless of whether they want to be saved. Hallelujah!

Again, after the message bar doesn't say Saving anymore, you can get back to work.

Using Autosave

Autosave is one of those features that seems like a fabulous idea. Until you find out what it really does.

Let's start at the beginning. What is Autosave? Autosave is an option that enables you to set Word to automatically save your file every few minutes or so. Sounds great, huh? Well, not exactly. You see, when Autosave saves, it's not really saving. I know it doesn't make sense, but it's the truth! I swear! All Autosave does is make a file that Word can use to recover from a disaster. You still have to save as you normally do.

Why use Autosave if it doesn't really save? If you're very bad about saving, then any kind of saving, even wimpy fake saving, is better than nothing. If you normally go 10 minutes or longer between saves, then turn this thing on. Minimally, it'll remind you to save for real. And it may even help out if you have a disaster and haven't saved lately.

To turn on Autosave and set it to 10 minutes:

1. Press Alt+**View** ➪ **Preferences** ➪ **Customize**.

2. Type **10** and press Enter.

From now on, every 10 minutes, you'll see the message bar flashing that your file is being Autosaved. That means it's time for you to press Alt+**File** ➪ **Save**.

When Autosave's timer says it's time to save but finds that you're merrily typing away, it'll politely wait until you've finished your thought before saving.

Saving As...

You may have bypassed the Save As command in the File menu. It's not as boring as it looks. There are four scenarios in which you'll see the Save As dialog box (see Figure 5-1).

Saving a new file

Whenever you save a file for the first time, Word pops up the Save As dialog box and simply insists that you give the file a proper name. After all, it can't be called Document1 forever! What would the neighbors say?

To make Word happy, you need to type a file name that is no longer than eight letters or numbers and has no spaces. Then press Enter. That's enough to satisfy Word. This is one of those great situations where, even if you accidentally type a space or something, Word'll just pop up another dialog box to tell you that `The filename or path is not valid`. Press Enter and try again. Try often.

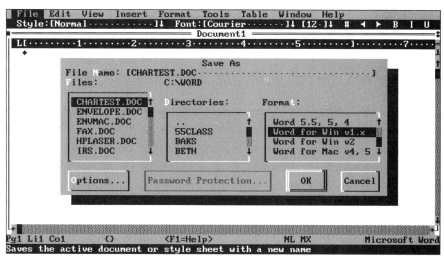

Figure 5-1: The Save As dialog box lets you clone files with new names, create Macintosh files, and password-protect your documents.

If you type a file name and Word asks, `Do you want to overwrite the existing file?`, Word is warning you that the "new" file name you just typed isn't as original as you thought. In fact, it's the same as another file name that's already on the hard disk. "Overwriting a file" is French for "erasing the file." Unless you know what you're doing, you should just say No and give the file a different file name.

File-naming convention

This isn't the sort of convention that takes place in Atlantic City. This convention is where we get together to put forth the basic rules for naming files.

First, a file name consists of up to eight letters or numbers, a period, then up to three more letters or numbers. Here are some examples of file names that fit into the pattern:

WHATSUP.DOC

DAFFY

A1.DOC

When you're naming a new file in Word, however, all you have to do is come up with the first eight letters or numbers (and that's *up to* eight letters; you can have fewer, if you want).

Word handles the period and the last three letters for you. That way, Word can consistently use certain file name endings to identify which file is what, such as the following:

DOC	Document file
GLY	Glossary file
STY	Style sheet
CMP	Dictionary

After you've successfully named and saved the file, you'll see its new file name up there in the title bar.

Saving an old file with a new name

Here's another one of those issues that sparks someone to ask, "Why would I want to save a file with a different name?"

There are a couple of reasons why you might want to do this:

✔ You have a letter named BOB.DOC that is, basically, the same letter you want to send to Susan, with a few minor alterations. Just load BOB.DOC and immediately Save As SUSAN.DOC. You'll still have BOB.DOC, and now you can make your changes to SUSAN.DOC and send it out.

✔ You are working on a report and you want to make revisions to the file, yet keep a record of the report before any revisions are made. The file is called REPORT.DOC. Now you can Save As REPORT2.DOC and have both copies.

Get the idea?

Here's how to do it.

1. Press Alt+**File** ➪ Save **As**.

2. In the Save As dialog box, just type the new file name and press Enter.

   If you make an error while typing the file name, press Backspace to erase and the left- and right-arrow keys to move around.

Saving a file with a new name leaves you with two files with different names. Renaming a file with File Management (introduced in Chapter 10), gives you one file with one new name.

Saving a file for another word processor

Sharing files between computers and word processors is so important that I gave it its very own chapter. Chapter 16 even tells you how (with an additional piece of software) you can get a PC to use a Macintosh disk!

However, if you just want to know the command to save your file as a Word for Windows file or as a Word for Macintosh file, with none of the frills, this is how to do it:

1. Press Alt+**File** ➪ Save **As** to get into the Save As dialog box.

2. Type a new file name for the Macintosh file.

   It's always a good idea to keep your original Word file intact.

3. Press Alt+Forma**t** and then use the up- and down-arrow keys to highlight the file format you want.

4. Press Enter.

The message bar tells you that Word is saving the file with the new file name. It usually takes longer to save the file in a new file format.

Version 6's Save **As** ⇨ Forma**t** is an expanded version of Word 5's Transfer/ Save/Format.

Saving a file with a password

Finally, you can safeguard sensitive files with password protection. Whenever a file has been secured with a password, only those who know the password are allowed access.

To save the current file with a password, do the following:

1. Press Alt+**File** ⇨ Save **As** to get into the Save As dialog box.

2. Press Alt+**P**assword Protection.

3. Type a password and press Enter.

Whatever you type appears only as dots on the screen (see Figure 5-2).

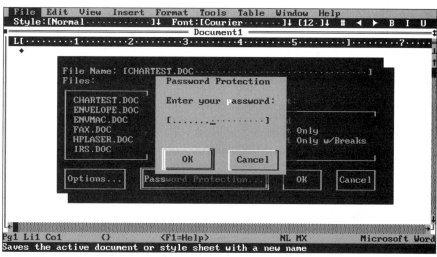

Figure 5-2: And the password is ... a bunch of dots? No, it's additional security so that no one can see what you're typing.

4. Type the same password a second time and press Enter.

Word has you type the password twice to make sure that the first time didn't contain a typo.

5. Press Enter in the Save As dialog box.

Word saves the file.

The next time you try to open that file, scan the file, or *anything* the file, Word demands the password. If you don't have the password, you don't get the file.

- ✔ If you later decide you want a new password, follow the same procedure used to password protect the file in the first place, except type a *new* password when prompted to type the password.

- ✔ If you want to unprotect the file, you can remove the password by again following the same procedure used to protect the file, but this time press Del when prompted for a password.

After you've password-protected a file, you cannot get into it without the password. Period. If you forget or lose the password — well, see the icon next to this paragraph? You get the idea.

When not to save a file

Always save your file, right? Well, not exactly.

As mentioned at the head of this chapter, not saving causes you to lose your work since the last save. But now I'll show you how losing can help you win. If, for example, you delete something major and can't bring it back, closing the file without saving restores the thing you deleted ... as long as your last save included that text. If you perform a disastrous search and replace and can't undo it, close the file without saving to restore its pre-search-and-replace condition (that's why we always save before a search and replace). And closing without saving can rescue you from the latest way to get into trouble — clumsy use of Typing **R**eplaces Selection may wipe out what you wanted to keep.

In short, anytime you've completely messed up the file, close without saving to put the file back the way it was in the last save operation. Saving often gives you a painless fall-back position so that you won't lose much if you do have to close without saving.

Heeding the **SAVE** *Warning*

Every now and then, you may see the SAVE warning appear in the status bar where <F1=Help> normally resides. When you see this message, save the file and quit Word. Don't try to type "one more thing."

The SAVE warning is Word telling you that it's about to crash. Just save, exit, and duck and cover.

Even if you save and the SAVE light goes out, exit Word anyway.

Quitting gives Word a chance to completely reset itself. Then you can get back into Word and continue working — unless you're working with a huge file.

The definition of what is, exactly, a "huge file" is a slippery thing because huge-ness is relative to *your* computer system. A safe size limit, one that is safe on any system, is to keep a single file to no more than 100 pages.

If you have a newer model computer with lots of RAM, you can pretty much do whatever you want. If you don't know how new your computer is or if you think RAM is a male sheep, keep your file to 100 pages. One way you know your file is too big is if you avoid saving because the process takes so long. Files should be short and snappy.

As you work with Word, it's constantly shuffling your text from a temporary file — a *buffer* — on the hard disk into the computer's memory. If you work for a long time, especially with big files or memory-intensive activities (like search and replace or mail merge), the buffer file eventually gets backed up like bad plumbing. When that happens, Word thinks it's out of memory and starts flashing SAVE. Even though you save the file, the flashing SAVE immediately returns because saving doesn't clear out the buffer. Only quitting Word gives the program a chance to reset itself. Isn't that special?

Chapter 6
Getting It Write

. . . .

. . . .

*W*ith the addition of the new and improved Grammatik grammar checker, Word provides a complete first-aid package for your prose. However, even if you've got the best spelling checker or the best grammar checker — or even if you've got Chubby Checker — *nothing* replaces human proofreading. For example, the phrase "Someday my price will come" will pass any checking system with flying colors. Unfortunately, the phrase should have read, "Someday my *prince* will come." What a difference an *n* makes.

Thinking with the Thesaurus

What transforms a mere idea into an outstanding concept? A thesaurus. Word's thesaurus can help bridge the gap between what's in your head and how you express yourself on paper.

Summoning the genie in the thesaurus is incredibly easy:

1. Put the cursor anywhere in the word you want to look up.

2. Press Shift+F7.

    This is going to be one of those function keys you actually remember. Put it on a Post-it Note and tack it to your computer.

    You'll get the Thesaurus dialog box (see Figure 6-1). The Definitions list box on the left reveals the various definitions of your highlighted word.

3. In the Definitions list box, highlight the definition you meant, and its synonyms appear in the box on the right.

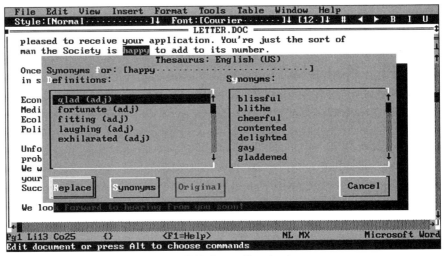

Figure 6-1: New words for old — press Shift+F7 to call up the thesaurus.

> ✔ As usual, press Tab or Alt+boldfaced letter to move between boxes, and use the arrow keys to highlight the word of your choice.
>
> ✔ Sometimes, if the word you're looking up is plural or past tense, Word may ask if the singular, present tense word is what you mean. For example, select *putting*, and the thesaurus asks whether you mean *put*. If *put* is "close enough," highlight it and press Alt+**S**ynonyms.
>
> ✔ If you don't get the dialog box in Figure 6-1, that means your word (as it's currently spelled) isn't in the thesaurus list. The consolation prize is the dialog box in Figure 6-2. At this point, either type a new word or, if you find your word on that list, highlight the word and press Enter to look up that word. Pressing Esc cancels the thesaurus operation.

4. Highlight the new word.

   Any highlighted word can be the basis for a new thesaurus search — Alt+**S**ynonyms. If you want to look up *puppy*, highlight it and then press Alt+**S**. Keep looking until you find what you want, and then highlight the word.

5. Press Enter.

   The highlighted word in the thesaurus replaces the word you looked up in your document.

> ✔ At any stage of the process, press Esc to cancel the operation.
>
> ✔ If you replace a word and then realize the error of your ways, you can always press Alt+Backspace (or Alt+**E**dit ➪ **U**ndo) to change the last thing you did.

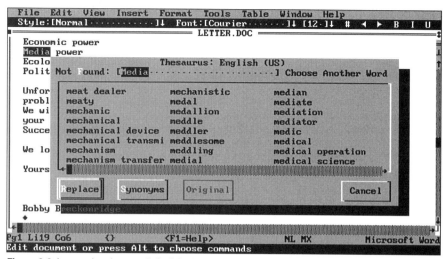

File Edit View Insert Format Tools Table Window Help
Style:[Normal············]↧ Font:[Courier······]↧ [12·]↧ # ◄ ► B I U
═══════════════════════════ LETTER.DOC ═══════════════════
Economic power
Media power
Ecolo   Thesaurus: English (US)
Polit Not Found: [Media················] Choose Another Word

Unfor   meat dealer   mechanistic   median
probl   meaty   medal   mediate
We wi   mechanic   medallion   mediation
your   mechanical   meddle   mediator
Succe   mechanical device meddler   medic
        mechanical transmi meddlesome   medical
We lo   mechanism   meddling   medical operation
        mechanism transfer medial   medical science
Yours

        [Replace] [Synonyms] [Original]   [Cancel]

Bobby Breckenridge

Pg1 Li19 Co6   {}   <F1=Help>   NL MX   Microsoft Word
Edit document or press Alt to choose commands

Figure 6-2: Interesting that *media* isn't in the thesaurus, but *meat dealer* is. Aren't they synonyms?

If you're not sure of the meaning of a word, look it up in the thesaurus. The synonyms can give you a pretty decent definition of your word.

After you start using the thesaurus, don't go overboard with fancy words. The point of the thesaurus is to make your writing more precise and interesting — not to turn your documents into vocabulary tests for your readers.

In Version 5, the thesaurus key was Ctrl+F6. Now it's Shift+F7. Just write it down, and you'll eventually get used to the new command.

Checking Out the Speller

Word's spelling checker compares your words with the words in its massive word list. When the spelling checker encounters a word in your document that doesn't match the list, a dialog box pops up and asks you to explain yourself. Basically, you can correct the word, leave the word alone, or add the word to the spelling checker's dictionary.

While it's checking your spelling, Word is also on the lookout for violations of basic capitalization and punctuation rules as well as double-word errors — when you typed the the same word twice. That kind of error can happen to the best of us.

Let's see how a basic spelling check session works:

1. Press F7.

   Get out another Post-It Note — we're starting another command with a function key. This is almost the last function key you need to memorize. Just think of F7 as the "word" key. F7 is the spelling checker and Shift+F7 is the thesaurus. The nonfunction-key approach to spell checking is Alt+**T**ools ⇨ **S**pelling (Thesaurus is in the Tools menu, too) — which is fairly clunky.

   After you press F7, the message bar says Loading dictionary, and Word starts searching from the cursor's position on down through the document for evil words and shameful punctuation.

   You'll get the Spelling dialog box (see Figure 6-3).

   Word already will have highlighted a suggested replacement for your word. In Figure 6-3, Word is suggesting we take out *Recepe* and replace it with *Recipe*. An excellent suggestion!

2. If you like Word's suggested change, press Enter.

   Pressing Enter tells Word to make the change and then continue the hunt for more bad words.

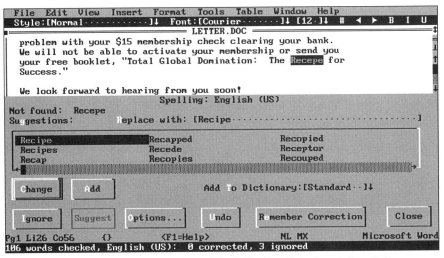

Figure 6-3: Press F7, and eventually you'll see Word's Spelling dialog box. Quite a thrill.

3. If you don't like Word's suggested change, here's what you can do about it (pick one):

   ✔ Move the cursor in the word list box, select the word you want, and press Enter.

   ✔ If you want to type a new word yourself, press Alt+**R**eplace With and, after typing the new word, press Enter.

   ✔ If Word is flagging a word that is correct, but just not in Word's vocabulary, press Alt+**I**gnore — no need to press Enter.

   ✔ If it's a correct — but odd — word that is used often (like your name), you may want to add it to Word's dictionary so that Word won't yell at you every time you spell check a document. To add the current word to the Standard dictionary, press Alt+**A**dd — no need to press Enter. Don't be shy about adding words to the dictionary; that's what it's there for.

4. If you make a mistake, press Alt+Undo.

   You can undo the last correction by pressing Alt+Undo. You'll be taken back to the previous dialog box and given the chance to make the correct choice.

You can run the spelling checker on a single word, sentence, paragraph, or any size block of text by highlighting the text first and then running the spelling checker. Word then processes only the selected text. This way, you don't have to check the whole document every time.

✔ The spelling check begins from the current position of the cursor and searches downward through the document. After reaching the end of the document, a dialog box pops up, asking whether you want to start from the very beginning.

✔ You can halt the spelling check process by pressing Esc.

✔ You can revoke an entire spelling check session by pressing Alt+Backspace (Undo).

When you have made a decision about a word and pressed Enter, it may look like nothing is happening. Do not assume that the first Enter didn't "take" and press Enter again. Put your hands in your lap and watch the message bar. If it says Checking document, everything is on track — Word is looking for the next error. Word makes the correction to the current word just before the *next* mismatched word appears. If you press Enter while Word is checking the document, Word applies those Enters to future word choices — you'll be accepting, in advance, some changes you may not want.

If you have a section of text with tons of technical terms or proper names or whatever that you know won't be in Microsoft's business English dictionary, you can tell Word in advance to "ignore" that region of text. All you have to do is highlight the text whose spelling you don't want to check, press Alt+Format ⇨ Language, select (no proofing), and press Enter. Use this only if you don't want to add these words to the dictionary. To turn off the "ignore" command, just press Alt+Format ⇨ Language, select English (US), and press Enter.

Customizing dictionaries

When you add words to the dictionary, they generally go into what's known as the Standard dictionary (catchy name, no?). However, endlessly adding words to the Standard dictionary eventually starts to slow down your spelling check. As an option, you can create a series of modular-type dictionaries to plug into various documents as needed. This method works well when your work is divided up into various projects, each requiring a special set of names and jargon. When the project is over, you can deep-six the dictionary.

The different kinds of dictionaries Word employs are outlined in Table 6-1.

Table 6-1	Word Dictionaries	
Dictionary Name	*File Name*	*When Applied*
Standard	SPELL-AM.LEX	Always used
User	SPECIALS.CMP	Always used, unless different user dictionary is chosen
Document	FILENAME.CMP	Used only with one particular document; created by user

You can select which dictionary receives your added words by going to the Add To Dictionary box and selecting from Standard, User, or Document.

✔ Use the User dictionary when you're working on a project that spans a number of documents and the project-specific terminology will never be used again after the project is over.

You can give your user dictionary a name other than SPECIALS.CMP by going into the Spelling Options dialog box. In Figure 6-4, you can see that the User Dictionary specified is DUMMIES.CMP. Guess what project I used that dictionary for?

✔ Use the Document dictionary only when the words are specific to the current document.

Forgetting about "Remember"

Warning: Remember Correction is *not* the same thing as "add to the dictionary." Whenever a change is Remembered, Word will — forever after — carry out that correction in every document *without asking you first*. It's like a permanent search and replace. In contrast, when you add a word to the dictionary, Word still asks you how to handle the word.

And, Word is more stubborn than any elephant when it comes to making it stop Remembering. To unremember requires editing or deleting the REMEM-AM.COR file, which can get pretty ugly. The safest approach is not to use this feature unless you really need it.

Changing options

You can make a few minor modifications to the spelling check process. Use Alt+Options from the Spelling dialog box to summon up Figure 6-4, the Spelling Options dialog box. You can turn off the punctuation checking if you want.

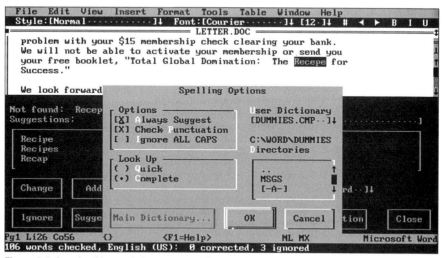

Figure 6-4: A techy thing to do is to use your Spelling Options to change the dictionary.

Also, the Look Up option lets you specify how much spelling help you need. If you're a know it all, select **Q**uick. Word assumes that you've got the first two

Parlez vous français? Sprechen Sie Deutsch?

In previous versions of Word, you could buy and install a foreign language dictionary — though I suppose that if you're from France, people in the U.S. are in the foreign country, but let's move on — and you still can with Word 6.

What's new in Word 6 is that if you do own a foreign language dictionary, you now can tell Word to use that dictionary on specific words or areas in the document instead of the English dictionary. To do this, just:

1. Highlight the word or words in the foreign language.

2. Press Alt+Format ➪ Language.

3. Highlight the language in which the text is to be formatted.

4. Press Enter.

letters right and runs the check on that basis. You get a faster response. The Complete look up assumes nothing — even providing phonetic words when appropriate.

In Version 5 the spelling check command was Alt+F6. Now it's plain old F7.

The Galloping Grammar Checker

Can you believe it — a separate manual for Grammatik, the grammar checker? Just breathe deeply into a paper bag while I explain why.

First of all, I promise you don't have to read the manual to use the grammar checker. Better?

One of the reasons they gave you a special manual for the grammar checker is because, unlike Word's spelling checker and thesaurus, the grammar checker is a separate program. It's not built into Word. You can use Grammatik with — you should pardon the expression — *other* word processing programs. In fact, if you don't use the grammar checker, you can even delete it from your hard disk.

But you probably won't want to.

The grammar checker, in addition to looking for split infinitives and that sort of stuff you forgot the moment the test was over, also has a spelling checker that's a bit smarter than Word's (but you can't just check one paragraph; it's all or nothing). You can edit your document while in Grammatik and make corrections based on its suggestions.

If you go completely nuts, you can even check your document's "readability" score — where it falls between a life insurance policy and a Hemingway short story, for example.

As Grammatik checks your document, suggesting changes and quoting rules, you'll find that it occasionally gives you really lame advice. Remember, Grammatik cannot read your material for sense. It can only compare the structure of your words with the rules set forth in its programming. It does an impressive job, though, and I think you'll find it invaluable.

Invoking Grammatik from within Word

Even though Grammatik is an independent program, they figured out a way to make it seem as though it's just another component of Word. All you have to do is remember to use a different command to start Word — and here's how:

1. Start both Word and Grammatik by typing **GMKWP** and pressing Enter.

   As near as I can figure, this alphabet-soup command means "**Gram**matik **W**ord **P**rocessor." Anyway, by typing **GMKWP**, you get the normal Word screen, just as though you had started Word the same old boring way.

2. When you're ready to do a grammar check, press Alt+**Grammatik**.

   Don't use Alt+G unless you're looking at the file you want to check.

   The Save As dialog box appears.

3. Press Enter.

   Clicking OK with the mouse does not work. If you click OK, the Save As dialog box goes away and nothing more happens — until you exit Word. Upon exiting, however, Grammatik suddenly starts up. When I was in the computer business, we usually referred to these types of screw-ups as "features."

4. Press I, for Interactive, after you get the Grammatik opening screen (see Figure 6-5).

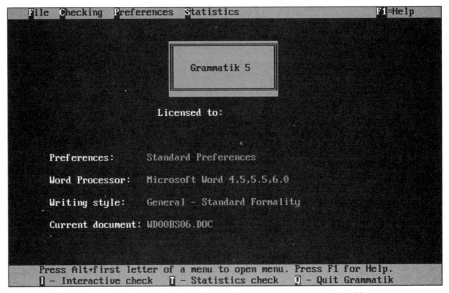

┌───┐
│ **F**ile **C**hecking **P**references **S**tatistics   **F1**=Help │
│   │
│   ┌──────────────────────────┐   │
│   │   │   │
│   │   Grammatik 5   │   │
│   │   │   │
│   └──────────────────────────┘   │
│   │
│   Licensed to: │
│   │
│   │
│   Preferences: Standard Preferences   │
│   │
│   Word Processor: Microsoft Word 4,5,5.5,6.0   │
│   │
│   Writing style: General - Standard Formality   │
│   │
│   Current document: WD00BS06.DOC   │
│   │
│   │
│   Press Alt+first letter of a menu to open menu. Press F1 for Help. │
│   **I** - Interactive check   **S** - Statistics check   **Q** - Quit Grammatik │
└───┘

Figure 6-5: The Grammatik opening screen. Typing **I** starts the grammar-checking process — typing **Q** lets you skedaddle back to Word.

The other way to invoke Grammatik is to go to the directory that contains your document files. Then type **GMK** and press Enter at the DOS prompt. When you get the opening screen, press I, and you receive a list of files to check. Highlight the desired file and press Enter.

Using Grammatik

After you've engaged the Interactive command, the screen splits, as shown in Figure 6-6. On the top is your text — the offending part highlighted. On the bottom, Grammatik explains why it stopped you and offers some suggestions.

After a problem is displayed, it's up to you to decide what to do.

With each new problem, an appropriate set of function keys appears at the bottom of the screen. I'm not going to list every conceivable function key that appears under every conceivable situation. However, here are the ones that'll get you going:

F10: *Next problem*. Tells Grammatik to ignore this problem — leave it alone — and go to the next problem.

Problem

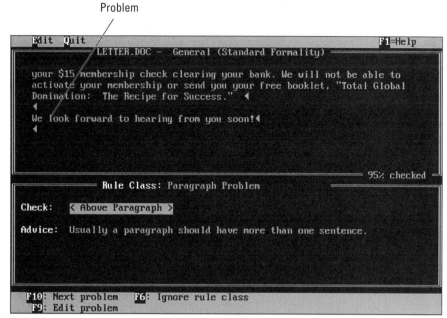

Figure 6-6: Your text is on top, Grammatik's complaints below. Use the function keys to move on or make changes.

F9: *Edit problem.* Puts the cursor in the text on the top screen. You can reword your text to fix the problem.

F6: *Ignore rule class.* Whenever Grammatik finds an error, it also rubs salt into the wound by telling you exactly what rule you're trouncing on. If you disagree with a particular rule, you can just turn it off with F6. That means the rule will not be used for the rest of the document.

When you end the session, if you've turned off a rule, Grammatik asks whether you want to keep the rule turned off on a permanent basis. If you say yes, you are launched down a road of various options to create a custom Writing Style. If this makes your hair stand on end, say no.

F3: *Replace/Next.* Take the Replacement suggestion and actually stick it in your document. Then go on to the next problem.

Exiting Grammatik

After going through the entire grammar-checking process, you get the chance to save and exit. You are returned to the main opening screen, where you can **Quit**.

Occasionally, however, you may want to stop the grammar check before you reach the end. To stop in the middle of a session:

1. Press Esc to exit and save.

2. Before you can exit, Grammatik wants to know:

```
Quit now, save work so far?
```

Your answer is Y.

3. The next million dollar question is

```
Save changes to this document?
```

All you have to do is press Enter.

If this isn't the first time you've checked this file, you also are asked whether you want to

```
Overwrite a previously saved backup?
```

You do, so press Enter.

If, however, you want to quit and not save the work you've done (maybe you realize something has been changed that you now regret):

1. Press Ctrl+C to exit and not save.

2. Grammatik asks, in an astonished tone:

```
Cancel checking and quit?
```

Press Y.

If you want to quit, but are planning to come back later to finish, you'll be glad to know you don't have to process — again — the material you've just gone through. You can place a "bookmark" in your document, which Grammatik will use as its start-up point when you work with the file again.

1. While in a grammar checking session, press B.

This stands for Bookmark. Grammatik asks you to save and such, as in a normal exit.

When you return later to finish work on the file, don't use the Interactive command to start the grammar checking. Press R to **R**esume.

Using other features

If you want some cheap thrills, when you get to Grammatik's main screen:

Press T   To display how many sentences, on average, are in each of your document's paragraphs, and more.

Press N   To compare your work to Hemingway and the dreaded life insurance policy — in terms of readability.

If you want to explore other options in Grammatik, you'll find the program to be comparatively friendly. Alt+boldfaced letters reveal the drop-down menus. Go exploring if you like.

Chapter 7

Formatting, Fonts, and Other Things That Go Bump in the Night

* *

In This Chapter

▶ Formatting text

▶ Aligning paragraphs

▶ Putting in page numbers

▶ Changing the margins

▶ Building Tabs

▶ Constructing headers and footers

▶ Formatting for three columns

▶ Getting what you're seeing

▶ Giving your pages a break

▶ Parting tips

* *

Focussing on Formatting

Formatting is the art of getting the material on the screen to look just right — and getting a printout to match.

Like any other art form, however, practice makes perfect. After all, it's a bit unrealistic to expect to wake up one morning and paint the Mona Lisa — unless, I suppose, you were Leonardo da Vinci in a previous life.

So, this chapter starts out with some basic connect-the-dot skills and builds toward Sistine Chapel-type efforts. You can bail out whenever you want — but come back later if and when you need to learn more.

Formatting etiquette

Before we start — just in case you've never met some of these terms before — formal introductions are in order. This is merely a get-acquainted moment — a mixer, if you will. We'll learn more about the behavior of each of these *objets d'formatting* in the pages that follow.

Character: In word processing, a *character* refers to a single letter, number, or symbol. When underlining and boldfacing and stuff like that, you're *formatting characters*.

Tabs: So far, we've used Tabs to move from item to item in a dialog box. Now we'll finally put Tabs to the use nature intended: moving the cursor forward a chunk of space at a time. As we shall see, the exact value of that forward motion can be adjusted to suit your fancy. Tabs are a key tool when it comes to lining up text properly.

Line Spacing: On a typewriter, *line spacing* comes in two flavors — single or double. In Word, the line-spacing choices are virtually infinite.

Page Breaks: Because the computer screen is not a piece of paper, Word has to decide, before printing the document, where one page will end and the next begin. The line of separation between one page and the next is called the *page break*. The act of deciding where the page break should be placed is called *pagination*. To Word, pagination is a matter of math — count out 50 lines of text — Boom! New page begins. When Word makes pagination decisions, it's called an *automatic* page break. A *manual* page break is where you, the human being, decide where the page meets its end.

Section: The *section* settings refer to the page size, margins, page numbers — not to mention columns and a whole grab bag of other items.

Section is the new word for Division. Plus, instead of pussyfooting around to Format/Division/Margins, Word 6 goes straight for Format/**M**argins. More straightforward, don't you think?

Spaces versus inches: Word eschews spaces for inches — and fractions thereof — when dealing with measurements in a document. You may have successfully dodged switching to the metric system, but there's no way to avoid trading in your spaces for inches. Gone are the days of indenting the first line of a paragraph "five spaces." In Wordspeak, it's indented half an inch, or, more specifically, .5".

There are two reasons "spaces" don't work as measuring tools in Word: First, a space between two humongous, poster-sized letters, for example, is not equal to the space between two fine-print, lawyer-type letters. Einstein said it best: A space is relative. Second, although ¹⁄₁₀ of an inch (the size of a "typewriter space") may seem small to you and me, printers measure things in much smaller increments. The Hewlett-Packard LaserJet 4, for example, boasts 600 dots per inch. Even the older laser printers get 300 dots per inch. Obviously, ¹⁄₃₀₀ of an inch is somewhat smaller than ¹⁄₁₀ of an inch.

Version 5 allowed the option of selecting how measurements were displayed (spaces, inches, points, and so on). In this version, your choice is inches or centimeters, so don't waste time looking for the Measurements command.

Margins versus Indents: A *margin* is the amount of blank space around the edge of the paper. (In Word, the normal margin is 1.25" on the left and right and 1" on the top and bottom — but you can change it to anything.) You use an *indent* to move a paragraph in on the left or right — in addition to the built-in margin.

Paragraph versus New Line: A *paragraph*, according to the official Microsoft party line, is "a series of characters terminated by an Enter." On the other hand, the New Line command — Shift+Enter — puts the cursor on the next line, but without starting a new paragraph. What that means is — never mind, all you have to know for now is that a paragraph and a new line aren't the same thing. We'll see the difference in action later on. I just wanted to let you know it was coming so that you could rest up for it.

Portrait versus Landscape: These terms indicate which direction the print will appear on the page. *Portrait* is normal. *Landscape* is sideways.

Ctrl-ing formatting

If this part of the book were a game show, the category would be "Things that begin with Ctrl," because every formatting command in this section begins with Ctrl.

It's possible to perform some baffling feats of formatting legerdemain with virtually no knowledge of sophisticated commands. Make sure that there's nothing up your sleeves and welcome to the world of *speed-formatting keys*, where men are men and women are women and children are above average.

Putting speed-formatting keys to work is as simple as:

1. Highlight the text you want to format.

2. Use the desired command from Table 7-1 or Table 7-2.

3. Press an arrow key to snap the cursor back into shape (or press Esc if in Extend mode and then move the cursor).

Can it be as simple as that? It is!

Table 7-1	Most-Used Character Formatting Commands	
To	*Highlight Text and Press*	*Or Click on the Ribbon*
Underline	Ctrl+U	U
Bold	Ctrl+B	B
Italic	Ctrl+I	I
Double underline	Ctrl+D	
Remove character formatting	Ctrl+spacebar	

Table 7-2	Most-Used Paragraph Formatting Commands	
To	*Highlight Text and Press*	*Or Click on the Ribbon*
Center	Ctrl+C	
Justified	Ctrl+J	
Indent text to next Tab	Ctrl+N	▶
Unindent text to preceding Tab	Ctrl+M	◀
Indent text on right and left	Ctrl+Q	
Hanging indent	Ctrl+T	
Double space	Ctrl+2	
Single space	Ctrl+1	
Remove paragraph formatting	Ctrl+X	

Figure 7-1 displays a collection of paragraph formats created by using the sexy Ctrl+speed-formatting keys.

✔ When formatting only one paragraph, you don't actually have to highlight the whole paragraph before formatting. Just put the cursor anywhere in the paragraph and then issue the command.

✔ You can combine commands. That is, after you press Ctrl+B to boldface, for example, you can press Ctrl+U to underline — then Ctrl+C to center. Or you can create a hanging indented paragraph with Ctrl+T and then add justification with Ctrl+J and then double space with Ctrl+2. You are the master of your format. In short, the Word is your oyster.

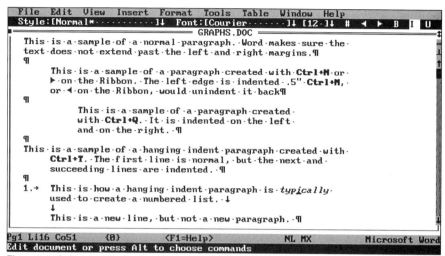

Figure 7-1: Ctrl+speed-formatting keys can create a cloister of clever configurations. Note that the Ribbon's I is boldfaced because the cursor is on an italicized word.

✔ The text formatting commands are toggles. Ctrl+B (or B on the Ribbon) turns on boldface. But if the text is already boldfaced, it returns the text to normal (always highlight text first).

✔ Take special note of the Ctrl+spacebar command. This command removes *all* character formatting. If you've got something boldfaced and underlined, highlight the text and press Ctrl+spacebar to remove both those attributes.

✔ Use formatting creatively. For example, if you like to print a document and make corrections manually on the page, with a real-live pen, you can use Ctrl+2 to print the document in double-space — allowing more space on the page for notes and edits. Later, turn the document back into single space (Ctrl+1), make the changes, and print a single-spaced final draft.

✔ The last paragraph in Figure 7-1 shows an instance where the New Line command (Shift+Enter) comes in handy. Using Enter to get to the next line would have started a new paragraph and the cursor would have gone all the way to the left instead of lining up under the text. Try it and see! Loads o' laffs.

The first step in all these commands is to highlight the text you want to change. Also, don't get so caught up in formatting that you forget to save!

Yes. All your speed-formatting keys have changed. Alt+C is now Ctrl+C, and so on. Sorry. They had to do it because Alt is what brings up the menu. Evolving from an Alt world to a Ctrl world may be a bit daunting at first. However, because there were so few Ctrl commands in Word 5, maybe it won't be as difficult as you think.

Formatting out of Ctrl

If you want to see how difficult life can be, try formatting a paragraph incorrectly. With the nonprinting symbols turned on (with Alt+View ➪ Preferences ➪ Show All), the evidence is in (see Figure 7-2). Maybe you can see some of your bad habits in there.

To get the Bad Example to line up like the Good Example, many Enters and spaces were called into play. Technically speaking, because Word's definition of a paragraph is a string of text that ends with an Enter, the Bad Example is actually composed of four paragraphs. The Good Example, meanwhile, was created with a mere flick of Ctrl+T.

The extra work compounds geometrically when words are added or deleted from the Bad Example (see Figure 7-3). The Good Example automatically reformats itself in response to any edits. The Bad Example requires much plastic surgery.

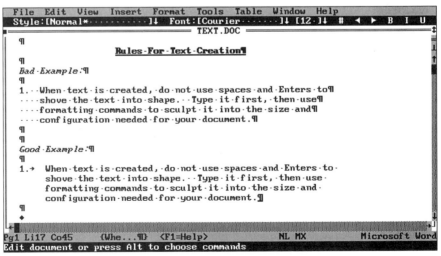

Figure 7-2: They may look the same — but one is the good 'graph and the other is the evil twin 'graph.

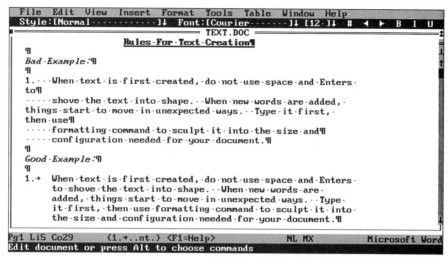

Figure 7-3: The evil will out. With editing, the bad 'graph falls apart and causes problems. The good 'graph, however, has enough self-esteem to stay flexible and adapt.

Then, just when the stuff is finally back into shape, some genius invariably says, "Hey, I've got an idea — let's not indent that paragraph." Now all the spaces and all the Enters have to come out. In the Good Example, a simple Ctrl+X removes the indent.

Formatting with dialog boxes

Thirsty for more? Okay, now we're going to have some big fun as we move into the grown-up world of formatting with dialog boxes.

As discussed in detail in Chapter 1, when you are in a dialog box, you can move to a command by pressing Tab until the desired destination is reached or by pressing Alt+boldfaced letter to jump right to the spot. Pressing the spacebar checks or unchecks a box or selects or deselects an option button. Press Enter when all selections are completed — or Esc to get out and forget any changes. Of course, a lot of Tabbing and Alt+ing can be avoided if you have a mouse and just click to turn on options and click OK to finish the transaction.

Formatting characters

In addition to the speed-formatting keys, you can format highlighted text with the options in the Character dialog box (see Figure 7-4).

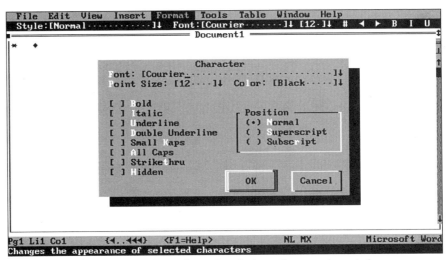

File Edit View Insert Format Tools Table Window Help
Style:[Normal············]↓ Font:[Courier········]↓ [12·]↓ # ◄ ► B I U
════════════════════════ Document1 ════════════════════════
*   ◆
                          Character
            Font: [Courier_·······························]↓
            Point Size: [12····]↓ Color: [Black·····]↓

            [ ] Bold
            [ ] Italic   ┌─ Position ──────────┐
            [ ] Underline   │ (•) Normal   │
            [ ] Double Underline   │ ( ) Superscript   │
            [ ] Small Caps   │ ( ) Subscript   │
            [ ] All Caps   └─────────────────────┘
            [ ] Strike thru
            [ ] Hidden
                                    ┌──────────┐ ┌──────────┐
                                    │   OK   │ │ Cancel │
                                    └──────────┘ └──────────┘

Pg1 Li1 Co1   {◄..◄◄◄}   <F1=Help>   NL MX   Microsoft Word
Changes the appearance of selected characters

Figure 7-4: Additional character formatting tools to further refine your character's appearance.

Follow these steps to format text:

1. Highlight the text you want to format.

2. Press Alt+Format ⇨ Character.

   In the Character dialog box, not only do the traditional Bold, Italic, and Underline make themselves available, but other, more esoteric choices also are there to provide you with options you'll never use. Maybe if you're a mad scientist, you can use the **S**uperscript and Subscript commands to better express your secret formulas. My philosophy is that if you don't understand what it is, you don't need it.

3. Select the formatting option you want.

4. Press Enter.

   ✔ If you want to apply the same formatting to another chunk of text, highlight the other text you want to format and press F4 to repeat the last command. You may do this as many times as you want as long as you don't perform another command — then F4 repeats *that* command.

Formatting fonts

Fonts — typefaces of different sizes and shapes (like in a magazine) — are included with the Word 6 package. Microsoft has thoughtfully provided Courier, Arial, Times New Roman, and two symbol fonts — Symbol and Wingdings. It may not seem like a lot, but in fact, it's enough to satisfy any basic office situation.

If you've never worked with fonts, go with the "less is more" philosophy when applying them to your document. Just use the Arial typeface for headings and Times New Roman for regular text and you won't go wrong.

The other new thing about fonts, if you've never used them before, is that you can format them to print in just about any size you want. Font sizes are measured in *points*. The TrueType fonts print in sizes ranging from 1 point to 127 points — about 1¼" tall. The normal point size is 12.

To apply a font to your text:

1. Highlight the text you want to format.

2. Press Alt+Format ⇨ **Character.**

3. Press Alt+down arrow.

   Scroll through the drop-down box to select the font of your dreams.

4. If you want to select a point size, press Tab.

   If you already know the point size you want, just type the number. If you don't, press Alt+down arrow to reveal the point size list and highlight the needed number.

5. Press Enter.

   ✔ Another way to get to the Format Character dialog box is by pressing Ctrl+F Ctrl+F. Ctrl+P Ctrl+P also takes you to the Character dialog box — at the **P**oint Size text box.

You also can use the Ribbon to select font names. With the keyboard, press Ctrl+F — for Font — and then Alt+down arrow to view the font name list. The Ribbon does not have to be turned on to use this shortcut. With the mouse, click the down arrow to the right of the Font text box.

✔ The font names in the drop-down boxes are not exactly in alphabetical order. To avoid scrolling endlessly in search of the desired font, press the first letter of the font's name. If you want Arial, for instance, type **A**. You'll be taken to the first font starting with the letter A. If it isn't Arial, press A again until you get there (see Figure 7-5).

✔ One thing about Ctrl+spacebar — the "remove the character formatting" keystroke — and fonts is that Ctrl+spacebar removes not only the formatting, but also the font formatting. Ctrl+Z removes the boldface or underline, but leaves the font formatting. If you use a lot of fonts, use Ctrl+Z instead of Ctrl+spacebar.

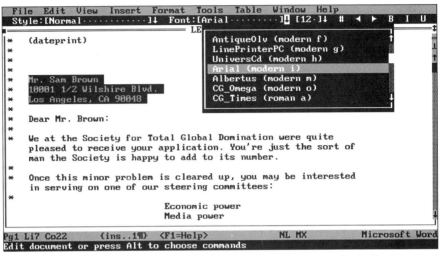

Figure 7-5: Use the mouse, or press Ctrl+F and then Alt+down arrow, to make the Font box drop down and offer its bounty of font names.

To turn on the Ribbon with the keyboard, press Alt+**V**iew ➪ Ri**b**bon (or Ctrl+Shift+F10, if you like a challenge). Turn on the Ribbon with the mouse by right-clicking the Ruler/Ribbon icon (⊥).

In addition to using the mouse to access the Ribbon commands, you can double-click the word Font on the Ribbon, and the Character dialog box appears. Aren't mice neat!

Printer troubleshooting

If you know that your printer is capable of using fonts or some other feature, but font names don't appear in the Font drop-down box, or the desired feature is dimmed and unavailable — do some investigating.

First, press Alt+**F**ile ➪ **P**rinter Setup and make sure that the proper printer is selected. If your printer isn't there, you need to install the proper *printer driver*. The printer driver is the software that tells Word what your printer can — and cannot — do.

Go find the original Word 6 disks and put the Setup disk in the floppy drive. Log onto that drive. (If your floppy drive is drive A, type **A:** and press Enter.) Then type **SETUP** and press Enter. Next you see a maze of multiple choice questions. Here are the answers: "Setup on Hard disk;" "Modify an existing version;" press Enter when the directory name is shown, and then "Install a printer driver." Find your printer and then "Complete the setup." This should get your printer going.

Searching and replacing fonts and formats

Just as you can search for and replace text, you also can search for and replace fonts and formats. This is a life-saver when you decide, for example, to change all your boldfaced text to underline.

To just search for a font:

1. Press Alt+Edit ⇨ **S**earch.

2. Press Alt+Search for Formatting Only.

3. Press Enter — the cursor is already on **C**haracter.

4. Select the text's characteristics.

   You see the Character dialog box. Your mission, should you decide to accept it, is to check the items you're looking for. Don't select or deselect every single item in the box. Just those items important in the hunt.

5. Press Enter.

To search *and replace* a font:

1. Press Alt+Edit ⇨ **R**eplace.

2. Press Alt+Search for Formatting Only.

3. Press Enter — the cursor is already on **C**haracter.

4. Select the text's characteristics.

   You see the Character dialog box. Your duty is to check the items you're looking for. Don't select or deselect every single item in the box. Just those items that need to be replaced.

5. Press Alt+Replace With.

6. Select the replacement text characteristics.

7. Press Enter.

   ✔ If you make a mistake, press Esc to close the dialog box and leave you exactly as you were when you started.

   ✔ You also can search for and replace all items in the paragraph dialog box — converting, say, all paragraphs indented half an inch into paragraphs that aren't indented at all.

Aligning paragraphs

In Figure 7-6, the four types of paragraph alignments — Left, Right, Justified, and Centered (the paragraph that apparently had more psychotherapy) — are on display. Virtually all the time, however, you'll use normal formatting. I use "normal" in a nonjudgmental way, of course.

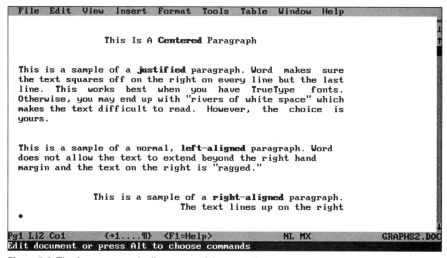

Figure 7-6: The four paragraph alignments of the apocalypse.

If you want to change the text alignment of your paragraphs, do the following:

1. Highlight the text you want to change.

2. Press Alt+Format ⇨ **Paragraph.**

   You see the Paragraph dialog box (see Figure 7-7).

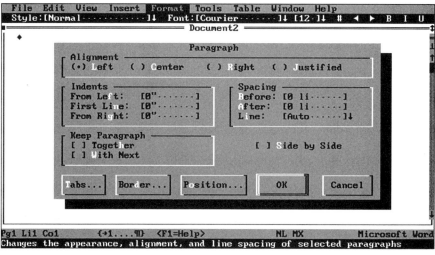

Figure 7-7: The Paragraph dialog box. So many choices, so little time.

3. Press the spacebar to select the alignment you want.

4. Press Enter.

> ✔ As with character formatting, after you've done the work of formatting a paragraph the "long" way, you can duplicate the format in other paragraphs by moving to another paragraph (or highlighting other paragraphs) and pressing F4 — the "repeat the last command" key.

Indenting paragraphs

Most of the indenting you'll need to do is covered by the speed-formatting keys. In fact, you can probably lead a scandal-free life without learning anything further about indenting. However, if the road less traveled calls to you, then the Paragraph dialog box provides all the latitude you require. Just follow this path:

1. Highlight the text you want to format.

2. Press Alt+Format ⇨ **Paragraph**.

3. Press Tab or Alt+boldfaced letter to go to the item you want to change.

   When putting numbers in the Indent box:

   > ✔ Remember that discussion we had about spaces versus inches? This is where you use that information. Word expects *inches*, so be sure to put decimal points where needed. For example, plain **5** means five inches, and **.5** means half an inch. What a difference a decimal makes.

   > ✔ If, after you press Enter, text suddenly reformats itself in a massively weird way, you probably forgot to put that decimal in. I won't say I told you so, but use Alt+Backspace to cancel what you did and try again.

   > ✔ The First Line measurement is used for indenting the first line of a paragraph.

   > ✔ If you put a number in the From Left box, you may put a negative number in the First Line box. That's how the hanging indent is achieved — with a **.5** in the From Left box and a **–.5** in the First Line box.

   > ✔ A negative number in the From Right box lets you sneak your text into the margin's forbidden zone.

4. When you are satisfied, press Enter.

   If you change your mind about the whole operation, don't press Enter. Press Esc to cancel, and all the numbers are put back the way they were.

Numbering paragraphs

This is a fun command. It's one of those things you always wanted computers to do for you.

Ever have a list of 50 items and then another item gets added or deleted, some-where in the middle — then you have to renumber everything after the change? Ta-da! Numbering paragraphs to the rescue! This feature isn't limited to just *numbering* items, either. Oh, no. You can A,B,C items, Roman numeral them, or even take the numbers away. To add — or update — numbers to a series of paragraphs, follow these steps:

1. Highlight the paragraphs you want to number.

2. Press Alt+T**o**ols ⇨ Numbering.

   This gets you to the Numbering dialog box (see Figure 7-8).

3. Press Enter.

   ✔ If you don't like what Numbering does, immediately press Alt+Backspace to put it back the way it was.

In case just pressing Enter doesn't produce happy results for you, try again — this time, try exercising one of the Numbering dialog box's exhaustive supply of options.

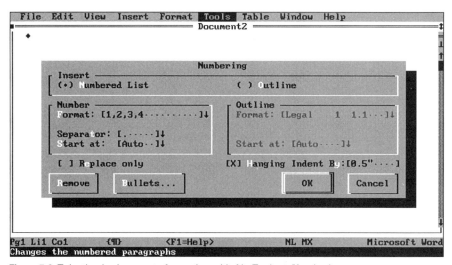

Figure 7-8: Take the drudgery out of counting with Alt+T**o**ols ⇨ **N**umbering.

✔ Press Alt+Format if you want to A,B,C or Roman numeral the list.

✔ Press Alt+Separator if you don't want the time-honored period after the number — pick another from the drop-down list, or invent your own. Never let it be said that Word didn't let you have any darn separator you wanted.

✔ Press Alt+Start At if you want the numbering to start with something other than 1 (or A).

✔ Pressing Alt+Replace Only lets you update existing numbers, without adding numbers to paragraphs in between the numbered paragraphs. So if item number 12 ends up with two paragraphs, the second paragraph won't be assigned a number.

✔ Press Alt+Remove to take away any numbers and, if the paragraph is indented, restore it to normal.

✔ Press Alt+Hanging Indent to number the paragraph and to create a hanging indent — which it normally does; uncheck this option if you don't like it.

✔ Press Alt+By to select the size of the hanging indent if Alt+Hanging Indent is checked.

Bulleting paragraphs

Bulleting paragraphs — putting little marks to the left of a paragraph to make it stand out — is a cool feature that's very easy to use as long as you can live with the defaults (see Figure 7-9).

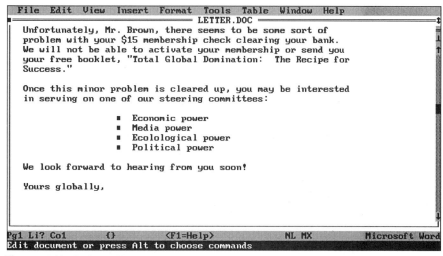

Figure 7-9: Yet further evidence of the violence of our times: bulleted paragraphs. Alt+Tools ⇨ **N**umbering is the prime suspect.

So for now, we'll live with the defaults — which isn't too shabby, considering that bulleting paragraphs without this feature is a massive pain in the petunia.

1. Highlight the paragraphs you want to bullet.

2. Press Alt+Tools ⇨ **B**ullets.

   You get the Bullets dialog box shown in Figure 7-10. Basically, the only thing you want to do here is highlight the **B**ullet Character of your dreams.

3. Press Enter.

   ✔ Press Alt+Backspace if you hate what happens.

   ✔ If you love your bullets, but they don't print out, highlight the bullet and try applying a different font format. For example, try CourierPC instead of Courier. Or use Pica instead of Courier. Eventually, you'll find which character format has the bullet character you want. (To learn the characteristics of all fonts in your system, see "Printing Out All Your Fonts," coming up.)

Keeping paragraphs Together and With Next

Keeping Paragraphs *Together* and *With Next* isn't some family values thing. It's one way that humans have some measure of control over how a paragraph is handled at the bottom of a page. Figure 7-11 illustrates when to use the With Next feature to avoid a page layout faux pas. We can tell Word not to break up a paragraph at the bottom of a page and, also, to treat certain paragraphs (a title and the succeeding paragraph, for example) as a unit.

Figure 7-10: These bullets may not make Clint's day — but they will make your paragraphs'.

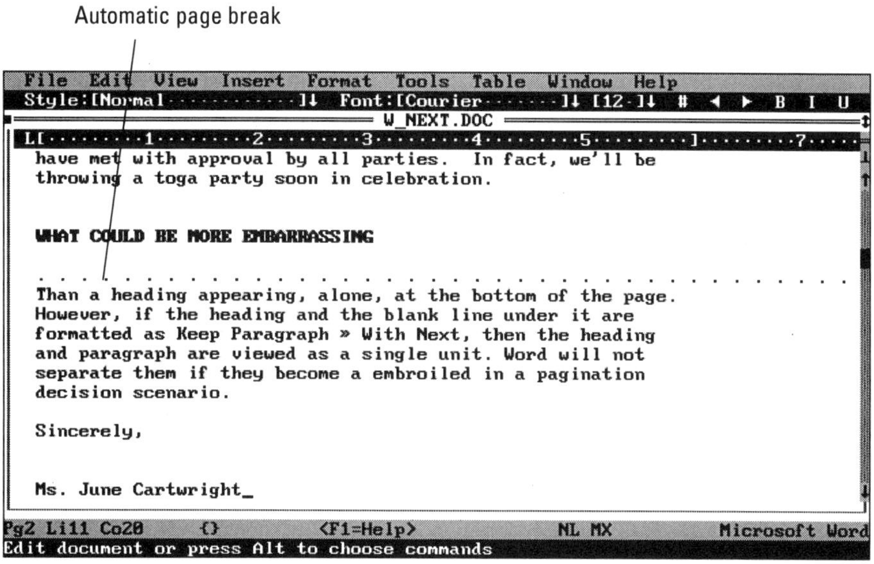

Automatic page break

```
 File  Edit  View  Insert  Format  Tools  Table  Window  Help
 Style:[Normal··········]↓  Font:[Courier·······]↓ [12-]↓ # ◄ ► B I U
========================= W_NEXT.DOC =======================≠
 L[········1········2········3·······4·······5········]·······7····
   have met with approval by all parties.  In fact, we'll be
   throwing a toga party soon in celebration.


   WHAT COULD BE MORE EMBARRASSING


   · · · · · · · · · · · · · · · · · · · · · · · · · · · · · · ·
   Than a heading appearing, alone, at the bottom of the page.
   However, if the heading and the blank line under it are
   formatted as Keep Paragraph » With Next, then the heading
   and paragraph are viewed as a single unit. Word will not
   separate them if they become a embroiled in a pagination
   decision scenario.

   Sincerely,


   Ms. June Cartwright_

 Pg2 Li11 Co20      {}        <F1=Help>          NL MX        Microsoft Word
 Edit document or press Alt to choose commands
```

Figure 7-11: Nobody likes to see a heading on one page and the paragraph on the next. Use Keep Paragraph ⇨ **W**ith Next to avoid this heartbreak.

1. Highlight the text you want to affect.

2. Press Alt+Format ⇨ **P**aragraph.

3. In the Paragraph dialog box, choose either or both of the following:

   ✔ Alt+**W**ith Next is used, mostly, to keep headings "attached" to their text — the "next" paragraph.

   ✔ Alt+**T**ogether prevents Word from breaking up the paragraph under any circumstances.

Putting in page numbers

You can tell Word to automatically print the proper page number on each page. This nothing-fancy technique for putting numbers on every page is as follows:

1. Press Shift+F10 to highlight the entire document.

2. Press Alt+**I**nsert ⇨ Page N**u**mbers.

   This command gives you the exciting Page Numbers dialog box (see Figure 7-12). The Page Number Position box lets you select where the page numbers will appear on the printed page.

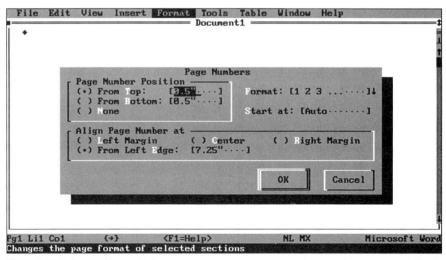

Figure 7-12: Using position and alignment, you can put a page number anyplace on a page. Total page-numbering control.

3. Press the spacebar to select the desired position.

4. Press Enter.

> ✔ Putting in a page numbering command creates a new section symbol — a row of colons — at the bottom of the file. Treat it just like an end mark — type above it and leave it alone.
>
> ✔ Just as paragraphs have format coding for the preceding paragraph, the section symbol carries the format instructions for the preceding document. If you delete the colons, you delete the formatting.
>
> ✔ The limitation of this method of page numbering is that the page number will appear on every single page, including the first. If you don't want page numbers on the first page, or if you want certain text to appear at the top of each page — then you need *headers* or *footers*, which are described shortly.

Changing the margins

Tired of that same old dingy white space around the edges of your documents? Want more? Want less? You can easily change the margins of your document by following these steps:

1. Press Shift+F10 to highlight the entire document.

2. Press Alt+Format ➪ **Margins**.

   Specify the desired margins in the Section Margins dialog box, as shown in Figure 7-13, where the **B**ottom margin has been changed to .5 and the **R**ight margin reduced to 1 (inch).

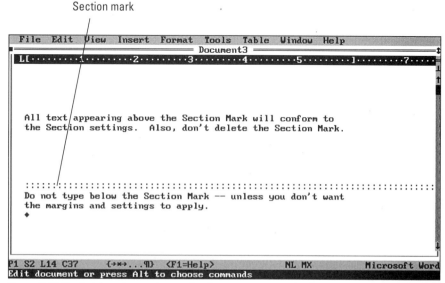

```
 File  Edit  View  Insert  Format  Tools  Table  Window  Help
                            Document3
L[ · · · · · · · · 1 · · · · · · · 2 · · · · · · · 3 · · · · · · · 4 · · · · · · · 5 · · · · · · · ] · · · · · · · 7 · · · · ·
  ◆
                              Section Margins
        Margins
         Top:       [1"· · · · · · ·]     Left:   [1.25"· · · ·]
         Bottom:    [.5_· · · · · ·]      Right:  [1· · · · · · ·]
         Gutter:    [0"· · · · · · ·]     [ ] Mirror Margins

        Page Size
         Width:     [8.5"· · · · ·]       Height: [11"· · · · · ·]

         Page Orientation:         (•) Portrait   (Normal)
                                   ( ) Landscape  (Sideways)

                                   [ ] Use as Default

         Section...                       OK          Cancel


Pg1 Li1 Co1       {→»→...¶}  <F1=Help>              NL MX        Microsoft Word
Changes the page format of selected sections
```

Figure 7-13: The Section Margins dialog box lets you change your left- and right-hand margins and a bunch of other stuff.

3. Press Enter.

> ✔ After you press Enter, a section mark appears at the bottom of the document. If you delete the section mark, your margin changes also are deleted.

> ✔ Be sure new text is typed *above* the section mark (see Figure 7-14).

Section mark

```
 File  Edit  View  Insert  Format  Tools  Table  Window  Help
                            Document3
L[ · · · · · · · · 1 · · · · · · · 2 · · · · · · · 3 · · · · · · · 4 · · · · · · · 5 · · · · · · · ] · · · · · · · 7 · · · · ·



     All text appearing above the Section Mark will conform to
     the Section settings.  Also, don't delete the Section Mark.




     : : : : : : : : : : : : : : : : : : : : : : : : : : : : : : : : : : : : : : : : : : : : : : : : : : : : : : : : :
     Do not type below the Section Mark -- unless you don't want
     the margins and settings to apply.
     ◆


P1 S2 L14 C37    {→»→...¶}  <F1=Help>              NL MX        Microsoft Word
Edit document or press Alt to choose commands
```

Figure 7-14: Don't delete the section mark unless you want section formatting — margins, columns, and page numbers — to disappear.

- ✔ Word 6 lets you go from **P**ortrait to Lan**d**scape — if your printer will do it — by clicking the appropriate Page Orientation option button. The page **W**idth and **H**eight change automatically.

- ✔ Items to ignore in the Section Margins dialog box: **G**utter and **M**irror Margins.

- ✔ Item to be careful with: **U**se as Default. This option allows you to *permanently* change the margins to new settings. You can always change them back — but avoid this option if you don't know what you're doing.

If you want to change section margins or page numbering, double-click the section mark symbol to pop up the Section dialog box.

You can have more than one section in a document — or even on a page. This is especially useful when dealing with multiple columns (see the next section). However, you cannot have both a landscape and a portrait page in the same document unless you have a PostScript printer. If you want a landscape page in an otherwise-portrait document — put it in its own separate file.

Building Tabs

The terrible Tabs. Tabs — who needs 'em? If you don't use fonts and never want to line up a column — you can probably avoid them.

You can set Tabs by pressing Alt+Forma**t** ▷ **T**abs and getting the Tabs dialog box (see Figure 7-15).

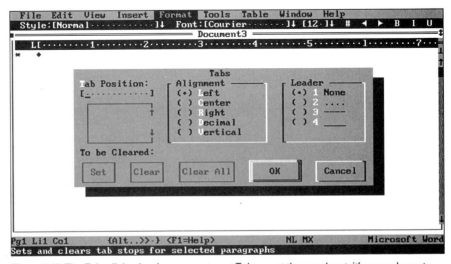

Figure 7-15: The Tabs dialog box is one way to set Tabs — at the very least, it's a good way to see all the Tab-setting options.

However, we're not going to use the clunky old dialog box to create Tabs. This may be a surprise, but you can set Tabs with the Ruler. Yes, the Ruler! And, even if the Ruler is normally turned off, it can be turned on for the duration of the Tab-setting ceremony.

A typical situation crying out for some Tab action is the — ahem — fabrication of the time-honored expense report (see Figure 7-16).

When dealing with Tabs, it's best to turn Line Breaks on with Alt+View ⇨ Preferences ⇨ Line Breaks. Line breaks are covered in the section "Seeing What You're Getting," later in this chapter.

Creating Tabs for an expense report

Create Tabs for an expense report by following these steps:

1. Go to where you want to set the Tabs (or highlight text to be tabbed, if the text is already entered).

2. Press Ctrl+Shift+F10.

   This turns on the Ruler and places a flashing cursor in it.

3. Using the left- and right-arrow keys, position the cursor where you want to set the first Tab.

   In the case of Figure 7-16, the first Tab, the one for the dollar sign, was set at 1.9". If you don't include a Tab for the dollar sign, they'll never line up.

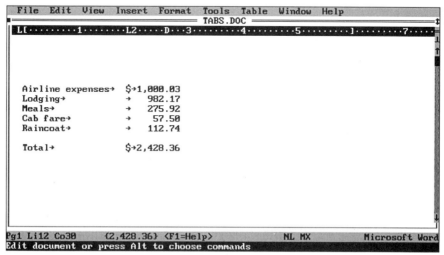

Figure 7-16: The expense report was typed with one Tab separating each item. The Tabs set are visible in the Ruler (L and D).

4. Press L.

This creates a *left-aligned* Tab — which is computerspeak for a normal, garden-variety Tab.

5. Move to the next Tab you want to set.

In the case of Figure 7-16, the second Tab, the one for the numbers, was set at 2.6".

6. Press D.

The letter D is the code for a *decimal* Tab. That means that when you type numbers in your document, the decimal point in the numbers will line up under this position.

7. When you are satisfied with your selections, press Enter.

> ✔ As you type your table, be sure to press Enter at the end of each line to clone the Tab settings to the next paragraph. If you've suddenly lost your Tab settings, go back up to the preceding line and press Enter — not the down-arrow key.
>
> ✔ Pressing Esc takes you out of the Ruler without setting any Tabs.
>
> ✔ Psst! This has nothing to do with Tabs, but if you want to add up a column of numbers, just highlight the numbers and press F2. The result appears in the Scrap — a result that you can Shift+Ins wherever you need the number. In case you don't remember it from the great F8 chart earlier in the book, the command to highlight a column of numbers is Ctrl+Shift+F8. More about calculating in Chapter 15.

Moving Tabs

You can move Tabs by following these steps:

1. Highlight the paragraphs containing the offending Tab setting.

2. Press Ctrl+Shift+F10.

3. Using the left- and right-arrow keys, position the cursor on top of the Tab setting.

4. Press Ctrl+right (or left) arrow, and drag the letter to the new position.

You see the text move as the Tab setting is moved.

5. When you are satisfied, press Enter.

Deleting Tabs

Delete Tabs by doing the following:

1. Highlight the paragraphs containing the offending Tab setting.

2. Press Ctrl+Shift+F10.

3. Using left- and right-arrow keys, position the cursor on top of the Tab setting.

4. Press Del.

5. When you are satisfied, press Enter.

Tactless Tabs

In most cases, being able to use the left and decimal Tabs will be enough to make you king of the hill. However, just in case you're consumed with curiosity about all those other kinds of Tabs visible in Figure 7-15, we'll run through them here. Two of the most popular Tab options are illustrated in Figure 7-17.

✔ In Figure 7-17, the first column of numbers (24, 7, and 365) introduces you to the exciting right-aligned Tab. This has nothing to do with politics — it has everything to do with how the numbers line up... on the right! Pretty exciting stuff, isn't it?

✔ Also, in Figure 7-17, see the dots between the Roman and the regular numerals? Those dots were inserted automatically by Word because that right-aligned Tab also had the Leader option selected. Other kinds of "leaders" are hyphens and lines. This is cool if you're doing a Table of Contents kind of thing.

✔ A weird kind of Tab — long thought to be extinct, but a few were recently discovered on the Galapagos Islands — is the Vertical Tab. You use the Vertical tab to draw vertical lines. It's much more reliable and flexible than using Line Draw, and maybe less complicated than making a Table. Like most Tab options, it's useful when you're using fonts.

✔ Finally, the mundane centered Tab centers text below it.

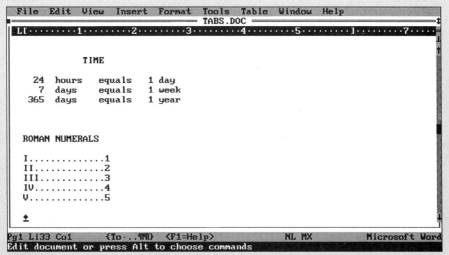

Figure 7-17: Tabs, Tabs, fanTABulous tabs — the key to properly lining up your fonted words! Right- and left-aligned Tabs — and even Tabs with leader characters!

The mouse can create Tabs as well. If the Ruler isn't on, left-click the Ruler/ Ribbon icon ($\bot$) to turn it on. Click the letter, initially an L, on the far left end of the Ruler. This letter is the code for the type of Tab you want. Keep clicking until it's the kind of Tab you want. Then point to the desired Tab location and click. You've just inserted a Tab. The Tab settings may be changed by dragging left and right. However, when dragging, the letter being "dragged" doesn't move until you release the mouse ear. If the setting is dragged downward, off the ruler, the Tab setting is deleted.

Constructing headers and footers

A *header* is text that appears at the top of every page of the document. A *footer*, logically, appears at the bottom of the page.

In correspondence, for example, it is common to have the name of the recipient and the page number appear at the top of the second and succeeding pages of the document.

To create such a header requires the following steps. It looks like a lot of stuff to go through, but there are actually two jobs being accomplished here: creating the header and installing a page-numbering command that is on the right.

Here's how to create our business header:

1. Go to the top of the document (press Ctrl+Home).
2. Press Enter twice and then up arrow twice.

   This clears two blank lines at the top of the document. Make sure that the cursor is at the top of the document. No blank lines can be above the cursor.
3. Type the name of the recipient of the letter.
4. Press Tab (once only).
5. Type the word **page**.
6. Press F3.

   Your page becomes (page).
7. Press Alt+Format ⇨ **Paragraph**.
8. Press R.
9. Press Enter.
10. Press Alt+F10.
11. Press Alt+Format ⇨ **Header/Footer**.
12. Press **Header**.
13. Press Enter.

    ✔ You should get something like Figure 7-18. The caret (^) to the left of Mr. Brown's name indicates that the line is now a header or a footer.

Header

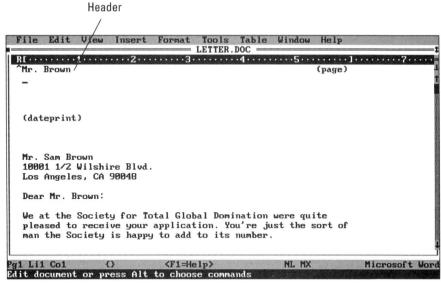

Figure 7-18: Hats off to headers — the caret (^) indicates which line will appear at the top of each page.

> ✔ Just for the record: Steps 1-2 created blank space in which to type the header, Steps 5-6 created the page number, Steps 7-9 put the page number on the right, Step 10 highlighted the text to be formatted as a header, and only Steps 11-13 actually created the header.
>
> ✔ If you want a footer, make that choice when the Header/Footer dialog box pops up (see Figure 7-19).

Figure 7-19: The Header/Footer dialog box offers a number of choices about how and where a header is printed. Pressing Enter gives you the most common choices.

> ✔ A document can have both headers and footers.
>
> ✔ Use the Alt+File ➪ Print Preview command to make sure that the header is working as expected.
>
> ✔ To remove a header, highlight the text to the right of the caret (^). If the caret appears on more than one line, highlight all the lines. Press Alt+Format ➪ Header/Footer ➪ None. Then press Enter.

Formatting for three columns

Making three columns out of your text is not too big a deal, actually. Just follow these steps:

1. Highlight the text you want to format.

2. Press Alt+Format ➪ Section.

3. Press 3.

   This gives you three columns.

4. Press Alt+Section Start and select Continuous.

5. Press Enter.

> ✔ Figure 7-20 shows a three-column layout in the Alt+File ➪ Print Preview mode.
>
> ✔ The column-break command is Shift+Ctrl. Then you press Enter.

Working with more than one section

Things start to get a bit techy here, but if you delve into three-column layouts, it's inevitable that you'll start thinking about sticking a title or masthead across the top of the page.

If you attempt to create a title with a page that allows only three columns, you'll quickly discover that the title won't go across the page — it'll only go one column wide.

The answer to this dilemma is to break the page into two sections — a normal section and a three-column section — by following these steps:

1. Move the cursor to the top of the document.

2. Press Alt+Insert ➪ Break.

3. Press S.

   This turns on the section break and automatically makes the break *continuous* — meaning, keep this section on the same page as the next section.

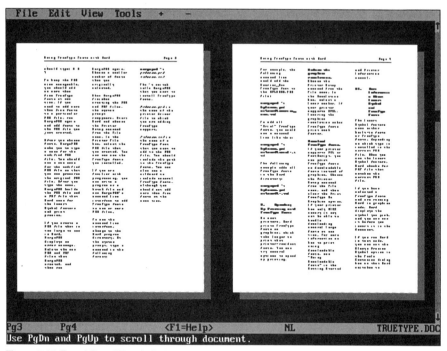

Figure 7-20: Extra! Extra! Read all about it! Microsoft Word baffles world by creating three-column layouts!

4. Press Enter.

   This gives you the traditional section mark — a row of colons.

5. With the cursor above the section mark, press Alt+Format ⇨ **S**ection.

6. Press 1.

7. Press Enter.

8. You may now type the desired headline above the three columns (see Figure 7-21).

   ✔ To see how it looks all put together, see Figure 7-22.

   ✔ Just because this example started with a one-column section and followed with a three-column section doesn't mean that's the only way to do it. You also can have several sections on a page. Once, for example, I started out with normal text, then went to a four-column list, and then back to normal text.

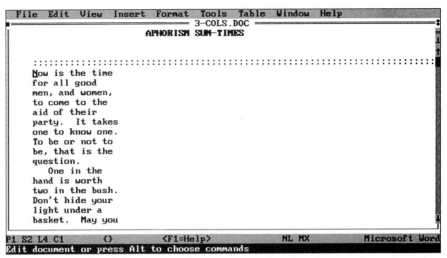

Figure 7-21: Tech alert! Before: A page with two sections. A single-column section on top and a three-column section below.

Figure 7-22: After: What the page looks like when printed out — title across the top and columns underneath.

Getting What You're Seeing

Ever feel guilty about the forest you're destroying while attempting to get a document to format correctly? Do coworkers glare meaningfully at the mountain of waste paper you create every day? One way to save time and trees is to take advantage of the many ways Word can show you — in advance — how the document will actually print out.

Previewing coming attractions

When you're in a movie theater and they show previews of coming attractions, you get to see a bit of what a new movie will be like. In Word, Print Preview enables you to see a miniaturized version of what your printout will look like. It's very cute (see Figure 7-23).

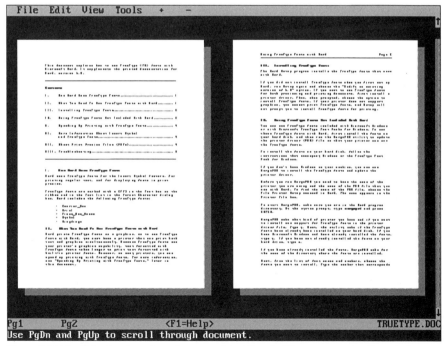

Figure 7-23: The Print Preview of coming attractions! Use the View command to Zoom in for close-ups. Mr. de Mille, I'm ready for my close-ups!

To view the current document:

1. Press Alt+**File** ➪ Print Preview.

   The shortcut key is Ctrl+F9.

2. Examine the document.

   Use PgUp and PgDn to move forward and backward through the document. Press Alt+**View** to adjust the manner in which the document is displayed — two pages at a time, one page, and so on. If you like what you see, then issue the Alt+**Print** command.

3. Press Esc when you are finished.

   ✔ Using Preview is an excellent way to make sure that headers or footers are working properly.

   ✔ While in Print Preview, the Zoom command lets you enlarge portions of the text for a more accurate look. You still can't edit the text, but you can see it better. You can either use the View command or press + or − to enlarge or shrink the display. Naturally, mousers can click the + or − instead.

Giving your pages a break

For some, the issue of where one page ends and another begins is fraught with passion and fervor. Others don't really care. However, somebody must think it's a big deal, because there are about 50 gazillion ways to create and see page breaks. Some are incredibly irritating, others are very helpful.

Entering manual page breaks

The end of a section in a report, the end of a chapter, the end of a title page — what do these things have in common? Well, each is the end of something and requires a page break command so that the new section begins printing at the top of the next page.

As you create these natural ending situations, enter a page break command so that Word formats the document properly, as in Figure 7-24.

To create a page break, simply press Ctrl+Enter, and a series of dots crosses the screen. To remove a page break, just press Del or Backspace over the dots like any other character. No secret password required.

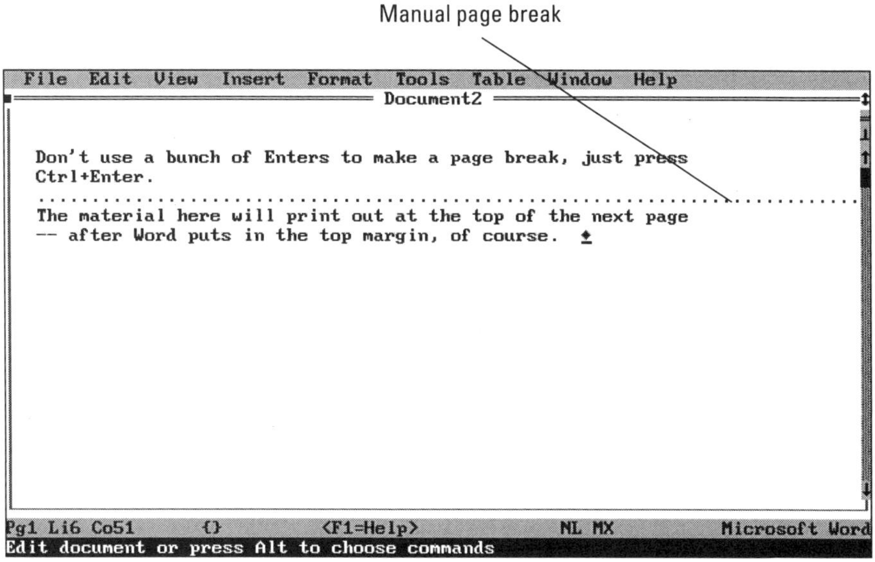

Manual page break

```
 File   Edit   View   Insert   Format   Tools   Table   Window   Help
========================== Document2 ==========================

 Don't use a bunch of Enters to make a page break, just press
 Ctrl+Enter.
 ..............................................................
 The material here will print out at the top of the next page
 -- after Word puts in the top margin, of course.  ±




Pg1 Li6 Co51        {}              <F1=Help>               NL MX          Microsoft Word
Edit document or press Alt to choose commands
```

Figure 7-24: A page break tells Word when to start a new page. We all have to start a new page some time.

Paginating in the background

If you want, Word can continually calculate the number of lines you've typed, and when you have enough to qualify as "a page," a line of dots magically appears on the screen, simulating the end of a page. Whether you appreciate the continuing feedback or find it intensely annoying is your choice. The process is called *background pagination*.

To turn background pagination on or off:

1. Press Alt+**V**iew ⇨ **P**references ⇨ **C**ustomize.

2. Check or uncheck the **B**ackground Pagination box to taste.

3. Press Enter.

   ✔ You'll know background pagination is on because, as you work, occasionally a dotted line appears across the screen, shoving your text around. The automatic page break dots are not as close together as the dots in the manual page break. Dots is not dots.

   ✔ If you want something to fall on the next page, don't press Enter to cross over the automatic page break threshold. Press Ctrl+Enter to create a manual page break.

Paginating interactively

Before printing, it's a good idea to take a few moments to work with Word to decide where the page breaks will be. Follow these steps:

1. Press Alt+Tools ⇨ Repaginate Now.

2. Press the spacebar to turn on Confirm Page Breaks.

3. Press Enter.

4. Word scrolls through the document, showing you where it proposes each page break. Your options, as displayed in the message bar, are to accept the page break by pressing Enter or to use the up-arrow key to reposition the location of the page break and then press Enter.

   ✔ Use of the down arrow is not allowed when paginating. If you really need longer pages, use the Alt+Format ⇨ Margins command to create smaller margins.

If you've already gone through the pagination process before, occasionally manually changing the location of Word's page break suggestions, it's a good idea to remove the old manual page breaks before the *next* pagination experience — so that you'll be starting with a "clean slate."

To remove manual page breaks, do the following:

1. Press Alt+File ⇨ Save to save the document.

2. Press Alt+Edit ⇨ Replace.

3. Type ^D.

   You create the caret (^) by pressing "capital 6" — Shift+6 (not the 6 on the numeric keypad). The D is just an ordinary D. That's the code for page breaks and section breaks. Make sure that the Replace With text box is empty and that Confirm Changes is on — we don't want to nuke any section marks.

4. Press Enter.

   Word finds and offers to remove each page break (line of dots) and section break (line of colons). Say Yes to the page breaks and No to the section breaks.

Viewing fonts with Line Breaks

Page breaks was all about where the page ended. And now — *line* breaks. I promise there's no such thing as a character break. However, at this point you may want to take a coffee break.

Some people want to see, on-screen, exactly where each and every *line* of text will end when they print the document. Sometimes this sort of information is helpful when formatting. And, sometimes, it's a sign of mental instability.

If you're not using TrueType — or any type of — fonts, then this probably isn't an issue.

Word cannot make the real fonts appear on-screen as they will be printed. The closest it can come to that is with Print Preview. However, Word can simulate the fonts by formatting the line breaks and page breaks just as though the real thing were visible.

It takes some imagination.

To turn Line Breaks on or off:

1. Press Alt+View ➪ Preferences.

2. Check or uncheck the Line Breaks box.

3. Press Enter.

If you've formatted your text with fonts, you're likely to get something like Figure 7-25.

Figure 7-26 shows how the page will look after you print it out.

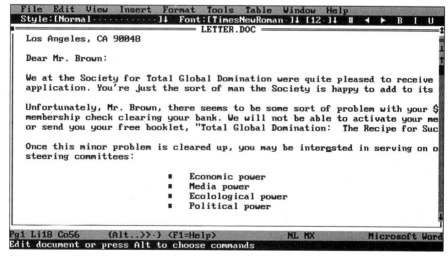

Figure 7-25: A typical screen when **View** ➪ **Preferences** ➪ **Line Breaks** are turned on — Word pretends there are fonts on-screen and everything runs off the end.

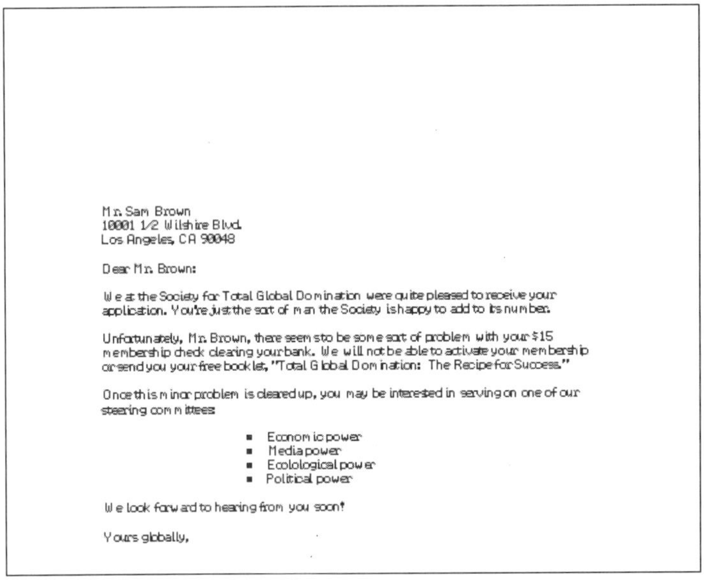

Mr. Sam Brown
10001 1/2 Wilshire Blvd.
Los Angeles, CA 90048

Dear Mr. Brown:

We at the Society for Total Global Domination were quite pleased to receive your application. You're just the sort of man the Society is happy to add to its number.

Unfortunately, Mr. Brown, there seems to be some sort of problem with your $15 membership check clearing your bank. We will not be able to activate your membership or send you your free booklet, "Total Global Domination: The Recipe for Success."

Once this minor problem is cleared up, you may be interested in serving on one of our steering committees:

- Economic power
- Media power
- Ecolological power
- Political power

We look forward to hearing from you soon!

Yours globally,

Figure 7-26: With the actual fonts in place, you can compare this to Figure 7-25 and see that it accurately reflected where the line breaks would occur. Mind-boggling!

Parting Tips

Removing automatic page breaks

After printing or previewing, Word dumps automatic page break lines throughout the document like so much digital flotsam and jetsam. For some reason, this really irritates me. Can you tell? I hate looking at those bloody dots! They may not bother you at all, but this is how I get rid of them.

1. Press Alt+**F**ile ⇨ **S**ave to save the document.

   Don't skip this step. What we're about to do could be dangerous, and if you save your file first, you can always retreat to the way it was.

2. Press Shift+F10.

   This highlights the document.

3. Press Shift+Del.

   This action deletes the entire document to the Scrap!

4. Press Shift+Ins.

   This step restores the document — minus those irritating automatic page break dots.

   > ✔ If, for some reason, you find that you've just deleted your document and you can't bring it back (sounds like a job for LifeAlert, doesn't it? — "I've deleted and I can't get it back!"), immediately press Alt+File ⇨ **C**lose and say No to saving changes. Then bring your document back with Alt+File ⇨ **O**pen.

Copying formatting

After you've got a piece of text looking just right, you may want to repeat that formatting elsewhere in the document. The F4 — repeat — command is helpful if the last function performed was the formatting. However, if it wasn't, you can try some other tricks.

✔ Put the cursor in the paragraph you want to copy, mindlessly press Alt+Format ⇨ **P**aragraph, and then press Enter. Then go to the paragraph where you want to apply the formatting (or highlight the paragraphs) and press F4.

✔ Because the paragraph symbol contains the formatting information, you can highlight the symbol and Ctrl+Ins it into the Scrap. Then go to the paragraph where you want to apply the formatting and place the cursor before the end of that paragraph and press Ctrl+Ins. You can only do this one paragraph at a time.

✔ The preceding trick also works with section marks, if you feel up to it.

✔ The easiest and ultimate way to copy formats for characters, paragraphs, and sections is with style sheets, which are covered in Chapter 11.

✔ Highlight the word where you want to apply the formatting. Then point to the word with the desired formatting and press Shift+Ctrl and click. This also can work with paragraph formatting. Highlight the paragraph to receive the formatting. Then point to the area to the left of the properly formatted paragraph, press Shift+Ctrl and click.

Printing out all your fonts

If you want to know what fonts your printer actually can print, you can get Word to print them all for you. To do this, we'll use one of the macros that was supplied by Word. As long as your computer was set up with the normal values, the following steps will work:

1. Press Alt+T**o**ols ⇨ **M**acro.

2. Press Alt+**O**pen Glossary.

3. Type **C:\WORD\MACRO.GLY**.

4. Press Enter.

    If you get a Files or directory does not exist message, make sure that you've typed Step 3 correctly — you've got your backslashes in the right direction, no spaces, and a period between MACRO and GLY. If you've done everything correctly and you still get Files or directory does not exist, it looks as though your setup is not the same as the default. Press Esc to exit the Macro dialog box.

5. After you're back in the Macro dialog box, press Esc.

    ✔ Now that you're back at your main screen, turn on the printer. This may take some time.

6. Press Ctrl+VC.

7. Watch your fonts print out.

    ✔ Now you can tell which fonts have which bullets and symbols.

    ✔ Be sure to keep the pages handy for future reference.

Chapter 8
The Sprint to Print

. . . .

In This Chapter

▶ Printing a document

▶ Printing more than one copy

▶ Printing a few good pages

▶ Printing wee bits o' documents

▶ Interrupting a printout

▶ Printing a group of files

▶ Printing problems

. . . .

A great deal of personal satisfaction can be associated with pressing the go button and watching the printer stir to life and finally grind out your document. There can also be a profound sense of relief.

Assuming you've written, formatted, spell-checked, and previewed your document, you're all ready to give birth to a new piece of paper.

Printing a Document ... Finally

All print commands follow the steps coming up. It's what you specify in the Print dialog box that varies the outcome.

To print one copy of the current document, follow these steps:

1. Press Alt+**File** ⇨ **Print**.

   You get the Print dialog box, where you can select various options, described in the following sections (see Figure 8-1).

2. Press Enter.

   The message bar counts down the pages as they are printed.

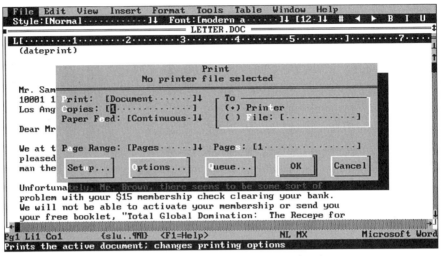

Figure 8-1: The Print dialog box allows you to specify what gets printed.

Printing more than one copy

When you initially give the Alt+File ⇨ **Print** command, the cursor ends up in the Copies text box. Type the number of copies you need and press Enter.

Printing a few good pages

When you don't need to print the whole darn thing, press Alt+Pages to jump to the Pages text box. Type your printout wish list:

Enter	To Print
1	page 1
1,4	pages 1 and 4
1-4	pages 1, 2, 3, and 4
1-3,8	pages 1, 2, 3, and 8

When you've finished with your list, press Enter.

✔ You must enter the numbers in ascending order. You can't ask for page 9 after page 10.

✔ You can Backspace to make corrections.

Printing wee bits o' documents

You can even print odd amounts (like a page and a half) if you want. That way, you can print things on a need-to-know basis if you're a spy.

1. Highlight the section you want to print.

2. Press Alt+**F**ile ⇨ **P**rint.

3. Press Alt+**Pa**ge Range.

4. Press S.

    The word Selection appears. That's what tells Word to print the high-lighted stuff only.

5. Press Enter.

Interrupting a printout

Although you can stop a document from printing, the response isn't exactly immediate.

As long as Word is still counting down the pages printing out (in the message bar), you can issue the cancel printing command by doing the following:

1. Press Esc.

2. A dialog box pops up, asking whether you want to continue printing or stop the presses and cancel.

3. Press Tab until you reach the Cancel option.

4. Press Enter.

    ✔ If the message bar isn't counting down pages, Word is no longer send-ing pages to the printer. You have stopped the printing.

    ✔ Word cannot, retroactively, retrieve what was already sent to the printer before you canceled printing. The printing may continue for a few more pages before it'll actually stop. Just relax and let the pages come out at their own pace and let the old print job run its course. Be sure to throw the pages into the recycle container. Then start again.

The shortcut key to printing is Shift+F9. You still have to take a look at the dia-log box to make sure that your preferences are selected.

Printing a group of files

Sometimes you need to print several files and it's a huge drag to open each file, print it, close it, open the next file, and so on.

Not to be denied the lazy way to do things, we can make an end run around the Alt+File ⇨ **P**rint command with a feature called File Management. File Management is covered in Chapter 13, but you don't have to know everything about File Management to print a couple of files. Just follow these steps:

1. Press Alt+File ⇨ File Management.

2. Use the arrow keys to get to the first file you want to print.

3. Press the spacebar.

   When you press the spacebar, an asterisk (*) appears to the left of the file name (see Figure 8-2). If you press the spacebar on the wrong file name, pressing the spacebar again takes away the asterisk. Spacebar is another one of those on/off light switch things.

4. Go to the next file you want to print and press the spacebar.

   If you accidentally press Enter instead of the spacebar, you'll be taken out of File Management and into the file. Don't panic. Just press Alt+File ⇨ **C**lose to close that file and start again from Step 1.

5. When you have selected all the files you want to print, press Alt+**P**rint.

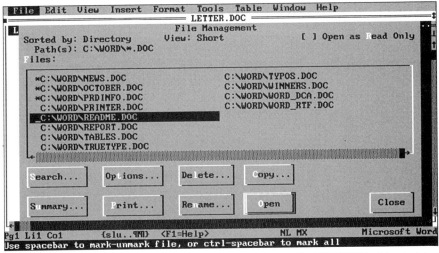

Figure 8-2: Use Alt+File ⇨ File Management to print marked files like NEWS.DOC, with asterisks to the left of their names.

6. When the Print dialog box appears, press Enter.

All selected (*) files will print.

> ✔ Printing a group of files is not the same as merging. Mail merge is covered in Chapter 11, in a little section called "Merging Mania" — if you're brave enough to tackle it.

> ✔ If you change your mind about using File Management, just press Esc to leave File Management and to go back to the main Word screen, safe and sound.

Printing while you work

Looking for someplace to unload some of your disposable income? Here's a suggestion: Buy a printer buffer.

What's a printer buffer? Well, first of all, it is not a whirling device that waxes and polishes your printer. A *printer buffer* is a fabulous little box that goes between your computer and your printer; that is, the cable that used to plug into the printer now plugs into the buffer and another cable comes out of the buffer and plugs into the printer.

"Why do I want this buffer thing?" you may ask.

Have you sat there, frustrated, while the computer and printer slowly grind out pages? Even if you have the world's fastest printer, it's not fast enough.

The reality is that the computer sends the stuff to the printer a whole lot faster than the printer can print — even if you have the world's fastest printer.

If you put the buffer between the computer and the printer, the computer sends the stuff to the buffer at computer speed and the buffer sits there and doles out the stuff to the printer at printer speed. For example, it normally takes 20 minutes for me to print a 120-page document. However, my computer can send it to the buffer in about 5 minutes. After the 5 minutes, my computer is freed up so that I can — what? — go back to work? Hmm ... maybe this isn't such a good idea.

Buffers are definitely cool and I highly recommend them.

However, for free, you can try out Word's print queue. It's kind of a buffer-on-a-disk. The older your computer and the smaller your hard disk, however, the worse an idea it is to use this feature. When you invoke the print queue, it robs some of your system's resources to do the printing job. Depending on your machine, you will notice a degradation in responsiveness, ranging from unacceptable to barely noticeable.

To turn on the print queue, press Alt+**File** ⇨ **Print** ⇨ **Q**ueue and make sure that the Use Print **Q**ueue box is checked. (Later, if you want to turn it off, just uncheck the box.) Print as you normally do.

You also can buy (there's that word again) a software *print spooler* that does what the print queue does — maybe a bit better. Often they require experimentation to get them in balance with your system.

The printer buffer, however, doesn't take any disk space; doesn't reduce your system resources; is very, very simple to install (you plug cables in); works with all your software; and never needs upgrading.

Maybe a loved one can buy you one for Christmas. Or something.

Printing Problems ... er, Challenges

That's what we learned in the 80s — new names for everything. All of our problems were replaced with challenges. Well, if you have a good printer with bad behavior, you may want to check out some of these helpful hints before you decide not to live up to your longevity potential.

Printer not ready

If Word tells you the Printer is not ready, it means that the printer isn't turned on, is out of paper, or is off-line.

- ✔ The out-of-paper and turned-off problems you know what to do about.
- ✔ The off-line/on-line thing may not sound so familiar.

On the front of your printer, someplace, is a little light that needs to be on if you want to print. Some printers label this light "On line," others call it "Select" or "Sel." Usually, it's next to another button that says "Form feed" or "FF." If the on-line button is not on, the computer and the printer are not talking. Press the on-line button.

Sometimes the on-line button gets turned off when you open the printer, change paper, and do that sort of thing.

Another thing to try is to turn the printer off, wait a few seconds, and then turn it back on. I've cured a lot of printer problems with that simple step.

No printer file selected

You get this kind of message from Word when you haven't specified what kind of printer you have, or have somehow deleted the name of your printer.

Press Alt+File ⇨ Printer Setup to get to the Printer Setup dialog box. You probably will see a couple of printer file names in the Files box (see Figure 8-3).

Press Alt+File to jump to the Files box. As you highlight a printer file, the names of the printers it represents appear in the Printer Name box. Select the right printer and press Enter.

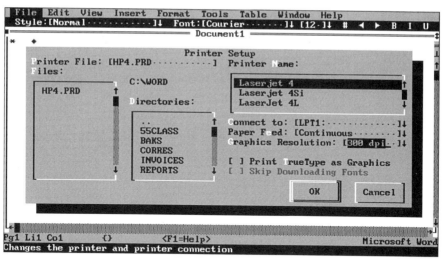

Figure 8-3: The Printer Setup dialog box is where everybody knows your printer's name. Find yours among the group to get back on line.

Nothing comes out

If nothing comes out immediately, and you have a laser printer, check your Form Feed or Data light. If it's flashing, then something is happening. If you're using fonts or printing a picture of some sort, your printer needs extra time to do the work. Have patience. If you've waited 20 minutes and still nothing comes out, you should reset your printer and try again.

If you print and nothing comes out but a blank page, and the message bar says `0 lines and 0 words counted`, press Alt+File ⇨ **P**rint. Take a look at the P**a**ge Range text box. It's probably set to Selection, and Word is printing out whatever text is selected in the document, which is probably none. Change P**a**ge Range back to All. Then, to print, press Enter.

Something weird appears on every page

If a line of text from one page magically repeats itself on every page of your print-out — what I call the "ghost of text past" phenomenon — then you've probably accidentally created a header or a footer (see Chapter 7 to learn how to make them on purpose). To get rid of the header or footer, do the following:

1. Press Shift+F10.

   This highlights your whole document.

2. Press Alt+Format ⇨ Header/Footer.

3. Select **N**one in the Format As box.

4. Press Enter.

5. Press any arrow key to remove the highlighting.

Chapter 9
Embracing Envelopes

*I*t used to be so simple to address an envelope.

Now, thanks to computers, an entire printing-an-envelope industry has sprung into existence.

Microsoft has been providing a little program to print envelopes with the last few versions of Word. Unfortunately, no one knew about it because it was buried in pounds of manuals and volumes of software! The version of this envelope-printing program — it's not a program, but a macro, actually — provided with Word 6 seems to be the best of the lot.

Now, you can just type an envelope on-screen and out it will come from the printer. Just like a typewriter. Almost.

Even though the macro is easy to use — all you really have to do is press Ctrl+EN — the setup required is not what you'd call intuitive. And the instructions in the manual are — the instructions in the manual.

Getting Ready

If you've let Microsoft set up Word 6 for you, then the macro and these set-up instructions will work. By the way, you need know nothing about what a macro is or does to make this work; all you have to do is follow the bouncing ball. (If you want to know about macros, see Chapter 11.) Follow these steps:

1. Press Alt+**T**ools ⇨ **M**acro.

2. Press Alt+**O**pen Glossary.

3. Type **C:\WORD\MACRO.GLY**.

4. Press Enter.

    If you get a Files or directory does not exist message, make sure that you've typed Step 3 correctly — you've got your backslashes in the right direction, no spaces, and a period between MACRO and GLY. If you've done everything correctly and you still get Files or directory does not exist, then it looks as though your setup is not the same as the default. Press Esc and go on to another chapter — or hunt down the person who's been messing with your computer and have him or her get this working for you.

5. After you're back in the Macro dialog box, press Esc.

Okay, now you should be back to your main screen. You're ready to try out the envelope macro.

Be sure to turn on your printer!

> ✔ You'll have to go through this process every time you get into Word and want to use the envelope program unless you make the setup permanent, as described in the last section of this chapter.

> ✔ This process loads not only the envelope macro, but all the macros that came from Microsoft. Virtually none of which you will use.

Printing an Envelope

If you've gotten this far, you're pretty much home free. All you have to do now is:

1. Stick an envelope in your printer.

2. Press Ctrl+EN.

    That means hold down — and keep holding down — the Ctrl key and then press E and then N.

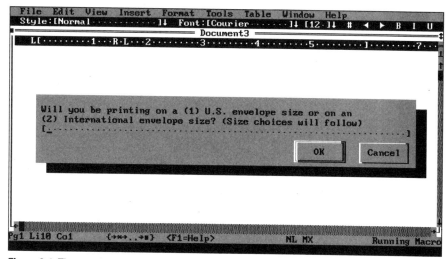

Figure 9-1: The envelope macro is running — all you have to do is answer a few questions.

It may not look like anything is happening at first, but the message bar says that the Envelope Macro is running. Relax while it sets itself up. This will be fun.

3. Respond to a series of dialog boxes, like the one in Figure 9-1, about the kind of envelope and printer you're using, whether you want a return address, how many lines long the address and return address are. All the questions are multiple choice — just pick a response and press Enter.

4. Impress your friends when the envelope prints out.

   ✔ If you want to cancel at any time, press Esc. You'll find several unfamiliar documents open; these were being used by the envelope program. Just close them without saving.

   ✔ Because you have the option to select an address from the screen, you may want to make a file with your commonly used addresses. Then you don't have to type the address every time — you just select it from the list.

Making the Envelope Macro Permanent

This gets a little involved. You may want to try using the envelope program a while and, if you like it, then it may be worth the steps required to make it permanent.

Here's how:

1. Go through the setting up process described in the section "Getting Ready."
2. Press Alt+T**ools** ⇨ **Macro.**
3. Press Alt+**Macros** and highlight the first macro, 1-README.
4. Press Alt+D**elete.**
5. Continue pressing Alt+Delete until the only thing left in the Macros box is
   ```
   Envelope <Ctrl E>N.
   ```
6. Press Alt+**S**ave Glossary.
7. Type **C:\WORD\NORMAL.GLY.**
8. Press Enter.

If you get confused about any of this, or get lost, or think you've made a mistake, just press Alt+**File** ⇨ **Exit** Word and do not save any changes except to your own documents.

- ✔ When you exit Word, you are asked whether you want to save the changes to MACRO.GLY. You *do not.*

- ✔ When you get into Word next time, try using Ctrl+EN. It should work without any additional setup.

If you want to print a bunch of envelopes, as in a mail-merge process, check out "Merging Mania" in Chapter 11, as well as Chapter 14, "Learning to Love Labels."

Pushing the envelope

If you don't know how to put an envelope in your printer, probably the only way to find out is to look in your printer manual. There is probably a picture someplace illustrating how it's done. Look up *envelope* in the manual's index. You may get lucky. Some laser printers have little pictures of envelopes etched into the feeder tray — try looking for that first. If you can't figure out how it's done, call the printer manufacturer and ask for help.

Even if you do get the envelope in the printer, it seems as though the printer can hardly wait to crush, crease, and otherwise mangle perfectly innocent envelopes. The printer may not actually be the villain. I have even found that environmen-

tal conditions (rainy days are the worst) will affect the treatment the envelope receives from a laser printer. Also, if you have envelopes printed on heavy paper, they may not work at all.

If you're feeding envelopes into a laser printer, the best thing to do is to run the end that's going into the printer between your thumb and index finger and flatten that end as much as possible. It'll make it easier for the printer to grab.

Also, if you're using a laser printer, be prepared for at least one envelope to get lost inside the printer during your lifetime. This is not the end of the world. You will have to open the printer to get it out, though, and you may need the manual for that.

Chapter 10
Defensive Computing

*I*t's 11 o'clock. Do you know where your data is?

You may think it's safely stored on your hard disk — but how safe is your hard disk? Did you know that, in addition to speed, manufacturers describe their hard disks in terms of "MTBF" — "mean time between *failures*?" Italics mine.

Are you prepared for the day when your hard disk — along with everything on it — suddenly takes a dive? If this were to happen tomorrow morning, would you be able to calmly restore your data — or would someone have to call 911 on your behalf?

Staying Clean

To avoid the embarrassment of being found in a fetal position under your desk, get into the habit of practicing *hard disk management* — which is very impressive-sounding computerspeak for deleting and copying files. The goal of hard disk management is to keep your hard disk as neat as your desk.

And, yes, I *am* talking about your desk and I *do* know what it looks like because I've got one just like it (and let's not even talk about the semicircle of worshipful file folders that lie at my feet).

Even so, the desk is still the perfect role model for good hard-diskkeeping because, chaotic though it may be, not every piece of paper you've ever held in your hand is sitting on your desk. There is a file cabinet or box or even a stack someplace *else* with lots and lots of *other* files that *aren't* on the desk. And, every now and then, the contents of the desk are evaluated and either filed — in both circular and permanent containers — or retained on the desk.

How long has it been since your hard disk has been subjected to that sort of scrutiny? Or, as with most people, does your hard disk contain every file you've created since the dawn of time? And, if you work in a large company, it may also contain all the files ever created by the dearly departed employee who used the computer before you!

Fortunately, Word has a way to make it easy to perform defensive computing — it's called File Management.

> ✔ Chapter 13 has some additional information about File Management that expands on the basic moves that follow.

File Management is the new name for Library Document Retrieval. After you're inside it, the options and moves will be familiar.

Backing Up

At the end of every day, you need to *back up* — also known as *copying* to a floppy disk — the files you have worked with that day. Doing this will take, maybe, one whole minute of your time. Follow these steps:

1. Put a floppy disk in the drive.

   Whether you use drive A or drive B is irrelevant. For the purposes of this example, I'll use drive A. If you're using drive B, just substitute drive letters as needed. And if your drive is the kind with a latch, be sure to close it. Also, it makes sense to designate a single disk as your daily back-up disk.

2. Press Alt+File ➭ File Management.

   You'll get the File Management dialog box, which contains a list of file names.

3. Use the up- and down-arrow keys — or mouse — to scroll through the list of files to the one you want to back up.

4. Press the spacebar to mark the file.

   In Figure 10-1, LETTER.DOC is highlighted; the asterisk (*) to the left was inserted by pressing the spacebar. This is called *marking a file*. The asterisk is your scent — you predatory beast, you — and you're marking your territory. You're going to star on the next episode of "Nature."

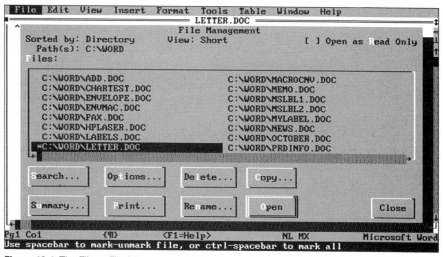

Figure 10-1: The File ⇨ File Management dialog box with the file LETTER.DOC *marked* with the tell-tale asterisk.

Unlike wild animals, though, you can unmark your territory. So, if you accidentally mark a file, or just change your mind, then highlight the file again and press the spacebar to make the asterisk go away.

5. Repeat Steps 3 and 4 until you have marked all the files you want to copy.

6. Press Alt+**C**opy.

You'll see the dialog box shown in Figure 10-2. Don't worry that your **P**ath Name may vary. Yours is perfect just the way it is.

7. Type **A:** and press Enter.

If you're using drive B, type **B:** instead of **A:**. After a few seconds, you'll be delivered back to the File Management dialog box.

8. Press Esc or click Close to return to the normal screen.

> ✔ You can use the same disk every day to back up your files. However, before Word copies the file, it'll ask:

> Do you want to overwrite the existing file?

Overwrite means erase. In this case, you do want to erase the old file in favor of the new file. If you're using your daily back-up disk, it's simply a case of "out with the old, in with the new." So finish the job by pressing Enter — or click OK — and Word races to carry out your command.

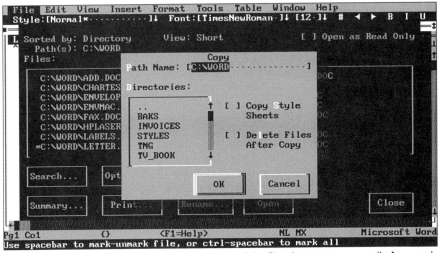

Figure 10-2: After you're in the Copy dialog box, just tell the file where to go — usually A: — and press Enter.

✔ Occasionally — just for fun — back up *all* your document files. To do so doesn't required highlighting and marking every last file one at a time. Word has a command to "mark 'em all" — Ctrl+spacebar. After they're all marked, proceed to Steps 6 and 7. (You also can press Ctrl+spacebar to *unmark* all previously marked files.)

✔ If you only want to copy one file, just highlight the file name; you don't have to actually mark it.

✔ If Word beeps at you and the message bar says Cannot copy a file, make sure that you actually put a disk in the drive and that you typed the correct drive letter in Step 7. If all that is correct, then the disk in the drive may not be *formatted* (see the sidebar in this chapter "Fooling with your floppy disks").

✔ If Word beeps at you and says Document disk is full, it means that the disk you're trying to copy onto already has a bunch of stuff on it. You need another disk.

These instructions are for backing up your Word documents only. You should also be backing up your entire system — including programs and everything. If you have never done this, please use either the DOS back-up program (MSBACKUP, which comes with Version 6 of DOS, is pretty good) or buy one of the many, many programs desperately competing for your hard-earned cash! Before you decide not to bother — just remember, the clock is ticking on your drive's MTBF.

Fooling with your floppy disks

Floppy disks can be a tremendous source of confusion — I guess as opposed to everything else about computers that makes so much sense. Perhaps the peak of confusion comes when you must purchase a new supply of these little darlings and you find out that they come in two physical sizes — 3.5" and 5.25" — and two *densities* — high density and double density.

The simplest way to make sure that you get the right thing is to take one of the disks you're currently using to the store and ask for more.

After you get the disks home, you need to format them — unless you bought some *preformatted* disks.

In the grand scheme of things, the *reason* for formatting disks is unimportant. Just know that you have to do it. Here's how:

1. This is not a Word command, so either exit the Word program or press Alt+**F**ile ⇨ MS-**D**OS Commands.

2. Type **FORMAT A:** and press Enter.

3. You'll be told to put a disk in the drive — even if there's one in there already — and press Enter.

4. Watch the percentage count as the formatting progresses. This is fun.

5. When it's finished, you'll have the opportunity to format another. Press Y to format another disk; press N to terminate the formatting cycle.

   ✔ If you're formatting a disk in drive B, substitute **B** for **A** in Step 2.

   ✔ When you get a new box of disks, it's a good idea to format all of them. That way, you won't get confused later about what is and isn't formatted. You can't tell just by looking.

✔ After a disk is formatted, you don't have to format it again.

✔ Most computers will even let you *unformat* a disk — in case you accidentally format a disk that you didn't mean to — as long as you haven't used it since the formatting. To unformat, use the same instructions as formatting, except type **UNFORMAT** in place of **FORMAT**.

Another important thing about formatting is that if you format a disk that already has stuff on it, you'll erase whatever's on the disk. Before you format an exotic disk of unknown origins, it might be good politics to find out whether it already contains some files. Although **F**ile Management can tell you what Word document files are on the disk, it's generally worthless when it comes to settling the issue of whether the darn thing is formatted.

Here's how you can find out:

1. Put the dubious disk in the drive.

2. Press Alt+**F**ile ⇨ MS-**D**OS Commands.

3. Type **DIR A:** and press Enter.

   ✔ If you get a list of files, then the disk is formatted and has stuff on it. If it's stuff you recognize, you may want to toy with the notion of slapping an identifying label on it. If you want to erase everything, then format it again. If no files are listed, it's a blank formatted disk!

   ✔ If you get:

`General failure reading Drive A. Abort, Retry, Ignore?`

Don't have a heart attack. Nothing is broken. First, check to make sure that you've got a disk in

(continued)

Fooling with your floppy disks (continued)

the drive and that the drive latch is closed (if you've got one). Also, if you typed **DIR A:**, make sure that the disk is in drive A. If the disk is in B, then you need to type **DIR B:**. After you've corrected any of these situations, press R for retry. If everything mentioned above is A-OK, then press A to abort the mission. Now you know you've got an unformatted disk.

Finally, if you work in an office littered with Macintosh computers, let them take a crack at the disk — it may have been formatted for a Mac and contain Macintosh files.

Doing the Delete

Beyond organizational reasons, deleting files from the hard disk actually promotes hard disk longevity. The more stuff on the hard disk, the more work the disk has to do. The more work the hard disk has to do, the sooner it breaks down. Conversely, the fewer files on the hard disk — the longer it will last. Besides, those extra files actually slow the whole system down.

Deleting and backing up

Can you believe it — you can actually delete and back up at the same time! Magic? No! Merely an example of better living through science.

Because Steps 1 through 6 for deleting and backing up are the same as Steps 1 through 6 for plain backing up, we'll just run through them quickly. (If you need more detail, it's in the preceding section.)

1. Put a floppy disk in the drive.
2. Press Alt+**File** ⇨ File Management.
3. Highlight the file you want to copy and delete.
4. Press the spacebar.
5. Repeat Steps 3 and 4 until all files to be copied and deleted are marked.
6. Press Alt+**Copy**.
7. Type **A:**.
8. Press Alt+Delete Files After Copy.

    By checking the Delete Files After Copy box, Word backs up the selected files on the designated floppy and then nukes 'em from the hard disk.

9. Press Enter.

After a few seconds, you'll be delivered back to the File Management dialog box.

10. Press Esc or click Close to return to the normal screen.

> ✔ This is the better-safe-than-sorry procedure. For the price of a few floppy disks, files can be *archived* — computerspeak for *filed away* — just in case you need them again after all.

Deleting

To just plain delete a file, most of the steps are the same as for copying — except for the surprise ending.

1. Put a floppy disk in the drive.

2. Press Alt+File ➪ File Management.

3. Highlight the file you want to delete.

4. Press the spacebar.

5. Repeat Steps 3 and 4 until all files to be deleted are marked.

6. Press Alt+Delete.

7. Verify that you want to delete the marked files by pressing the traditional Enter.

You cannot delete a currently open file. If you open a file to look at it, you have to close it before Word will let you delete it.

Undeleting — resurrecting the dead

If you accidentally delete something, it isn't necessarily a huge disaster because most computers nowadays have the capability to resuscitate a deleted file.

In addition to what's built into the system, there are programs out on the market that deal with recovering from a disaster on a much higher level. Chances are, if things get that messed up, you won't be in charge of recovery operations.

Undeleting isn't major surgery — it's just a simple Heimlich-type maneuver to get the computer to cough up your file. Lovely metaphor, huh?

Let's say you just accidentally deleted a file — knock on wood that this will never happen — but, let's just say. Then let's just say you immediately realize your error. (The longer you wait, the

(continued)

Undeleting — resurrecting the dead (continued)

more files you work with, the more likely the file will be gone for good.) To bring the file back, cross your fingers and — no, wait, you can't type with crossed fingers — so, uncross your fingers and then:

1. Press Alt+File ⇨ MS-**D**OS Commands.

2. Type **UNDELETE** and press Enter when you get the MS-DOS Commands dialog box.

    Eventually, you'll see Undelete (Y/N) on the right hand side of the screen (see Figure 10-3). To the left of that question is a bunch of numbers and stuff and, we hope, the name of your file with a question mark in place of the first letter of the file name.

    In Figure 10-3, you can see ?AT.DOC — which used to be CAT.DOC. The computer, meanwhile, is waiting for an answer to the question — Undelete (Y/N)?

3. Press Y if you want to undelete.

    If you press N, then the next undeletable file name appears. Eventually, and with any luck, the file you want will be found and you'll get to press Y.

4. You're asked for a letter to replace the question mark. In this case, I'd type **C**.

5. After a few seconds, if your karma is good, you'll see the words File successfully undeleted.

6. Next, you are prompted to press a key to resume Word.

7. Party.

   ✔ Test your computer's UQ — undelete quotient — before it becomes a life-or-death question. Just delete something you don't care about and then try to bring it back. If you can't do it, then run, do not walk, to a software store and invest in a file-recovery program such as Norton Utilities, or even MS-DOS Version 6, if you don't have it.

   ✔ If you see a Bad Command or File Name error message after Step 2, your computer will not undelete. Go buy some software, per the preceding suggestion.

   ✔ If you get something about Not enough memory to run, exit Word and then try Steps 2 through 5.

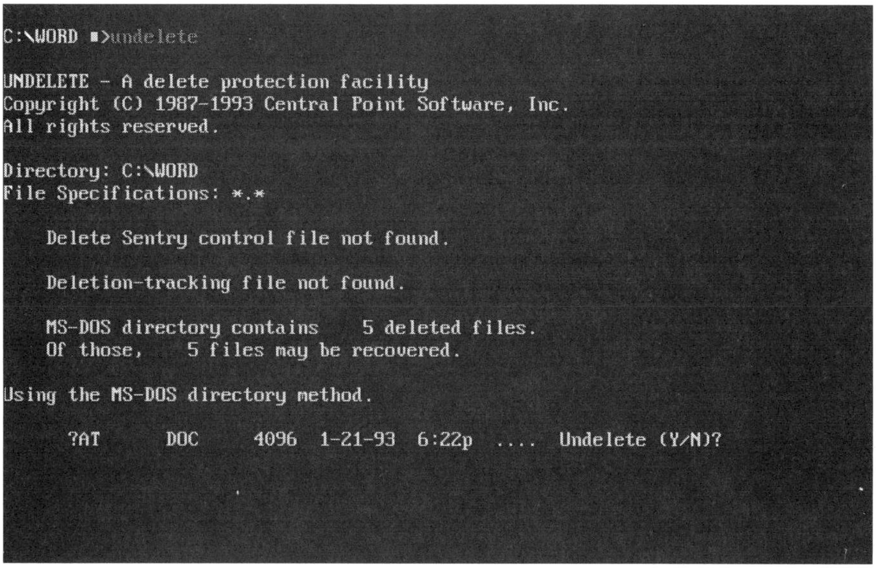

```
C:\WORD ■>undelete

UNDELETE - A delete protection facility
Copyright (C) 1987-1993 Central Point Software, Inc.
All rights reserved.

Directory: C:\WORD
File Specifications: *.*

    Delete Sentry control file not found.

    Deletion-tracking file not found.

    MS-DOS directory contains     5 deleted files.
    Of those,     5 files may be recovered.

Using the MS-DOS directory method.

     ?AT      DOC     4096  1-21-93  6:22p  ....  Undelete (Y/N)?
```

Figure 10-3: The Undelete screen. The bottom line is the bottom line. Press Y to undelete the file, press N to move to the next one, and keep repeating your mantra.

Part III
Life in the Fast Lane

"These kidnappers are clever, Lieutenant. Look at this ransom note, the way they got the text to wrap around the victim's photograph. And the fonts! They must be creating their own- must be over 35 typefaces here...."

In this part . . .

*F*irst of all, if you bought this book *only* to get the basics —
immediately make a U-turn and stay in the pages behind
this one. Turn back now! If you dare to proceed, if you defy
my warning and look upon the titillating, intoxicating, and
forbidden commands coming up — like style sheets, macros,
Glossaries, sorting, mail merge, borders, reverse printing, and
more — you risk being turned into a pillar of silicon!

Chapter 11

Features You've Secretly Wished You Understood

*T*hey're creepy and they're kooky, mysterious and spooky. They're altogether oooky. They're the features covered here.

Okay, so it doesn't exactly fit the rhyme. Sue me.

What does fit is all these swell features in one nonthreatening chapter. This chapter features the type of things computers absolutely love to do — repetitive tasks. And, continuing the *...For Dummies* tradition, we've cut to the chase on these normally complex features. Basically, this chapter is the tip of the iceberg on all four topics.

Even so, never underestimate the power of the tip of an iceberg — just ask the Titanic.

If, however, you go mental on one of these features and need more, more, more! — you'll have learned enough by then to negotiate the manual for yourself.

Now *that's* oooky.

Stylin' with Sheets

The good news is that if you can format a character, paragraph, or section, you already understand 80 percent of all there is to know about style sheets. Honest. (If you need a refresher on formatting, you might want to reminisce in Chapter 7.)

Remember how much fun it was to use the speed-formatting keys in Chapter 7? Being able to press Ctrl+T and instantly get a hanging indent was pretty cool. Well, one of the far out things about style sheets is being able to create your own, personalized, speed-formatting keys.

For example, pretend that the reports you create have two kinds of paragraphs — a normal one and one that's indented *and* italicized. It quickly becomes a major drag to use Alt+Forma**t** ⇨ **P**aragraph blah+blah+blah... and press Enter every time you want to switch from one type of paragraph formatting to the other. Wouldn't it be swell if you could record the paragraph formatting — otherwise known as a *style* — and assign it a *key code* — a speed-formatting key?

Then, in the future, just press the key code and, voilà, you're instantly indented, italicized mode. Another key code and, shazzam, you're back in normal mode.

A style *sheet*, then, is a collection of saved Forma**t** **C**haracters, Format **P**aragraphs, and Forma**t S**ections, each with a key code.

If you need to produce many different kinds of documents, you can create many different style sheets to match the specifics of each type of document. Or, if you have simple needs, you can have one set of styles that are always there, no matter what.

Using style sheets keeps formatting consistent, regardless of who is doing the work. Plus, you can have one person doing the formatting and recording of the style — and a person who only knows when and how to apply a style doing the actual typing.

It gets better.

The pièce de résistance is that if you change the formatting in the style sheet — say you decide that you don't want that paragraph italicized after all — all the paragraphs formatted with that key code will automatically change as well. No search and replace, no highlight, no nothing. Change the style sheet and the document will follow. Instantly.

On the other hand, if your documents are like snowflakes — no two look alike — then style sheets aren't for you. You can skip this section.

Building a style sheet

You build a style sheet, basically, with paragraphs. One brick at a time. One way to get a running start at style sheets is to open a document that already has several different kinds of paragraph formatting. Hopefully, it's a type of document that you create on a regular basis — a report, a proposal letter, or a certain kind of memo. Whatever.

Recording your first style

To record a style, follow these steps:

1. Place the cursor someplace within the body of a paragraph that has formatting you want to record.

2. Press Alt+Format ⇨ **R**ecord Style.

   You'll get the Record Style dialog box, which has an overabundance of computer-looking stuff in it (see Figure 11-1). You can ignore all of it except for the **K**ey Code text box.

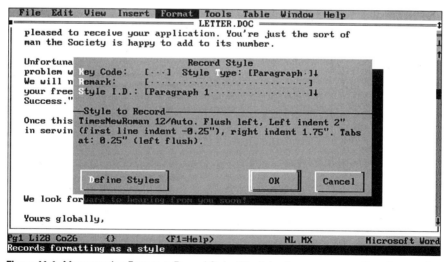

Figure 11-1: After pressing Format ⇨ Record Style, this dialog box pops up — all you have to do is supply the key code — the Style to Record gobbledygook is supplied by Word.

3. Type a key code.

For your first style sheet, let's just use one-letter codes. Later, if you start doing killer style sheets, you can use two-letter codes. In the example in Figure 11-1, I'm creating a style for an indented paragraph, so I'll give it the key code of **I** — for "Indented."

4. Press Alt+**R**emark.

5. Write an identifying phrase.

To help you always remember what this style should be used for, type something like **Indented list**.

6. Press Enter.

You now have your first style.

Congratulations.

Now, put the cursor in another paragraph and create another style.

✔ Don't forget to record the style of your regular-looking paragraphs as well as the unusual ones.

✔ If you have headings, create a style for them, too.

✔ You also can record a style for a character by highlighting the character you want to record and, when you're in the Record Style dialog box, use Alt+Style **T**ype to specify the type of style — character — to be recorded.

✔ You also can record the current section by simply selecting Section as the Style Type. If you have more than one section in your document, you can put your cursor on the section mark you want to record and then record the style. But if you've got more than one section in your document, I'll be calling you up for advice.

✔ If you want a specific style to be the default, you need to assign it the **S**tyle I.D. called Normal. Press Alt+**S**tyle I.D. and Alt+down arrow to reveal Normal, which appears at the top of the list.

Naming

After you've got a few styles safely hidden away in your sheet, you need to save and name the whole thing. To do that, we'll have to look at what has been created — actually view the entire style sheet. It's accessible by pressing Alt+Format ⇨ **D**efine Styles and then Enter. Word opens another window and sticks the style sheet in it. You'll get something like the screen shown in Figure 11-2.

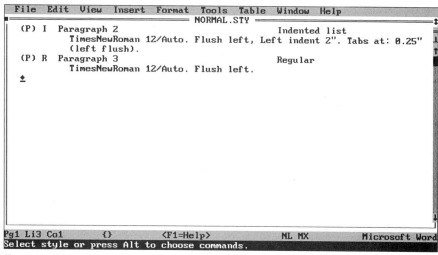

Figure 11-2: Your first style sheet — one small step for a person, one giant leap for personkind.

After you've got the style sheet on-screen, the options in the menus change. Although it looks the same, the menu bar has been secretly revamped — temporarily — to apply to style sheets. If you don't believe me, pull down the Format menu, for example: the last third of the commands are now gone because they no longer apply. Isn't Word smart?

Okay, now let's save the style sheet before something happens. When you have the style sheet on-screen:

1. Press Alt+**File** ⇨ Save **As**.

   This gives you the Save As dialog box — tailored toward style sheets (see Figure 11-3). Style sheet names, you may notice, end in STY. Right now, the style sheet you've just created is called NORMAL.STY. If you don't change that name, then every single time you start Word, that style sheet will be active. That may be good, it may be not-so-good. It depends on your situation. For now, we're going to give it a new name.

2. Type a file name.

   Like, type **REPORT**, for example, if the style sheet is going to be used for reports. You may name it whatever you want — as long as you don't get long winded and exceed the eight alphanumeric-character limit.

3. Press Enter.

4. Press Alt+**File** ⇨ **Close**.

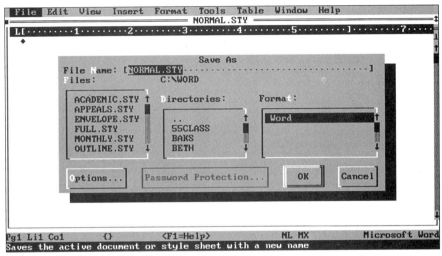

Figure 11-3: The Save As dialog box tailored for style sheets.

That closes the style sheet window and puts you back at your normal Word screen.

Congratulations, you have now created and saved a style sheet.

> ✔ If you want, you can keep the style sheet file open. Word treats it just like another file window. Ctrl+F6 flips you back and forth between style sheet and document. Actually, Ctrl+F6 cycles you through all the open files. But if all you have open is one document and its style sheet, then Ctrl+F6 toggles you between the document and its style sheet.

In Version 5, the Gallery — a whole separate place in the program — was used to edit and print style sheets. In Word 6, the style sheet is treated as though it were just another document. The same Forma**t** ➪ **C**haracter you use in edit mode is how you format characters in a style sheet. It feels kind of strange at first. But it's a much more sensible, streamlined approach. The biggest difference comes in applying the style — Version 6 uses, gulp, Ctrl+Shift+key code instead of Alt+key code, as you'll see in the sections that follow.

Using styles

Now that you've created a style sheet, let's see whether it was worth all this effort.

Attaching a style sheet

When you start a new document and you want to employ the styles in a particular sheet, the first step is to *attach* the style sheet:

1. Press Alt+Forma**t** ⇨ **A**ttach Style Sheet.

   The Attach Style Sheet dialog box displays the various available style sheets — including the samples that come with Word (see Figure 11-4).

2. Type the name of the desired style sheet. Or highlight it, or click it — you know the drill by now.

3. Press Enter.

   > ✔ After pressing Enter, it *looks* like nothing has happened. There's nothing on the screen to say, "Yo, the style sheet's here!" But it's there, or Word would've kicked if you made an error attaching it.

   > ✔ You can print an attached style sheet by pressing Alt+File ⇨ **P**rint ⇨ Alt+**P**rint S S and then pressing Enter. This way, you can have a list of the key codes.

You only have to attach the style sheet once per document. After gettin' hitched, the document and style sheet are married for better or for worse.

Even though the term is "attaching a style sheet," the style sheet isn't really "attached," in a physical sense, to the document. This distinction becomes important only when you copy the document to a floppy disk. Basically, a

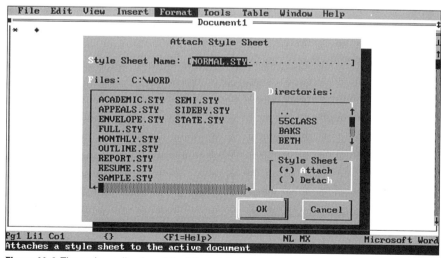

Figure 11-4: The spring collection of the latest styles!

document without the style sheet is like Wayne without Garth. The style sheet is what makes sense out of the document. If you copy a file with File Management, take advantage of the Copy Style Sheets option in the Copy dialog box (visible in Figure 10-2).

Using key codes

To apply a key code, press Ctrl+Shift+key code. For example, I made an indented, italicized style and assigned it a key code of I. To use it, then, I would press Ctrl+Shift+I.

If you want to apply the code to text that's already been typed, just highlight the text and press the code.

- ✔ Remember that plain Ctrl+I was the speed-formatting key for italics. Using Shift with Ctrl is what tells Word to use the style sheet.

- ✔ If you accidentally give a paragraph the wrong style, it's no problem. Just apply the right style, and it'll supplant the preceding one.

- ✔ You also may use the Style box in the Ribbon to apply a style. Press Ctrl+S to get your cursor in the Style box and then press Alt+down arrow to drop down the various style options. Alternatively, just click the down arrow with the mouse. Select the desired style and press Enter.

Viewing the style bar

Due to popular demand, nonprinting symbols for the various styles can be displayed so that you can actually see which style you've assigned to a paragraph.

To turn on or off the style bar:

1. Press Alt+View ➪ Preferences.

2. Press Alt+Style Bar.

   Check the Show Style Bar box if you want to see the style bar. Uncheck it to turn it off.

3. Press Enter.

In Figure 11-5, the document has its style bar turned on. See the letters to the left? Each letter represents a style. C is for character name, D is for dialog, A is for action. Not that I expect everyone to go out and write a screenplay — but it's a type of document that's got markedly different-looking paragraph styles.

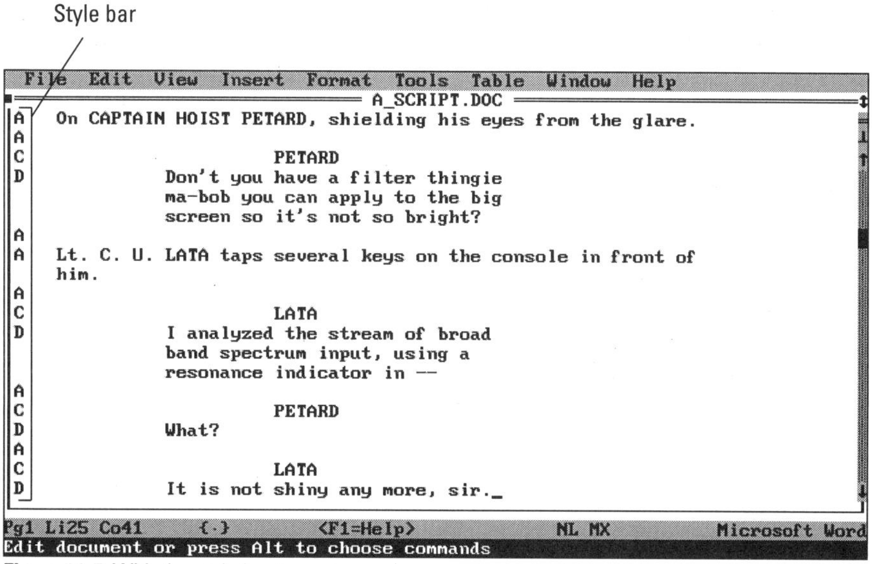

Style bar

```
 File  Edit  View  Insert  Format  Tools  Table  Window  Help
══════════════════════════ A_SCRIPT.DOC ══════════════════════════
A  On CAPTAIN HOIST PETARD, shielding his eyes from the glare.
A
C                        PETARD
D              Don't you have a filter thingie
               ma-bob you can apply to the big
               screen so it's not so bright?
A
A  Lt. C. U. LATA taps several keys on the console in front of
   him.
A
C                        LATA
D              I analyzed the stream of broad
               band spectrum input, using a
               resonance indicator in --
A
C                        PETARD
D              What?
A
C                        LATA
D              It is not shiny any more, sir._

Pg1 Li25 Co41     {·}        <F1=Help>          NL MX      Microsoft Word
Edit document or press Alt to choose commands
```

Figure 11-5: With the style bar turned on, you can see which styles are in use.

Editing styles

If you decide to make a change — in font, in margins, in whatever — you'll need to edit one of your styles. This just means using Format Paragraph on your styles — it's not a big deal.

Assuming that you're in the document that uses the style sheet to be edited, follow these steps:

1. Press Alt+Format ⇨ **D**efine Styles.

   This makes your style sheet visible.

2. Highlight the style you want to change.

   Use the up- and down-arrow keys to travel through the style sheet.

3. Press Alt+Format ⇨ **P**aragraph.

   Make the changes to the style.

4. Press Enter.

5. Press Alt+**F**ile ⇨ **S**ave.

6. Press Alt+File ⇨ **Close**.

   ✔ You can delete a style by highlighting it and pressing Del.

If you change a style sheet in one document, the change also affects every other document that is sharing that same style sheet. If you want to change just the one document, then, after making changes to the style, use Alt+**File** ⇨ Save **As** and give the style sheet another name.

Glorifying the Glossary

One of the many reasons computer terms are so confusing is because they *look* like English — but they're really not. In the preceding section, we discovered that *attach* doesn't mean attach. And, in another section *Autosave* doesn't save. Now a *Glossary* isn't a glossary. I suppose we'll have to take comfort in the fact that "a kiss is still a kiss and a sigh is still a sigh." At least *those* fundamentals still apply.

In Word, a Glossary is, in essence, a permanent Scrap.

Instead of highlighting text and deleting it to the Scrap — where only the last thing deleted can be retrieved — the Glossary lets you name and save the text. Later — and I mean anytime later ... even days, weeks, or months later — you can invoke the magic name the text was saved under and the associated text reappears.

I already know the next question: Why would anyone want this?

Let's do a f'rinstance.

Most of your correspondence ends with the same closing: "Sincerely yours, and let's do lunch and so forth." If you had saved all that obsequious sincerely stuff to the Glossary and named it simply "Sin," then typing **SIN** and pressing F3 (the "expand Glossary key") would cause the entire closing to type itself for you.

In addition to "Sincerely," you can store your boilerplate paragraphs, your legalese, your whatever. Basically, anything you can highlight you can save in the Glossary and invoke with a few keystrokes.

Now does this sound interesting?

Making a Glossary entry

Start out by getting into a document that contains some of your favorite phrases.

1. Highlight the text you want to save in the Glossary.

2. Press Alt+**E**dit ⇨ Glossary.

   This puts you in the Glossary dialog box (see Figure 11-6).

   You can see in Figure 11-6 that some of the text highlighted before the Glossary command was invoked is visible in the Selection section.

3. Type a Glossary name.

   This is where you decide what the code name will be for your text. You can be verbose, if you want, but it's better to type a two- or three-letter shortcut code. Like **Sin**, for example, for the "Sincerely yours" stuff. After something is typed into the **G**lossary Name box, the **D**efine command button comes to life.

4. Press Alt+**D**efine.

   If you've chosen a shortcut code that has been used previously, you'll get a warning box that asks whether you want to overwrite the previous defini-tion. Say OK if you know what you're overwriting. If you don't know what will be overwritten, say No. Go back to Step 3 and try another Glossary name.

   You are returned to the normal screen.

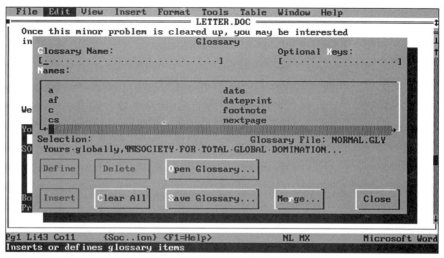

Figure 11-6: The Glossary dialog box, where you can save oft-used text.

To save the Glossary:

1. Press Alt+**E**dit ➪ **Gl**ossary.

2. Press Alt+**S**ave Glossary.

   You see the Save Glossary dialog box, which assumes that you want to name your Glossary file NORMAL.GLY (see Figure 11-7). This implies that you can have several Glossary files — which you can — and that the one named NORMAL is the set of shortcuts you get just by starting Word. All of which is fine; we don't have to make a federal case out of it.

3. Press Enter.

   If you saved your Glossary as NORMAL.GLY, all your shortcuts will be there every time you start Word.

   ✔ If you saved your Glossary as something other than NORMAL.GLY, you'll have to load your oddly named Glossary before you can use your shortcuts. Use Alt+**E**dit ➪ **Gl**ossary ➪ Alt+**O**pen Glossary. Specify the name of the Glossary you want to open and press Enter.

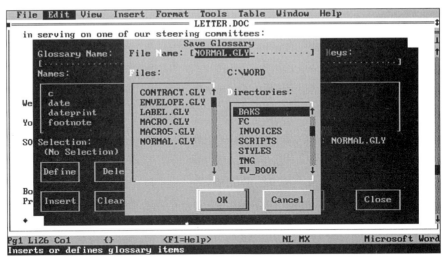

Figure 11-7: The Save Glossary dialog box enables you to give your Glossary a different name — without going to court.

✔ Leave Merge Glossary alone unless you know what you're doing. This command commingles two Glossary files. Things can get weird.

✔ You can print out the Glossary file by pressing Alt+File ➪ **Print** ➪ Alt+**Print** and then pressing G and Enter. This way, you can have a list of the key codes. It'll show each shortcut and what text it'll generate.

✔ You can delete a Glossary entry by going into the Glossary dialog box, highlighting the offending entry, and pressing Alt+Delete. Be sure to save your Glossary after you make changes to it.

Using a Glossary

Finally, to use the Glossary shortcuts:

1. Type the shortcut you've defined.

2. Press F3.

   Your text magically appears. (Watch out, David Copperfield!)

Even if you don't want to make any Glossary entries yourself, you can use the built-in Glossary entries Microsoft has so graciously provided, which are described in Table 11-1.

Table 11-1	Built-In Glossary Entries
Type	*And Press F3 To*
page	Have Word calculate and print the appropriate page number on the pages
date	Place the current date on-screen
dateprint	Have Word reflect the date of printing on the document
time	Place the current time on-screen
timeprint	Have Word reflect the time of printing on the document
Note: All time commands are as good as your computer's clock.	

Making Macaroni of Macros

So far in this chapter, we've talked about saving and playing back formats (style sheets) and saving and playing back text (Glossaries). A *macro* is a saved set of keystrokes. It's a sort of "speed dial" for your computer. It's a way of making your own commands.

If you find yourself repeating a set of instructions, you may want to codify them into a macro. Making a macro is pretty straightforward.

Creating macros

The basic moves for creating a macro go like this:

1. Press Ctrl+F3.

   This is the "turn on the keystroke tape recorder" command. If you want to mouse it, use Alt+T**o**ols ⇨ **R**ecord Macro.

   Naturally, you get the Record Macro dialog box (see Figure 11-8). I swear, Word is becoming absolutely predictable!

2. Type an identifying name for the macro.

   Be as long-winded as you want. Just don't use any spaces. If you really need spaces, try substituting underlines.

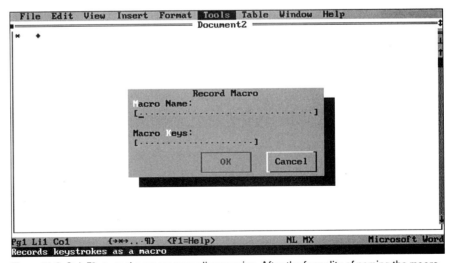

Figure 11-8: Ctrl+F3 starts the macro recording session. After the formality of naming the macro and selecting a hotkey, you're on your way.

3. Press Alt+Macro **K**eys.

Type the key or keys that you want to trigger the macro. You can use just about anything you can type. You can even override Word's preprogrammed function keys. If you happen to hit one of the few unallowed key combinations, Word'll let you know.

4. Press Enter.

The macro recording feature is now turned on — the MR on the status bar confirms it.

5. Carry out the process you want to record.

Everything has to be done with keystrokes. The mouse won't cut it here. And by the way, you can relax and take your time. No matter how long it takes you to create the macro, Word'll play it back at top speed.

6. When you are finished, press Ctrl+F3.

7. To save the macro file to disk, press Alt+T**o**ols ⇨ **M**acro.

This brings up the Macro dialog box.

7. Press Alt+**S**ave Glossary.

8. Press Enter.

This saves the macros in the NORMAL.GLY file — which means the macros will automatically be there for you when you first get into Word. You don't even have to ask nicely.

- ✔ When you record a macro with your own set of commands, follow the blueprint in this section.

- ✔ From now on, as you work with Word, pay attention to those commands or operations that you use time and again. Those procedures are all good candidates for macros.

- ✔ You can print the Glossary file by pressing Alt+**F**ile ⇨ **P**rint ⇨ Alt+**P**rint and then pressing G and Enter. This way, you can have a list of the macro hot keys. It'll show each hot key and what text it'll generate.

- ✔ If you assign a hot key to a macro that's the same as a speed-formatting key — Ctrl+I, for example — the macro will override the speed-formatting key. You can still use the speed-formatting key if you press Ctrl+A first. To use Ctrl+I for italics, you would press Ctrl+A Ctrl+I.

Macros and Glossary entries are both saved in Glossary files. Word assumes that you always want to use the contents of NORMAL.GLY. Until you feel comfortable with macros and glossaries and bears, oh my — just keep everything in NORMAL.GLY. Life will be much simpler.

Although the macro dialog boxes and such haven't changed that much from Version 5.5 to 6, there is no longer a Macro menu item. Recording and editing macros are now under the Tools menu. There is no particular Macro Edit... command. Just T**o**ols ⇨ **M**acro, which gets you to the Macro dialog box — where you can edit, run, delete (and so on) the macros.

As you can see, Version 6 offers more on-screen guidance through the terrifying macro-making process than Version 5. Note that the record-a-macro command is now *Ctrl*+F3 — not Shift+F3.

Typing an actual macro — step by step

It's likely that you're still feeling a bit unsure about macros. To breach any lingering macro insecurity you may be feeling, I'm going to walk you through the creation of a macro. Just follow the instructions, and you, too, will have a swell macro. Guaranteed. And finally, if you don't like the macro — hard to imagine — just don't save it. No harm done.

This macro copies all your files to a disk in drive A, so please stick a blank disk in the drive before actually creating this macro. Otherwise, you'll end up with unwanted keystrokes and badly-behaved macros.

1. Press Ctrl+F3.

    This step starts the macro recording process.

2. Type **Save_All_to_drive_A** (don't forget the underscores).

    This names the macro.

3. Press Alt+K.

    This moves cursor to the Macro **K**eys box.

4. Press F9.

    This makes F9 the hotkey for this macro.

5. Press Enter.

    This closes the Record Macro dialog box and signals the beginning of the actual recording.

6. Press Alt+F F.

    This is the first command in the macro — goes to **F**ile Management.

7. Press Ctrl+spacebar.

    This step tags all files.

8. Press Alt+C.

   This step activates the Copy command button.

9. Type **A:** and press Enter.

   This tells Word to send the files to drive A. Study meditation or do your target practice while Word performs this task.

10. Press Esc.

   When it's finished copying, this takes us back to the main screen.

11. Press Ctrl+F3.

   This turns off the record-a-macro function.

   > ✔ If you want to keep this macro permanently, you have to save the Glossary by pressing Alt+**S**ave Glossary and Enter.
   >
   > ✔ If you don't want to keep this macro, then don't save the Glossary when you exit.

To have Word *run* the macro, press F9. Because this macro copies all files to a floppy disk in drive A, be sure to put a disk in the drive before pressing F9.

Using a macro

To use a macro, just press the hotkey you created. In the preceding example, the hotkey is F9.

When a macro is running, the message bar says `Running Macro` where `Microsoft Word` usually sits. If something goes wrong, you can stop a macro in its tracks by pressing Esc.

Editing a macro

If you created and played back the macro in the preceding example, you may have noted an irritating — at least *I* think it's irritating — flashing of menus as the macro was executed.

You can get rid of those flashing menus by editing the macro and inserting a few special macro-programming words. The business of programming a macro — rather than recording a macro — can get very serious very quickly. So, we're going to do very little of it. You can do a lot of it in Chapter 20, though.

However, you should have an idea of how to make some simple changes in case you make a typo while recording — or want to get rid of the flashing menus.

1. Press Alt+T**o**ols ➪ **M**acro.

2. Highlight the macro you want to edit.

   In this case, edit the Save_All_to_Drive_A macro.

3. Press Alt+**E**dit.

   The macro appears in your file in this form:

   ```
   <menu>ff<ctrl space><alt C>a:<enter><esc>
   ```

4. Add the "turn-off irritating flashing menus" command to the beginning of the macro and make any other correction as needed:

   ```
   «set echo="off"»<menu>ff<ctrl space><alt C>a:<enter><esc>
   ```

   Create the « and » by pressing Ctrl+[and Ctrl+].

5. Highlight the whole macro.

6. Press Alt+T**o**ols ➪ **M**acro.

7. Highlight the Save_All_to_Drive_A macro.

8. Press Alt+**D**efine.

9. Just say Yes when asked whether you want to replace the existing macro.

   You'll be dumped back to your main screen.

   ✔ Be sure to save the Glossary file.

A shortcut to editing a macro, which eliminates Steps 1-3, is to type the name of your macro — in this case, **Save_All_to_Drive_A** — on a blank line in any open document and then type a caret (^) and press the F3 key.

Merging Mania

I hope I don't destroy any fantasies here, but you aren't the only one getting letters from Ed McMahon. We're all victims of *mail merge* every day.

Mail merge is basically a fill-in-the-blank command.

Mail merge empowers you to send the same letter — each addressed to a different recipient — without having to type the letter over and over again just to change the name and address of the recipient. The letter is created with blanks that the computer fills in with the real names and addresses, listed in another file.

You can send notifications, invitations, invoices, collection letters, and even obnoxious Christmas letters with mail merge. The concept here is: Many addresses, one letter.

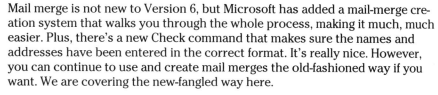

Mail merge is not new to Version 6, but Microsoft has added a mail-merge creation system that walks you through the whole process, making it much, much easier. Plus, there's a new Check command that makes sure the names and addresses have been entered in the correct format. It's really nice. However, you can continue to use and create mail merges the old-fashioned way if you want. We are covering the new-fangled way here.

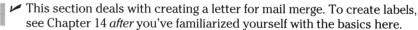

> ✔ This section deals with creating a letter for mail merge. To create labels, see Chapter 14 *after* you've familiarized yourself with the basics here.

Preplanning your merge

When you flip through your Rolodex cards or address book, notice that the cards consist of a series of familiar units: Title (like Mr. or Ms.), First name, Last name, Company name, Street address, City, State, and ZIP code.

In the preplanning stage, you decide what units — or *fields* — you want to use in the mail-merge letter. Maybe you want to include spaces for spouse's names or phone numbers or even pet's names.

Not every address needs to use every field. For example, let's say you have a field named Company. Not every address will need to use that category and it's okay to leave it blank when entering your data. On the other hand, suppose that somebody's address has an "in care of;" you can stick that in the Company slot — if it's not being used.

In any case, examine the addresses you'll be using from the perspective of what they have in common.

After you've built an address model that works for all your addresses, you can initiate the process of constructing a merge event.

Doesn't that sound impressive?

Setting up

Word will help us create the *data file* — which will have the names and addresses — and a *main document* — which will contain the basic letter you want to send to all your victims.

Creating the data file

The first step in creating a data file is, bizarrely, to get into a new blank file that will end up being your main document file. If you've already written part of the letter, then get into that file and follow these steps:

1. Press Alt+**File** ⇨ Print **M**erge.

   You see the Print Merge Setup dialog box (see Figure 11-9).

2. Press Alt+Attach/Create **D**ata File.

   After you select this option, Word needs to know whether you want to create a new data file or use one that's already in existence. We'll assume that you don't have a data file already and want to create one.

3. Press Alt+**C**reate.

   When you choose Create, Word gives you the Create Data File dialog box (see Figure 11-10). This is where you type the field names you came up with during the preplanning session.

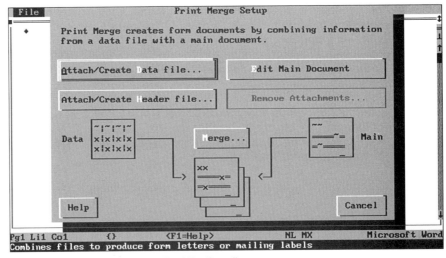

Figure 11-9: The friendly "front end" to Word's mail merge generator.

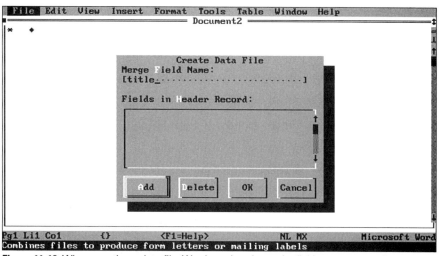

Figure 11-10: When creating a data file, Word needs to know the field names to use. Do not type Ebbets or Wrigley.

4. Type each Field Name and press Enter.

   One set of Field Names may be (press Enter after each field name): **Title**, **First_name**, **Last_name**, **Company**, **Address**, **City**, **State**, and **Zip**. You can use different field names. But no matter what, don't use any punctuation other than underscores in your field names and don't start the field names with numbers. Oh, and no spaces either.

5. When you have finished entering all your field names, choose OK.

   You then see a Save As dialog box. This is where you name your data file.

6. Type a name for your data file — like DATA.DOC — and press Enter.

   After a few seconds, you'll get something like the screen shown in Figure 11-11, with your field names on the top line — called the *header record* — and a data grid all laid out so that you can start entering your names and addresses.

   It's okay if you can't see all your field names on the screen at the same time. Word scans to the right as you type the names and addresses.

7. Type the appropriate information in each box and press Tab to advance to the next box.

8. After you reach the end of the line and have filled in the last field, press Tab — *not* Enter — to go to the next line. Pressing Tab prompts Word to add a new row to the grid.

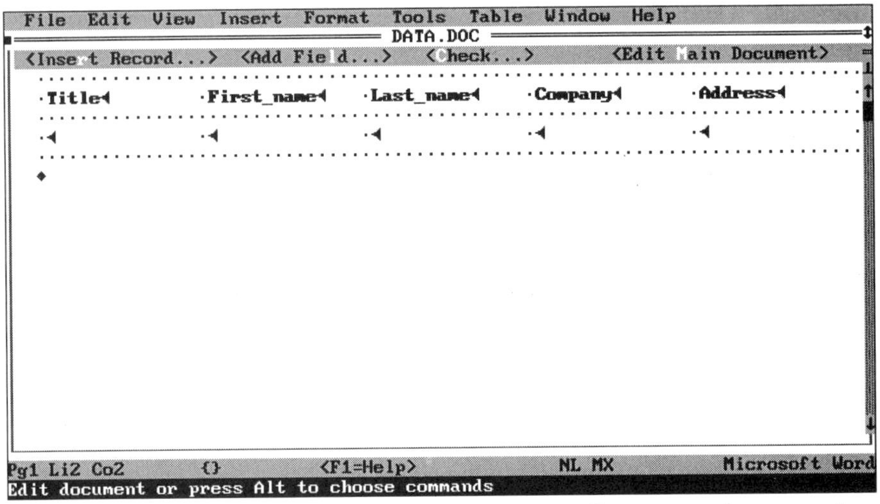

Figure 11-11: New to Word 6! A data file grid for easy data entry. No more counting commas!

Figure 11-12 shows the data grid with three *records* entered. Did you happen to notice the Merge Buttons underneath the title bar? If you did, good for you! We'll be using them shortly.

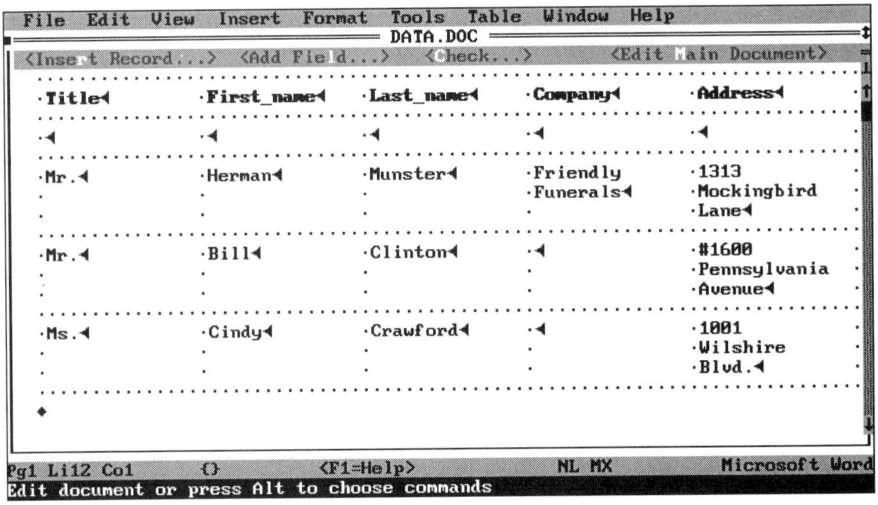

Figure 11-12: The dawn of a new database! The City, State, and Zip fields are hanging off to the right, just out of sight.

9. After you have entered all your records, save one more time. (You *have* been saving all along, haven't you?) Then use Alt+Check to make sure that you have followed the rules for data document creation. If you let Microsoft set up the data document for you, it's pretty hard to make a mistake.

   Pressing Alt+Check brings up the Database Diagnostic Tools dialog box in Figure 11-13. As in the example, select the items to be checked and then press Enter.

   If DDT finds a mistake, a dialog box pops up, giving you a clue about what you did wrong.

10. When you have finished double-checking, press Alt+Edit **M**ain Document.

    ✔ Because typing names and addresses is so boring, you may have made a few typos. Run a spelling check before printing. Although it'll be a bit tedious — Word will stop at all those proper names — it may catch a few typos.

    ✔ After you have a data document, you can use it with any number of main documents. All you have to do is press Alt+Attach/Create **D**ata File in Step 3 — and tell Word the name of your data file.

    ✔ The data grid is nothing more than a table. While you're in the data document, all the table commands apply. More about tables in Chapter 16.

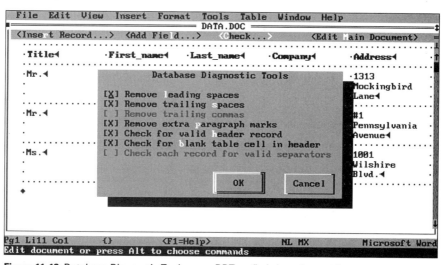

Figure 11-13: Database Diagnostic Tools — or DDT — finds bugs in your data entry.

✔ If you have a previously constructed data document, where the fields are separated by commas or Tabs, it's perfectly usable. Just make sure that there's a header record at the top.

Creating the main document

Because we're following the pathway set forth by Word's merge-building process, the main document is created after the data document. You can, however, rough out a main document first. It may help you better focus on what kind of data you need in the data document.

In any case, here we are.

At the top of the file is a line that looks something like this:

```
«DATA C:\WORD\DATA.DOC»
```

Don't delete this line — it tells Word where the names and addresses are. Which is kind of important.

Okay, now you need to write your letter. Remember to place field names where you normally type a person's name or address.

If you can't remember your field names, that's okay. Word will type them in for you — as well as some other things.

Let's make a letter:

1. Put the cursor where you want the person's address to appear.

   The first thing we need is the addressee information — who the letter's going to.

2. Press Alt+Insert Merge Field.

   You get the dialog box shown in Figure 11-14. Your very own field names should be in the box on the left.

3. Highlight the field you want to insert.

   The first one is Title (for Ms. or Mr.).

4. Press Enter.

5. Repeat Steps 3 and 4 until you have inserted all required fields.

   Figure 11-15 illustrates a main document that's ready to be merged. Notice how the «City» field in the body of the letter can be used to further personalize things? You could even scatter a «First_name» here and there throughout the document.

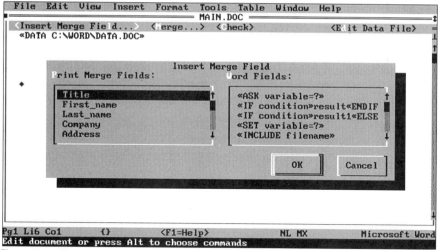

Figure 11-14: The Insert Merge Field — the IMF? — dialog box offers the field names you typed in the data document. Pick one at a time to populate your letters.

6. Enter any IF statements you need.

   An IF statement is used when not all the records use all the fields. For example, some of your addressees may have a company name in their address. Some may not. If there's a company name, you want to use it. But

An IF statement

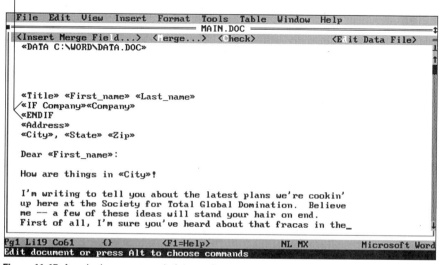

Figure 11-15: A main document ready for merging.

if there isn't, Word has a nasty habit of leaving a blank line where it would have appeared.

Figure 11-15 contains an IF statement dealing with the company name issue. Copy that format exactly. The Insert Merge Field box helps you by providing some sample IF statements.

7. When you think everything's in shape — *think* being the operative word here — use Alt+Check to see whether Word shares your opinion.

Check makes sure that you typed things correctly — at least from a technical standpoint. If you, as impossible as this may seem, made a mistake — Word tells you that Some errors have been found, and if you press Enter, a blooper document with your errors is displayed. You can print the blooper file and compare it to your main document.

Make your corrections and run the fabulous Check again until you get an all clear. When you see the message No errors have been found, you get a chance to **V**iew Sample — to see how the document will look in final form.

Figure 11-16 is an example of a merged sample, using the first record in the data document we've been playing with.

- ✔ Create the left and right *chevrons* — Wordspeak for the funny brackets — with Ctrl+[and Ctrl+].

- ✔ If you need to make corrections, you can always jump back to the data document with the Alt+E**d**it Data File command.

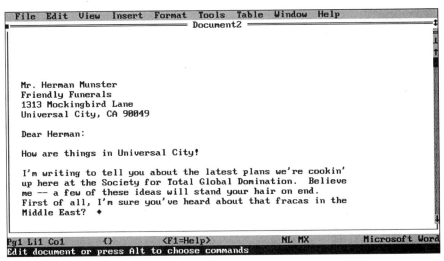

Figure 11-16: A modern masterpiece entitled, "Sample document — merged." Picasso would be envious.

Merging — finally

As with most things computer, setting up something the first time is always the worst. After you've done it, it gets easier. I think it's a corollary of the law that says it always takes longer to drive *to* a place than to drive home *from* that same place.

Anyway, now that your data document and main document are whipped into shape, you are ready for the big time. Merging!

1. From your main document, Press Alt+**M**erge.

   The Print Merge dialog box appears (see Figure 11-17).

2. Press Enter to print all records.

   You also can specify which particular records will be printed. Do you want records 1-3? Or more?

3. You get the normal Print dialog box. Make your selections, if any, and press Enter.

4. The message bar starts flashing Merging, Printing, and so on, until all pages are finished.

Several rules: If you have a long merge, do a test run of the first 20 or 30 pages to make sure that everything is working out. And remember to use the crummy paper for merge tests. Don't print on nice, expensive stationery until you're sure it'll all be okay.

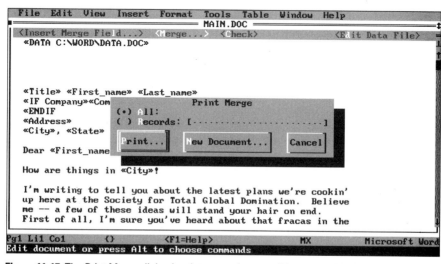

Figure 11-17: The Print Merge dialog box lets you print everything or specify which records to print.

Merging is one of the few things you can do that can really test the limits of your computer system. To make sure that Word has all the system resources it needs, before you merge, save all your files and quit Word — this clears its memory buffers. Then when you get back into Word, open only the main document. Don't open the data document. The data document does not need to be open to print merge; all it does is gobble up memory. These two steps may make the difference between a successful merge and a hung-up system.

More merging

There's another kind of merging.

It's used when you have a series of files you want to print with continuous page numbers. For example, suppose that you've written the Great American Novel. Now you want to print your 20 chapters.

Start out by creating a main document and simply list all the files that your book comprises — each on its own line. You can place page breaks between the chapters to make sure that the following file starts on a new page. Be sure to remove any page numbering or section commands from the various chapters. The main document governs the look of the whole document — your page number and section commands belong in the main document.

Then, in front of each file name, type an open chevron — Ctrl+[— and the word **INCLUDE**. After each file name, type a close chevron — Ctrl+]. You should end up with something like Figure 11-18.

The word **INCLUDE** is basically the "fetch" command. When we merge this document, it'll print each file in the order of the list.

After the whole thing is set up, press Alt+File ⇨ Print **Merge** ⇨ **Merge** to print your Great American Novel.

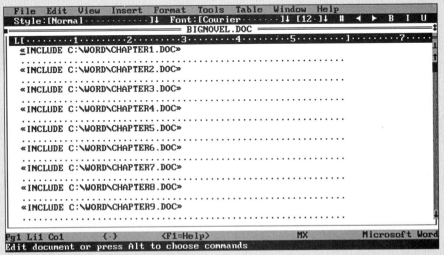

Figure 11-18: Alt+File ⇨ Print **Merge** a document with INCLUDEs to string together a number of sections.

Chapter 12
Sprucing Up Your Documents

- -

In This Chapter

▶ Revealing borders, lines, and shades

▶ Waiting tables

▶ Inserting symbols

▶ Inserting pictures

▶ Working in Layout mode

▶ Sketching with Word

▶ Adding to your fonts

- -

I will admit to having spent many hours of my teenage years hunched over a mimeograph machine, cranking out newsletters and the like. In fact, I was grousing to someone just the other day that these days people don't know about all the suffering we went through in the old days to produce the simplest graphics when I suddenly realized that already I was sounding like Andy Rooney. Heaven knows what I'll be like in 25 years.

Anyway, they didn't call it *desktop publishing* "back then," but that's what it was. Nowadays, Word lets us — nay, *encourages* us — to turn our proposals and letters into singular sensations.

Don't shy away from this chapter if you don't have a laser printer. Although not every printer can print everything described, most printers can do most of the stuff. So, don't touch that remote!

That reminds me. When I was growing up, we didn't have remotes. We had to actually get up and turn a dial on the TV to change the channel — and no cable, either — it was brutal, I tell you, brutal. And we didn't have phone answering machines, either ....

In case you didn't think to grab a minor in graphic arts when you were in college, here's a suggestion: Start a folder right now called "Graphics Ideas." Every time you get a newsletter or bulletin that looks appealing, stick it in the folder. You can even get ideas from magazines and newspapers — just start looking at them in terms of lines and borders. When it comes time to produce your own material, you'll have a reference folder full of "inspirations."

Guarding Borders, Lines, and Shades

Figure 12-1 shows a few examples of borders, lines, and shades so that you can see what this section is all about. All this, and more, can be yours by learning to manipulate two formatting commands: Border and Paragraph. Format **Paragraph** you already know how to use (see Chapter 7), so you're halfway there already.

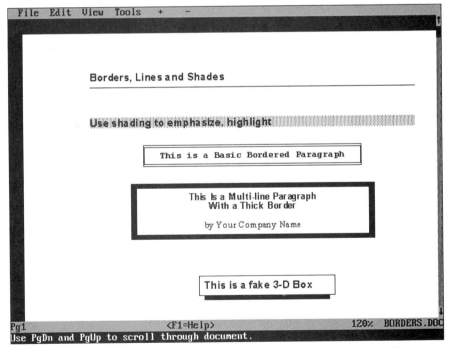

Figure 12-1: Adding some simple graphic elements can do to your text what caffeine does to your body.

The other command, our new friend Mr. Forma**t B**order, allows us to transform daunting masses of text into organized text that reflects our keen insights. And, if you're fresh out of keen insights, you'll need all the fancy borders and boxes you can get your hands on.

Preplanning

Before we start telling Word what we want — borderwise — it's a good idea to understand what choices are available. That way, when you're confronted with the dreaded dialog box whining "what do you want," you can proceed with confidence!

If all you want is a regular box, you can skip the following and just choose Box when the question presents itself.

Border Type: The first mind-shattering realization is that you don't have to select "just a box." It shouldn't be news that a box is composed of four sides. You can decorate your text with any side of a box. In other words, you can put a line above the text, or below the text, or even to the left or right of the text — or any combination thereof. In Figure 12-1, the first paragraph uses a line at the bottom. Sometimes a simple line is all that you need.

Line Styles: In addition to selecting *where* your lines will appear, you also can specify how the lines will *look*. Figure 12-1 demonstrates a few: double lines for the "Basic Bordered" paragraph, and a thick line for the "Multi-line" paragraph.

One paragraph, one border: We're going to resurrect the infamous definition of a paragraph here: A paragraph is a string of letters or numbers terminated by an Enter. That little bit of info is critical here, because sometimes you'll want more than one line of text inside a box — like the "Multi-line" box in Figure 12-1. A title, a subtitle, and additional information are examples.

However, if a paragraph is formatted with a box and you press Enter, you don't get a bigger box. You get two boxes. Two Enters, two boxes.

To duplicate the paragraph in the example, you must use the New Line command — Shift+Enter — at the end of each line *instead of* Enter. This creates a new line, without adding another Enter — or paragraph — to mess up the works.

Let's say, however, that you simply must have a single box to go around several paragraphs. You can do this, with a little effort, by formatting with lines. Format the top paragraph with left, top, and right lines. This creates the top of the box. Format the in-between paragraphs with lines on the left and on the right. Then the bottom paragraph gets a line on the left, the bottom, and on the right — to create the bottom of the box.

Background Shading: Word lets you create more shady characters than Damon Runyon. In addition to, or instead of, the box and lines, you can assign a certain percentage of shading to the text, as you can see in the infamous Figure 12-1.

We're getting serious mileage out of this one figure, aren't we?

Color: Unless you have a color printer, *color* means shades of gray. Normally, the lines appear in black, but you can select among several shades of gray, if your printer supports it. The command is dimmed if it doesn't.

✔ Shades appear only in Print Preview mode only and in your printout.

✔ You have to play with the background shading numbers to see what you like. A practical approach is to make half a dozen sample paragraphs with various degrees of shading applied and print them for comparison. Keep the sheet as a handy chart for later.

✔ Shading looks great on the printout. However, if you plan to photocopy the material for general distribution, you also should find out what your photocopy machine is going to do to the shade. Things can get lost in the translation. Sometimes the shade completely disappears or comes out unevenly. Adjust the shade accordingly. The same applies if you're going to be using colored paper.

✔ If you're using text with shading, it's a good idea to boldface the text to keep it dominant.

Creating borders, lines, and shades

Making a border works just like any other Format command in Word — highlight text you want to format and issue the formatting command.

By the way, if you intend to use a particular border or shade throughout a report, why not record it as a style so that you can use a speed-formatting key to save some work?

Wait a minute. A computer saving you work? I think I'm starting to hallucinate.

Beginning borders

1. Highlight the text you want to border.

2. Press Alt+Format ➪ **Border**.

   You get the Border Paragraph dialog box, displaying all the now-familiar options available (see Figure 12-2).

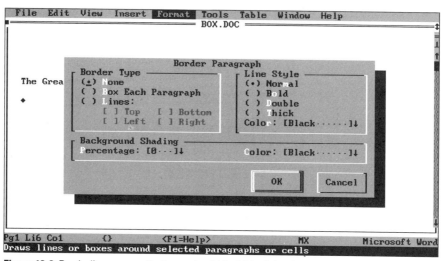

Figure 12-2: Borderline personality types should find this dialog box particularly appealing.

3. Press Alt+**B**ox Each Paragraph.

   This selects the basic, normal, nothing-special box.

4. Press Enter.

Now you've got a box around your text. That was simple, wasn't it?

- ✔ Explore the various options in the dialog box. As always, Alt+boldfaced letter, or Tab, moves you to the various options. Check the options you want. Press Enter when you're finished with your selections.

- ✔ In the first example paragraph, in Figure 12-1, I used Alt+Lines, Bottom.

- ✔ In the Shading example paragraph, still Figure 12-1, I just used the Alt+**P**ercentage command to select shading.

Fine-tuning borders, lines, and shades

Having the border is great, but it may not be quite what you had in mind, as illustrated in Figure 12-3, which shows what the preceding beginning border command produces — the text is on the left and the border stretches the width of the page.

This is where the Format **P**aragraph stuff comes in — it sizes the box and moves things around.

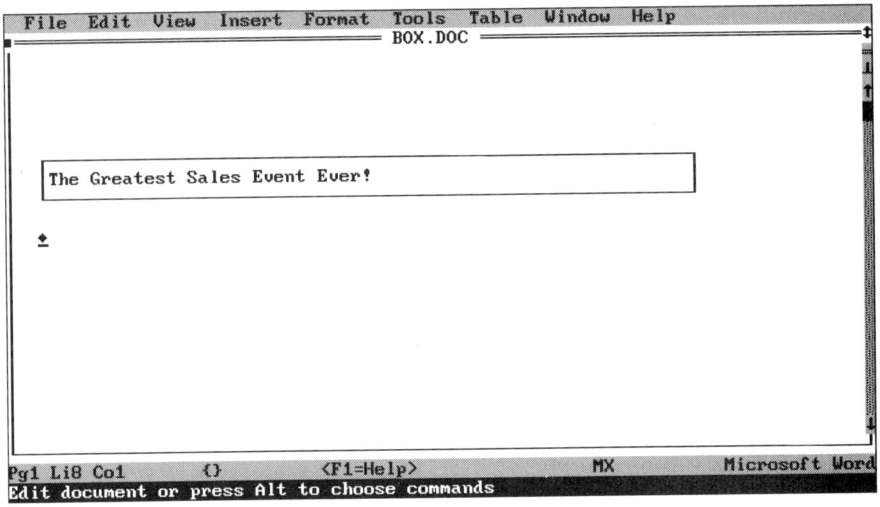

```
 File  Edit  View  Insert  Format  Tools  Table  Window  Help
                           BOX.DOC

  ┌─────────────────────────────────────────────────────┐
  │ The Greatest Sales Event Ever!                        │
  └─────────────────────────────────────────────────────┘

  ±




Pg1 Li8 Co1         {}           <F1=Help>              MX        Microsoft Word
Edit document or press Alt to choose commands
```

Figure 12-3: The basic results of a Format ⇨ Border command, sans fine-tuning.

Let's apply paragraph formatting commands to our pathetic-looking bordered paragraph.

1. Highlight the text to receive the formatting.

2. Press Alt+Format ⇨ **P**aragraph.

   This brings up our old friend, the Format Paragraph dialog box.

3. Press Alt+**C**enter.

   You also can choose any of the other alignment options, of course. Try **R**ight sometime, for an interesting look.

4. Press Alt+From Le**f**t.

5. Type **1**.

6. Press Alt+From Ri**g**ht.

7. Type **1**.

8. Press Enter.

   ✔ Depending on the size and look you want, you probably will need to adjust the numbers in Steps 5 and 7.

   ✔ If you want extra space above and below the text in this box, place the cursor on the first letter of text and press Shift+Enter — the New Line command — to put blank space above the text. Then go to the end of the text and press Shift+Enter again to put blank space below the text.

> ✔ If you're in the Format Paragraph dialog box, please note that there's a wormhole command button at the bottom that'll take you straight to the Format Border dialog box.

Quick-and-dirty box formatting:

> ✔ Put cursor in the box.

> ✔ Press Ctrl+C — the speed-formatting key for centering.

> ✔ Press Ctrl+Q — the speed-formatting key to indent on both sides.

Getting fancy

By the way, did you notice the 3-D Box in the example in Figure 12-1? Can you figure out how to make it? If you want to know how, send five dollars . . . no, just kidding again.

The effect is created by adding a thick, indented line *underneath* the boxed paragraph. Then I indented that line a bit on the left and on the right to cast the shadow. The step-by-step instructions follow. There are a lot of steps because we're formatting *and* indenting.

1. Make a normal boxed paragraph, as described previously.

2. Put the cursor in the paragraph *beneath* the boxed paragraph you just created.

   There should be no text on this line, just the Enter.

3. Press Alt+Format ⇨ **Border.**

4. Press Alt+**Lines.**

5. Check Top.

6. Press Alt+**Thick.**

7. Press Enter.

8. Press Alt+Format ⇨ **Paragraph.**

9. Press Alt+**From Left.**

10. Type a number that is .1 more than the indent for the boxed paragraph.

    If the boxed paragraph isn't indented, type **.1**. If it is indented by 1 inch, you type **1.1**.

11. Press Alt+**From Right.**

12. Type a number that is .1 more than the right indent for the boxed paragraph.

13. Press Enter.

> ✔ When you're finished, it won't look "right" unless you print out or use the Print Preview mode.

The point to take away from this is that you can be creative. Mix and match. And, above all, don't be afraid to try things. And more than that — don't forget to save often!

Printing white on black

You can, if your printer allows it, "print" white letters on a black background, as illustrated in Figure 12-4.

The basic technique is to format a paragraph with a black background (or you can use a shade of gray, if you want), using the steps described previously.

Then highlight and Format ⇨ Character your text in the color white. It is usually best to also format the text as bold. It'll make the text stand out more.

Alternatively, you can print gray letters on a white background. Again, a little experimentation is required.

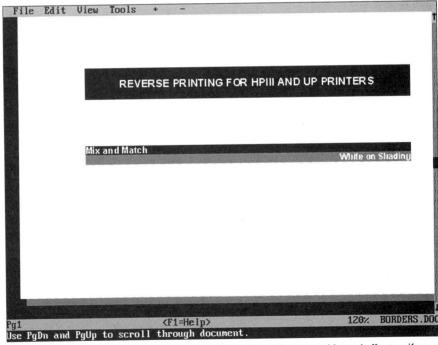

Figure 12-4: Format white letters with black background shading to get this cool effect — if your printer supports it.

Waiting Tables

When you hear the word "table" — and it's not mealtime — your mind's eye conjures up something like Figure 12-5, which looks much like an Excel spreadsheet. If you're into that sort of thing. However, a "table" can also be something like Figure 12-6.

If you can remember the first three letters in "table" — TAB — you're already ahead of the game in negotiating with tables. First of all, tables can replace dealing with Tabs in some situations — like columns of numbers. Also, to move the cursor around within a table, you use the Tab key.

However, let's start at the beginning.

Preplanning a table

If you did the mail merge, you've already seen and worked with a table. Basically, a table is a grid of rectangles — called *cells* — in which you may imprison any sort of information you want.

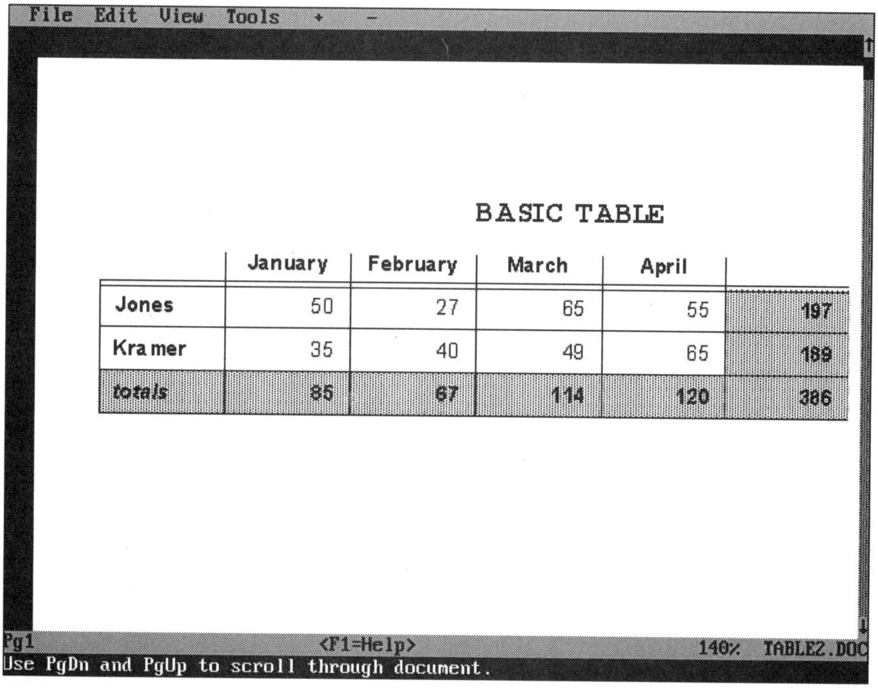

Figure 12-5: Using Word's Table command, creating an attractive spreadsheet-like array is possible.

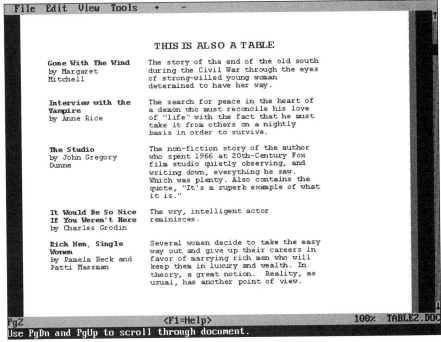

Figure 12-6: You also can use the Table command to create independent, side-by-side paragraphs — and more.

A cell can be as large as a page or as small as one character. You can have as many as 50 cells across and unlimited cells down. Remember Figure 12-6? It was only two cells across. Figure 12-7 shows the behind-the-scenes table — embarrassing gridlines and all.

When creating a table, the first thing Word wants to know is how big you want it to be. Although you can change the size of the thing later, you need to have some sort of a starting place in mind.

Creating a table

To create a table, position the cursor where you want the table to make its debut — and it can't be inside another table.

```
 File  Edit  View  Insert  Format  Tools  Table  Window  Help
══════════════════════════ TABLE2.DOC ══════════════════════════
 L0[········1·········2]⊤·······3········4·······5·······6·⊤·····7···
  ¶
                      THIS IS ALSO A TABLE¶
  ¶
 ················································································
 ·Gone With The Wind↓  ·The story of the end of the old south
 ·by Margaret         ·during the Civil War through the eyes   ·
 ·Mitchell◄           ·of strong-willed young woman            ·
 ·                    ·determined to have her way.◄            ·
 ·                    ·                                        ·
 ················································································
 ·Interview with the  ·The search for peace in the heart of    ·
 ·Vampire↓            ·a demon who must reconcile his love      ·
 ·by Anne Rice◄       ·of "life" with the fact that he must     ·
 ·                    ·take it from others on a nightly         ·
 ·                    ·basis in order to survive.◄              ·
 ·                    ·                                        ·
 ················································································
 ·The Studio↓         ·The non-fiction story of the author      ·
 ·by John Gregory     ·who spent 1966 at 20th Century Fox
 Pg2 Li15 Co12    {¶}        <F1=Help>              MX      Microsoft Word
 Edit document or press Alt to choose commands
```

Figure 12-7: The "book table" with the gridlines visible.

The coolest way to make a Table is with the Ribbon and the mouse, as in Figure 12-8. Drag the # sign on the Ribbon, and the little graphic will appear, indicating how many cells wide and tall the table will be. When you've got it the right size, let go of the mouse button and, after a few seconds, the empty Table shows up, as in Figure 12-9.

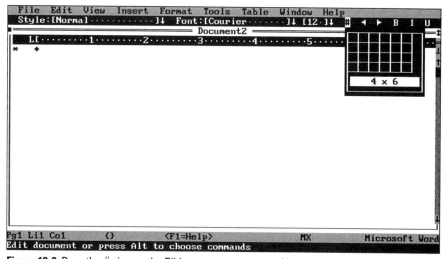

Figure 12-8: Drag the # sign on the Ribbon to create a new table.

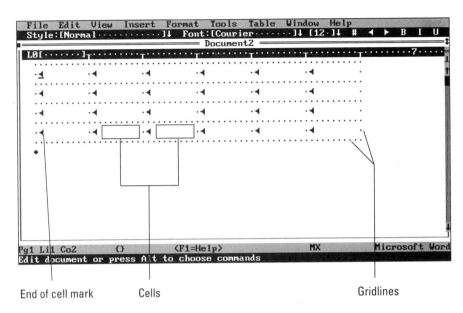

File Edit View Insert Format Tools Table Window Help
Style:[Normal ....]↓ Font:[Courier ....]↓ [12·]↓ # ◄ ► B I U
══════════════════════════ Document2 ══════════════════════════
L0[........]..7....

End of cell mark   Cells   Gridlines

Figure 12-9: An empty table — waiting to be filled with your knowledge.

The boring (keyboard) way to make a table is as follows:

1. Press Alt+**Ta**ble ⇨ **I**nsert Table.

   This gives you the — what else? — Insert Table dialog box (see Figure 12-10).

2. Type the Number of **C**olumns and Number of **R**ows you want and press Enter.

   Columns are the vertical cells (like a column in a building). *Rows* are the horizontal cells. Four columns and six rows, for example, give you a grid four cells wide and six cells tall.

   The Column **W**idth refers to the size of the individual cells within the table. The cells in Figure 12-5, for example, are smaller than the ones in Figure 12-6. Make life easy on yourself and leave it on Auto — meaning it will adjust to whatever amount of text you enter. As usual, you can change this later on down the road.

3. After a few seconds, the empty table appears, as in Figure 12-9.

   ✔ If you don't want to look at the gridlines, press Alt+**Ta**ble ⇨ **G**ridlines to toggle it off. If you don't like looking at those end of cell marks (◄), you can nuke those too by pressing Alt+**V**iew ⇨ **P**references ⇨ Alt+**P**aragraph Marks. Okay, are you satisfied now? Sheesh.

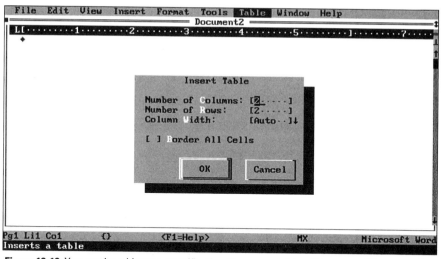

Figure 12-10: You can be a bit more specific about how your table will be created if you use the Insert Table dialog box instead of the Ribbon.

Typing in tables

Typing in tables is a little strange at first. Keep in mind the following:

- ✔ Press Tab (or point and click) to move among the cells. If you want an actual Tab in a cell, you have to press Ctrl+Tab.

- ✔ Press Tab in the last cell of the last row to create another row — duplicating the formatting.

- ✔ You may press Enter within a cell to start a new line — though consider using Shift+Enter instead if you're planning on using any paragraph formatting.

- ✔ When you use the Del key, you delete text — but not the cell itself.

- ✔ If you use the Shift+Del command, however, you delete both text and cell — and you can Shift+Ins the cells to another part of the table. You also can use drag and drop to move rows and columns.

- ✔ Alt+Home takes you to the left side of the table. Alt+End goes to the right side.

Shrinking and expanding tables

There are two basic approaches to changing the size of a table. One is to delete or add rows and columns. The other is to shrink or expand the size of the cells within.

Changing the numbers of rows and columns

When you get to the end of the last row in the table, pressing Tab automatically takes you to the beginning of the next line — rolling out a new row of cells for you like a visiting dignitary gets a red carpet.

You also can highlight a row or a column and press Shift+Del to delete a row or a column, and then Shift+Ins to add on to the table.

However, you also can use the Table menu to insert and delete rows and columns. How that works depends on what you've got highlighted.

✔ If you highlight a row or column where you want to add or delete a row or column and then press Alt+Table, you find that the first two commands revealed are the options to Insert or to Delete. Pick the one for you.

✔ You can control the number of columns and rows created or deleted with Insert or Delete by the number of cells you highlight before issuing the command. Highlighting two columns is the first step to either creating or deleting two columns. It's the same old story: Highlight first and then take action.

✔ If the cursor is just pathetically sitting in a single cell when you press Alt+Table ⇨ Insert or Delete — Word asks whether you want to delete the *row* the cursor is in or the *column* the cursor is in.

Changing the size of cells

Sometimes old Auto just doesn't do the job to our liking. Automatic sizing of the cell may cause the text to wrap in a funny way — or it's just ugly and you don't like it.

You can change the height or width of the cells on a row-by-row or column-by-column basis. You cannot make one cell a different size from all the other cells in a table. To change the height or width of the cells:

1. Put the cursor in the row you want to change.

2. Press Alt+Table ⇨ Row **H**eight.

   You get the Row Height dialog box (see Figure 12-11).

3. Press Alt+**H**eight of Row.

   This takes you to the text box where you can type in the desired height.

4. If you want to change the size of other rows of cells, you can press Alt+**P**revious or Alt+**N**ext to travel up and down through the table.

5. And, of course, press Enter when you're finished.

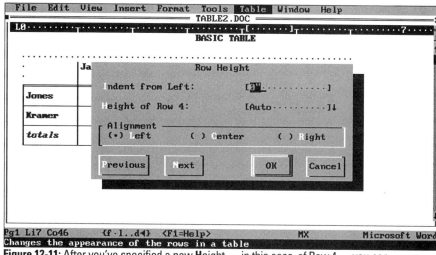

Figure 12-11: After you've specified a new **H**eight — in this case, of Row 4 — you can Alt+**P**revious to adjust the tallness factor of Row 3.

> ✔ The Alignment in the dialog box refers to the alignment of the whole table. Use normal paragraph formatting to align individual cells.

If it's the column width you want to change, it works the same way, just press Alt+T**a**ble ⇨ Column **W**idth to get Figure 12-12.

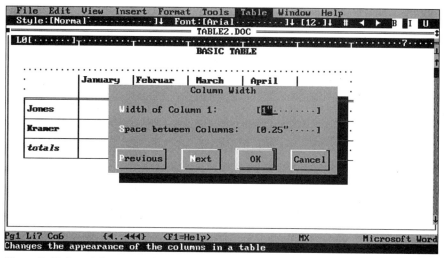

Figure 12-12: Step right up, ladies and germs! Select your column width and then move right on to the next column!

The easiest way to change the column width is with the Ruler. The Ruler, visible in Figures 12-10 and 12-11, has special marks — that look like the letter "T" — for each cell in a table. Just click and drag the "T" with the mouse to reposition the cell width as desired.

Formatting cells

Formatting cells in a table is truly a peak experience. It's a conglomeration of Format **P**aragraph and Format **B**order commands with lots of "which side of which cell should have what sort of line" kinds of decision making designed to gobble up hours of your time with endless fine-tuning.

Let's remind ourselves of the basics that'll still work here for those of us with normal needs.

✔ Text in a cell may be formatted just like any other text. You may want to center and boldface your titles, or format numbers with a right alignment.

✔ If you want to center or align the entire table to the right or left, you must use Alt+Table ➪ Row **H**eight and select the desired alignment (see Figure 12-11).

✔ If you want to apply some uniform type of formatting to the table — like a font or something — put the cursor in the table and press Alt+NumPad 5 (that's the 5 on the numeric keypad) to highlight the entire table in one magnificent gesture.

✔ If you want extra space between the rows, you must use the Format **P**aragraph spacing commands. To add one line of space between the rows, press Alt+Format ➪ **P**aragraph. In the resulting dialog box, enter a **1** in the **A**fter text box.

Okay, now the tough part.

To format cells with lines, borders, and shading requires some thought before-hand. Do you want to box or shade one cell, the row of cells, two columns of cells, the whole table? The variations are endless.

If you're a spreadsheet kind of person, this will all be second nature to you. Already I need an Excedrin. Two.

1. Highlight the cells you want to format.

2. Press Alt+Format ➪ **B**order.

   Because you're in a table, you get a different sort of Border dialog box (see Figure 12-13). This is basically a revamped version of the Border Para-graph dialog box, designed to meet the needs of the table.

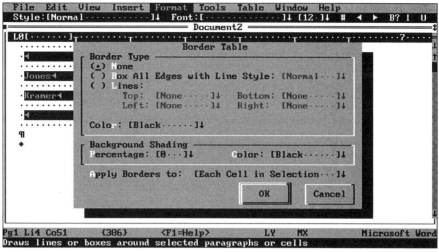

Figure 12-13: The Border Table dialog box.

3. Select the **B**ox and **L**ines of your choice.

   The choices here reflect the fact that we're dealing with a table consisting of a number of cells. The concepts here, however, are the same as the Border Paragraph commands — just carried out to the *n*th degree.

4. Press Alt+**A**pply Borders To.

   This is where you decide which of the **B**ox and **L**ines drop-down choices will be carried out.

Inserting Symbols

Enough with this serious stuff. Let's do something fun! And easy.

Inserting a symbol doesn't sound like either. But it is. Both.

Earlier — many pages back, in a galaxy far, far away — I mentioned that Word comes with three text fonts and two symbol fonts. The two TrueType symbol fonts are called Symbol (duh, wonder where they came up with that name?) and Wingdings (ditto).

The Symbol font is mostly things like trademark symbols and other business things. The Wingdings, however, are a bunch of little drawings: scissors, mailboxes, floppy disks, zodiac signs, and much more. You can put all of these pictures into your document to emphasize a point or whatever.

To put a symbol in your document, follow these steps:

1. Put your cursor where you want the symbol to appear.

2. Press Alt+Insert ⇨ **S**ymbol.

   You get the Symbol dialog box, which is shown in Figure 12-14, but with the default Printer symbols on display.

3. Press the down-arrow key until `Wingdings` appears in the Symbols **F**rom text box.

4. Press Alt+**S**ymbol.

   If you get a message that indicates `A symbol has not been selected`, blow past it with an Enter or OK.

5. Cursor on down to a symbol name.

   The little box on the right shows you a picture of what the printout will look like.

6. When you've got the symbol you want, press Enter — or click OK.

   You are returned to your regularly scheduled document.

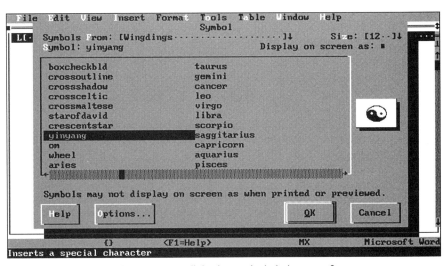

Figure 12-14: Who wouldn't want to put a little yinyang in their document?

Changing your bullets

All those symbol fonts can be used, automatically, in the bulleting paragraphs command! Here's how:

1. Press Alt+**T**ools ➭ **B**ullets.

2. Press Alt+**N**ew Bullet.

Surprise! You're now in the Symbol dialog box, just like Figure 12-14. Select whatever you want for your bullet symbol and then press Enter. It'll now appear in the Bullet Character box.

✔ You do not see the symbol on-screen as you write. You get a square. However, if you look at your document through Print Preview, you can see the little guy in all his glory. Naturally, it'll show up in the printout.

✔ When the symbol is first dropped into your document, it is formatted as a Courier character — and that is fine in most situations. However, if you want to make your symbol bigger or smaller, you won't be able to, unless you highlight the symbol, press Ctrl+F, type **WINGDINGS**, and press Enter. Now you can format the symbol to any size you want and in any color your printer allows.

✔ When you first get into the Symbol dialog box, you get the Printer symbol set — which works for 99.9 percent of printers. However, if you always use Wingdings, use the **O**ptions command button in the Symbol dialog box to select a different default.

Inserting Pictures

In case you didn't know, you can insert photographs and artwork into your documents.

However, the first step in this process is to *get* some photographs or artwork to insert. There is a huge industry out there waiting to fulfill your every artistic whim with electronic artwork. We used to call it *clip art* — now it's called *click art*.

Alternatively, you can spend even more money and buy a scanner, which takes your own artwork and turns it into something the computer can deal with.

Anyway, after you have some artwork to insert:

1. Press Alt+Insert ⇨ **Picture**.

   This gives you the Picture dialog box (see Figure 12-15).

2. Press Alt+**Files**.

3. Highlight the name of the picture file.

   Word senses what format it is, so you don't have to worry about that. And, from my experience, you'll do all the size adjustments to the graphic after you've inserted it.

4. Press Enter.

   You get something like this in your document.

   ```
   C:\WORD\RIBBON.SCR;6.5";4.537";Capture
   ```

   By changing the numbers on the graphics instructions, you can easily size the picture. The first number is the Width, the second is the Height.

   ✔ Again, the graphic is visible in the Print Preview mode.

   ✔ You also can put a border around the graphic by formatting the graphic instructions line and using the Format **B**order command just as though it were text.

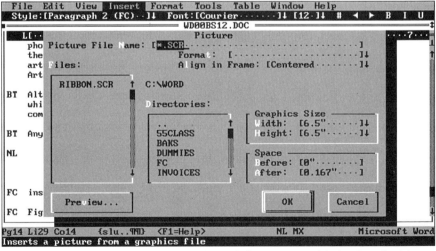

Figure 12-15: The Picture dialog box lets you size and align your artwork before inserting it into the current document.

Hanging Out in Layout Mode

Layout mode is a kind of bogus editable Print Preview mode. When invoked, the text does its darndest to position itself exactly where it will appear on the printed page. You can edit and work with the text pretty much as normal.

However, every time you change something on the screen while in Layout mode, it triggers a *screen refresh* — which manifests itself as a flashing screen and in sluggish response times.

There are times when it's a helpful feature — when you're working in columns or Tables, or formatting with Tabs, or in other elaborate formatting scenarios. I don't know anyone who could live with it turned on all the time.

Layout mode is a toggle switch — it's either on or off.

1. Press Alt+View.

   If there is a dot to the left of the word Layout, then it's already turned on. No dot means it is off.

2. Press Layout.

   This turns it on or off.

   > ✔ You know Layout mode is on by the LY in the message bar to the left of the words Microsoft Word.

   > ✔ If you flip back and forth between Layout and non-Layout mode a lot, this is a good candidate for a macro.

Sketching with Word

This isn't new. But they did move the Etch-A-Sketch command from the Utilities menu to the Tools menu (I wonder how many meetings that took?). Now you know where to find it, in the unlikely case that you actually have a use for the Line Draw command.

As for me, I've never found a way to work it into my daily routine. And in fact, if you do use it, let me know. I'd be curious as to how and why. The only thing I can think of is using it to create a form.

No matter, it's fun to try once. To make your cursor keys into little line-drawing robots, press Alt+Tools ⇨ Line Draw. You may now draw up, down, left, and right with your arrow keys. When you're finished "drawing," press Esc — or click the left mouse ear.

Although the default Line Draw "look" is just a straight line, you can actually make it anything you want. Use Alt+**Tools** ⇨ **Customize**. Press Alt+**Character** and use Alt+down arrow to see the preprogrammed choices — or just type anything. Press Enter to finish.

Adding to Your Fonts

The Word is out — you can buy Windows TrueType fonts and use them in Word 6! It doesn't make any difference if you don't now use, or ever have used, Windows.

What they never tell you in advance, though, is what you have to do to coax Word 6 into *using* those new fonts. Also, Microsoft hints that it is the only manufacturer of TrueType fonts. Wrong. There are others.

I'm not going to try to cover any actual installation procedures here. There are just too many variables. For example, Microsoft wants you to use MERGEPRD — a program that is as miserable as it sounds — to update your printer information. However, MicroLogic Systems — another font manufacturer —takes care of the MERGEPRD business *for* you while you eat a candy bar.

No matter whose fonts you've purchased, the first step is to protect yourself. That's what I'm going to walk you through.

Before changing your printer setup, make sure that you have a copy of it on a floppy disk. If something goes wrong with the installation, you'll be able to return to the status quo. Although eliminating "potential doom" from the equation kind of takes the kick out of trying something new, it's all part of growing up.

To back up your printer file:

1. Put a formatted floppy disk in drive A (or B, if you prefer).

2. Press Alt+**File** ⇨ **Printer Setup**.

3. Write down the `Printer File:` — it ends in PRD. And, underneath it, but above `Directories:`, you'll find the path — probably `C:\WORD`. Write that down, too.

4. Press Esc.

5. Press Alt+**File** ⇨ MS-**D**OS Commands.

6. Press Alt+**Multiple Commands**.

   This puts you at the system prompt.

7. Type **COPY C:\WORD\MW.INI A:** and press Enter.

   If your Word program is somewhere other than C:\WORD, use that drive and directory name instead.

8. Type **COPY C:\WORD*YOURPRD.** A:** and press Enter.

   Make sure that C:\WORD matches the path you wrote down from Step 3 above. Substitute the printer file from Step 3 for *YOURPRD*.

9. Type **EXIT** and press Enter to return to Word.

That's it. Proceed with your font installation.

If something happens to mess up your printer setup, you can fall back on these files to restore your printer.

1. Press Alt+**File** ⇨ MS-**D**OS Commands.

2. Press Alt+**M**ultiple Commands.

   This puts you at the system prompt.

3. Type **COPY A:MW.INI C:\WORD** and press Enter.

   If your Word program is somewhere other than C:\WORD, use that drive and directory name instead.

4. Type **COPY A:*YOURPRD.** C:\WORD** and press Enter.

   Make sure that C:\WORD matches the path you wrote down from Step 3 when you backed up. Substitute the printer file from Step 3 for *YOURPRD*.

Chapter 13

Tricks You Didn't Know You Needed to Know

. . . .

In This Chapter

▶ Wild cards

▶ Finding files

▶ Finding text

▶ Deleting unneeded files

▶ Launching Word with a twist

▶ Making spaces and hyphens

▶ Searching for nonprinting symbols

. . . .

*I*n man's prehistory, the required survival skills were obvious — get food, get fire, and when you hear a low growling sound, get going.

With computers, it's a big enough challenge to know how to do the "obvious" things — how are you supposed to know the things you don't know? I mean, you really have to know a lot to know what you don't know. You know?

This chapter gets a little technical. But, in the words of our ancestral cavepersons, "That which does not kill you makes a good dinner."

Nothing up My Sleeve — Wild Cards

If you don't know about *wild cards*, it's a good time to be introduced to the concept — especially because it comes up time and again in this chapter. Although wild cards aren't as much fun as a raucous poker party, they are extremely useful.

As we covered in Chapter 5, every file name must follow a certain pattern. It can be *up to* eight characters long, followed by a period, and then have *up to* three more characters.

The following are examples of acceptable file names:

REPORT1.DOC

REPORT1

RPT

If it becomes necessary to take some action with those three files, it can become very boring to give a command three times so that three files can each be handled. Often, you may want to do something with a dozen files. Does that mean you have to issue the command 12 times? No. Ta-ta-ta-dah! Wild cards to the rescue!

If you did well with that song on Sesame Street about "what do these things have in common ...," you are born to be wild.

We'll play that game here. So what *do* those previous three file names have in common? What matches?

How about — they all start with the letter R! It's as simple as that. Believe me, you don't have to unravel the mystery of the pyramids to get this right.

After you've determined what the files have in common, you can issue commands that affect only "... the files that begin with the letter R."

If, instead, you wanted "... all files that begin with RE," you'd only be including the first two files.

Unfortunately, DOS does not accept commands in conversational English — you have use a secret formula. But I'll tell you the secret.

In DOS, the way to specify files beginning with R is **R*.***. The "RE" files are **RE*.***. The asterisks are the *wild cards*. Wild cards mean, literally, "anything" — or "I don't care." As in, "Begins with R and then after that, I don't care." When you use wild cards, you have to satisfy the file name pattern — something, period, something.

If you want to identify "files that end in DOC," you use ***.DOC**. Or, for "files that start with the letter F and end in DOC," use **F*.DOC**.

The one fine-print detail to asterisks is that after you use an asterisk, you can't put in any characters after the asterisk — unless they follow the period. Huh? Look, here are some examples:

CAT*.DOC	okay
CAT*.D*	okay
CAT*5.DOC	not okay

Okay? The reason we care about wild cards in the first place is that you can apply wild cards technology in the Open dialog box, in File Management, and in MS-DOS Commands — and on and on. You'll use wild cards so often you'll start seeing them in your sleep.

Finding Philandering Files

Have you ever tried to open a file, only to discover that the file — and, in fact, *all* your files — are gone? Completely vanished?

Then, just as suddenly — about the time you finish preparing your favorite recipe from *Final Exit* — the files reappear. After chalking up the incident to a case of UFO abduction, you move on with your life, grateful the files were returned unharmed and that you didn't have to try out that recipe.

One of the most confusing problems — and important tricks — is figuring out where you, and your files, are on the hard disk.

Think of it this way.

You're in a huge darkened house. You can't even see your hand in front of your face. You have no idea how big the house is, how many rooms it has, or even whether it's got more than one floor. But none of this bothers you because you know all you need to know: Take three steps forward, and you get a treat. So you do. Every day, you take three steps forward and you get a treat. So far, so good.

One day, you mistakenly take only two steps forward and are surprised when you find no treat. You're sure you took three steps forward. You've been doing it every day. But where's the treat? The treat is gone! It's disappeared! You go from completely confident to utterly baffled in a nanosecond.

Because the house is pitch black and you know nothing about its size or configuration, you have no way of knowing that you're only one step from the treat. What you feel is completely lost. What you now know is that your ability to deal with any situation other than the norm is nonexistent. What you'd like is a floor plan and a flashlight.

Fortunately, Word provides you with all the help you need, if you know where to look and how to interpret the signs. Oh, if you didn't figure it out yet, the house was a metaphor for your computer's hard disk.

Preplanning

When you get lost, it's helpful to at least know where you — and your files — are *supposed* to be. Every good parent makes sure that their little darlings can recite their street address. You should be equally equipped. It's important to know how to describe — in computerspeak — where home base is on your hard disk. You don't have to understand it, you don't even have to like it — but you *do* have to know what it looks like. To find out where your home base is, begin by pressing Alt+File ⇨ **O**pen to get the Open dialog box.

If, when inspecting the Open dialog box, the file names listed are your familiar files, then you are at home base. Huzzah! Write down what the *current path* is — you'll need it later — Figure 13-1 indicates where you can find your current path.

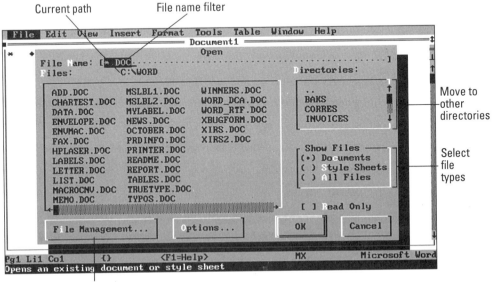

Figure 13-1: The Open dialog box does more than list your files — it works as a glass-bottom boat that travels anywhere on your computer, including floppy drives, to view what's there.

Traveling your computer

In basketball, you get a penalty for traveling. Not so with computers. You can travel all you like. The only issue is how and where.

Before you can decide where to go, you sort of have to know where you *can* go. Your hard disk is compartmentalized into sections known as *directories* — sort of like rooms in a house — where files are stored. For example, when Word installs itself, it automatically creates a directory called WORD, which, naturally, holds your Word program and files. You probably also have at least one other directory — named DOS — that contains the files that run your computer (your computer dealer probably set it up for you). You may have another directory for games.

Now that we know about directories, let's see how to solve the case of the mysterious missing files. We'll return to the scene of the crime by starting Word and pressing Alt+File ⇨ **O**pen and discovering all the files missing, as shown in Figure 13-2. To solve the mystery, the first step is to look at the current path. Does it match your home base path? Probably not.

Okay, so you're in the wrong place. Lost. Now what?

Instead of panicking and eating a gallon of ice cream, take a look at the list box on the right — **D**irectories. This shows you a list of all directories *underneath* the current directory. By selecting a directory, you can transport yourself to that directory and have *its* files displayed.

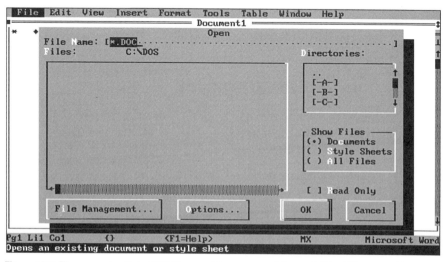

Figure 13-2: The current path is C:\DOS — and there are no Microsoft Word files stored here. A change in *path* is in order.

Or, select the two dots (. .) — the first choice in the **D**irectories box — and travel *up* one level.

How can you go "up" and "down" on a hard disk?

Well, you see, the directories are laid out in an "upside-down" tree structure — try to imagine an inverted tree. You start out at the top and then follow a branch that leads to another branch, and so forth. If you want to go to another branch, first you have to travel up to the beginning — the top — and then go back down. I don't know why they made it that way, but that's the way it is.

Isn't it fun being a pioneer? At least you won't die from a snake bite.

All right, in Figure 13-2, the **D**irectories box displays a few symbols. The [- A -] and [- B -] refer to the floppy drives, meaning that you can travel to drive A or drive B and see what files are there — even open one or print it out. The [- C -] is the hard disk. Selecting [- C -] returns you to the hard drive if you've been visiting one of the floppies.

If the directory you want to go to is not displayed in the box, you should move up the tree until you get to the top. You know you're there when the path says C : \ and there are no more . . in the Directories box. Then you can start moving down to the Word directory.

By moving up and down, you can get to any place on your hard disk. After you're in the correct directory — and you see your files again — you can select a file to open.

If you know the name of the directory you want to go to, you can warp straight to your destination by typing it in the File **N**ame box. For example, type **C:\WORD** and press Enter to move directly to the WORD directory — and the appropriate files appear automatically.

Finding missing files

After you get into the right "room" (directory), the next problem is finding the right file. Usually, you use the Alt+**F**ile ⇨ **O**pen dialog box, see your normal document files, load them, and think nothing more about it.

What you haven't been concerned about, up to this point, is that each of your document files ends in DOC. And that in the lower right corner of the Open dialog box is a Show Files box, illustrated in Figures 13-1 and 13-2, where the type of file to be displayed is set to Do**c**uments. When you can't find the file you need, and you know you're in the right directory, the search starts here.

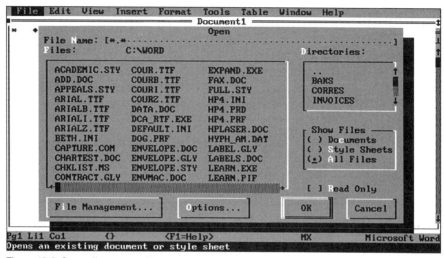

Figure 13-3: Same directory as Figure 13-1 — but a whole bunch of different files. What gives? It's show **A**ll Files!

Selecting **A**ll Files suddenly transforms your polite little list of document files into something wild and woolly like Figure 13-3, in which every file in the whole directory is unveiled. This is the first step in any file recovery effort.

Recovering a lost file

After **A**ll Files are available, take a look at the file names. You may have accidentally renamed your file or saved it with an ending other than DOC. I've seen a lot of wacky file names in my time.

Another thing to do is to see whether your file name is there, but with an ending of BAK rather than DOC (such as REPORT.BAK instead of REPORT.DOC). This is a major hint from Word that the file you want has been deleted and only this version now exists.

Finally, if you still can't find your file, look for a file starting with MW and ending in TMP. If you have any TMP files, open them. One of them is probably your missing file.

In all cases, after you've found your file, press Alt+**F**ile ⇨ Save **A**s and save the file as a DOC file.

In case of emergency...

If something just cannot be found, try quitting Word and typing **UNDELETE**. There's a *chance* DOS can recover the file. If you're really in desperate straits, go buy a file-recovery program like Norton Utilities — a Rescue 911-type program for your computer — from your local computer dealer. As long as you have any hopes of recovering the file, never create a new file with the same name as the missing file. Also, do not use the computer until you get the file-recovery program. Things can be brought back from the dead surprisingly often, as long as you keep your wits and follow instructions.

Expanding your horizons

Normally, in the Open dialog box, you see the files for the current directory.

The reality is that many of us store files in more than one directory and it gets to be a bother to move from one directory to another all the time. Call it lazy, but it's a fact of life. There is a way, using File Management, to display files from several directories in a single list all at once.

The only catch is that you need to know the exact path name for the directories you want to display. After you've got the path names to be listed, here's an example of how to do it:

1. Press Alt+File ⇨ File Management.

   This puts you in the File Management dialog box

Temporary insanity

As you work with a file, Word creates a temporary *swap file* on your disk, which is the current version of the file in use. When you exit Word properly, Word saves the file under the normal file name and deletes the TMP file. If, however, you don't exit Word before turning off the computer — or the power goes out — then the TMP file is left behind on the hard disk. That's why, if the power goes out, you may be able to find your file disguised as a TMP file.

All things being equal, though, you should not be collecting TMP files. They should be deleted. Unless you're looking to recover from a crash, TMP files just take up space and slow down the computer.

2. Press Alt+**S**earch.

   This gives you the Search dialog box — which contains many search options — most of them have nothing to do with our current mission: To display more than one directory.

   For now, let's pretend that the two directories we want to display are C:\WORD — the normal Word directory — and C:\WORD\INVOICES — a directory underneath Word that contains a bunch of invoice files.

3. In the Search **P**aths text box, type the following:

   C:\WORD, C:\WORD\INVOICES

   Your Search box should look something like Figure 13-4. Don't forget the comma between the two directories.

4. Press Enter.

   Now as you scroll through the files in the File Management dialog box, you see files from *both* directories, living in peaceful coexistence — ready to be copied, deleted, printed, and manipulated ruthlessly (see Figure 13-5).

5. When you're finished with File Management, press Esc.

   ✔ Whatever search path you choose remains the search path until you specify a new search path. Word remembers it from session to session.

   ✔ You can search through as many paths as you can type in.

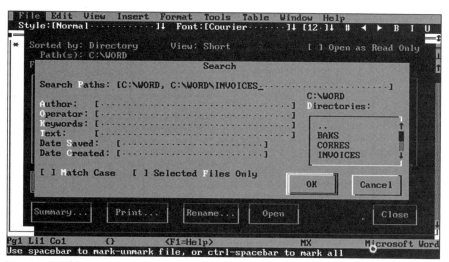

Figure 13-4: Expand your horizons by searching through multiple paths. Don't forget the comma between path names.

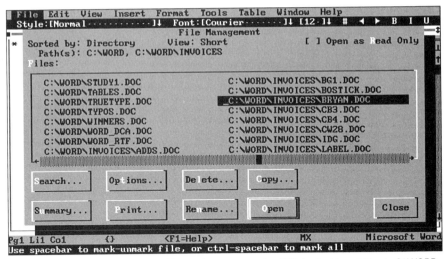

Figure 13-5: Who says you can't be in two places at one time! We're looking at files in C:\WORD *and* C:\WORD\INVOICES.

✔ You also can use Search **P**aths to select which *files* to display. For example, **C:\WORD*.DOC** shows only Word's document files. **C:\WORD\F*.DOC** reveals only the document files starting with the letter F. You can even ask for more than one file name to be revealed (see Figure 13-6).

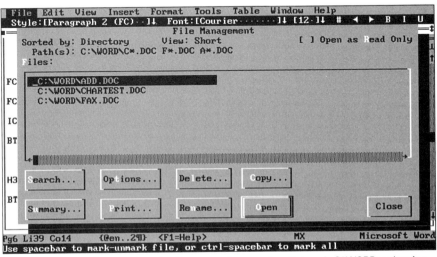

Figure 13-6: Just to show you how far this can go, the search path here is C:\WORD and we've requested that only files beginning with C, F, and A be shown. Note the spaces in the search path to keep the search in one directory. Whew!

Although the features are the same, in Word 5, this was called Library Document Retrieval/Query.

Searching for files containing certain text

Everyone, at one time or another, has the frustrating experience of wanting to find a particular passage, but not being able to remember which file it's in. Did you know that Word can scan through your documents and find which one (or ones) contain the words or phrase you're pining for? Here's how to track down that elusive verbiage:

1. Press Alt+**File** ⇨ **File Management**.

   This puts you in the File Management dialog box.

2. Press Alt+**Search**.

3. Make sure that you've got the right search path.

   If it isn't the right search path, just type a new one. The default search path is C:\WORD.

4. Press Alt+**Text**.

   This takes you to the Text box.

5. Type the unique word or phrase of your dreams.

   In Figure 13-7, we're searching for "oak desk."

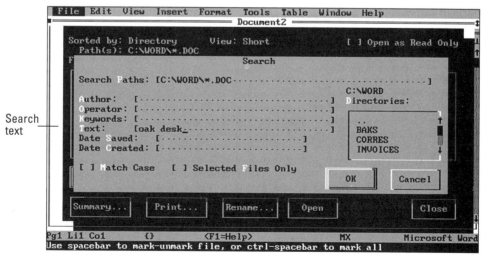

Figure 13-7: Quicker than you can say "x-ray vision," File Management's Search box can scan through your files to find the file that uses a particular word or words.

6. Press Enter and let the search begin.

Word reports (at the bottom of the screen) that it is `Searching Documents....` This shouldn't take too long (unless you've got a slow system and you're searching through lots of big files).

7. When the search is over, the screen flickers and the files listed in the File Management window are reduced to only those containing the desired phrase.

The next step is to open the file (or files) and use the Alt+Edit ⇨ **Search** command to find the exact place where phrase appears.

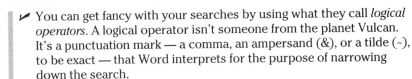

- ✔ You can get fancy with your searches by using what they call *logical operators*. A logical operator isn't someone from the planet Vulcan. It's a punctuation mark — a comma, an ampersand (&), or a tilde (~), to be exact — that Word interprets for the purpose of narrowing down the search.

- ✔ For example, if, in Step 5, you enter **Luke,Solo** as your search text, Word shows you documents that contain either Luke or Solo (the comma means "or"). **Luke&Solo** displays those files that contain *both* Luke *and* Solo. Finally, there's the tilde, which is the "not" command — **Luke~Solo** finds files containing Luke, but with no mention of Solo.

- ✔ You also can use wild cards in your text search. If you can't remember whether the client's name was Johnson or Johnsen, you'd search for **Johns*** — meaning that the name starts with *Johns*, but anything after that is okay.

- ✔ You also can search by other items in the Search box — as long as you've been diligently filling out the Summary Sheet when you save the file (see the sidebar "Summary Sheets").

- ✔ **Keywords** is not to be confused with **Text**. A *keyword* is a predesignated word that you have chosen and entered in the Summary Sheet.

Summary Sheets

If you've got a lot of files or lots of people creating lots of files, you probably will want to use the *Summary Sheet* to track the work flow. If your life isn't that complicated, then you can pass on Summary Sheets.

Basically, a Summary Sheet is a dialog box, which pops up when you save a file (see Figure 13-8).

If you don't have a popping-up Summary Sheet, you need to turn it on with Alt+Tools ⇨ Customize and then select Prompt for Summary Info. Then, as you go about your exciting daily life, fill out the appropriate information as needed.

Then, when you need to, File Management will let you sort by any of the summary profile elements.

By selecting the Options command button, you can have the files organized by author or project title. Or you can search for a file written by a particular person but typed by someone else.

And by the way, just because the slot says Title or Author, it doesn't mean you're tied down to that definition. If you're always the "author," why not use the slot for something useful — like the due date. The computer won't know. If you do use the slot for something other than the "suggested" use, remember to be consistent so that your searches will work.

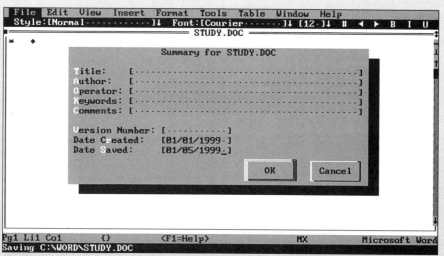

Figure 13-8: You can create a detailed rap sheet on your files with the Summary Sheet. It makes it easier to track down the file later.

Flushing Unneeded Files

In Chapter 10, I outlined how to nuke document files with File Management. Granted, if all you do is follow those directions, you'll be doing better than most.

However, there's something else you need to know. Little elves are constantly running around inside your computer, making duplicates of your files. It's true. For every document (DOC) file you create, Word automatically creates a back-up file — distinguished by its BAK file name ending. Plus, if you're using the grammar checker, it's also busy making backup files — this time ending in GBK. Not to mention the scandal of unwanted TMP files discussed elsewhere in this chapter.

Here's how to get File Management to show you all your BAK, TMP, and GBK files — and then how to delete them:

1. Press Alt+**File** ⇨ **File Management**.

2. Press Alt+**S**earch.

3. Make sure that the right path is displayed in the Search **P**aths text box.

   Remember, you're supposed to know where your home base is. Usually it's C:\WORD.

4. Press the right-arrow key.

   This moves the cursor to the end of the search path, so you don't have to type everything from scratch.

5. If there is no backslash (\) at the end of the search path, add one. Then type ***.BAK,*.TMP,*.GBK**.

   The Search **P**aths text box should look like this:

   ```
   C:\WORD\*.BAK,*.TMP,*.GBK
   ```

6. Press Enter.

These steps filter out all files except for the ones created by the elves that end in BAK, TMP, and GBK. If you see any files with endings *other* than those three, go back to Step 5 and double-check your typing.

When the BAK, TMP, and GBK files are listed, it's hammer time:

1. Press Ctrl+spacebar to select all the files on display.

   If, for some reason, there is a file or two you don't want to delete after all, deselect those files by highlighting them and pressing the spacebar.

2. When you're ready to proceed, press Alt+Delete.

3. Verify that you want to delete the marked files by pressing your basic Enter key.

   All marked files are deleted.

Finally, because it's a bit unsettling to see no files listed in your File Management display, the final step is to restore order in the universe:

1. Press Alt+**S**earch.

2. Press the right-arrow key.

3. Backspace over the file name endings until you have the normal `C:\WORD` (or whatever your normal home base search path is).

4. Press Enter.

Now, having made your hard disk safe for democracy, your DOC files will again be listed in the File Management dialog box.

> ✔ Deleting these unneeded files is an ongoing task, because every time you work on a file, at least one duplicate is created. You wouldn't let weeds take over your lawn — don't let these extra files over run your hard disk.

Visiting the Wizard of DOS

Okay, you're in the middle of a Word session and you need to copy a file or format a disk or do some other DOS sort of thing. On the other hand, you're in the middle of something with four or five files open and the last thing you want to do is quit.

Here's a timesaver. With Word's MS-DOS Commands, you can temporarily suspend your Word operations, attend to your DOS function, and then resume Word without missing a beat.

That's what Alt+File ⇨ MS-DOS Commands is all about. We've actually used it previously in this book, but didn't really cover the hows and whys of it — not that there are that many options. But the main thing is to know what DOS command you want to perform.

1. Before carrying out any DOS command, save all your files (press Alt+File ⇨ **S**ave or Alt+File ⇨ Save All) as a precaution.

2. Press Alt+File ⇨ MS-DOS Commands.

   You get the MS-DOS Commands dialog box (see Figure 13-9).

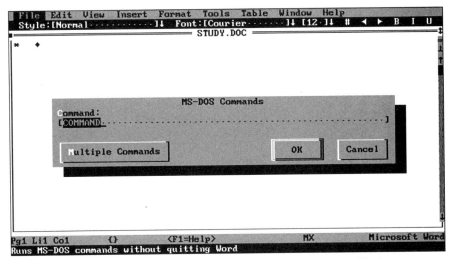

Figure 13-0: Use MS-DOS Commands to leave Word without actually leaving Word.

3. If you want to perform one DOS command — like FORMAT — just type the command and then go to the next step. If you want to perform a number of commands, skip to the next step.

4. Press Enter.

Word 6 has the **Multiple Commands** option, which, basically, dumps you at the command line until you ask to return to Word.

5. If you're using the **Multiple Commands** method, then when you're finished DOSing around, type **EXIT** and press Enter.

If you're using the one-command method, you go back into Word automatically.

✔ You may get a `Not enough memory` error message if you try to use a big program while you're in command mode — even though Word isn't on the screen, it's still taking up a lot of memory. Use command mode for minor excursions into DOS, not major safaris.

✔ Another time you'll get a `Not enough memory` message is if you space out and forget you're in command mode and then try to start Word again. Just type **EXIT** and press Enter to get back into Word.

✔ Some MS-DOS commands you might want to use: **COPY A:*filename.doc*** (to copy a file from drive A), **FORMAT A:** (to format the disk in drive A), **UNDELETE** (to bring back a recently deleted file), **DIR A:** (to get a list of files on drive A).

This command replaces Word 5's Library/Run command.

Launching Word with a Twist

Most of the time, you get into Word with your basic, ho-hum **WORD** and Enter. However, there are some jazzier, and useful, ways to start up Word.

Starting switches

A *command line switch* sounds imposing, but in Chapter 1 we saw two of them at work: typing **WORD** *filename* and pressing Enter starts Word and loads the named file; and typing **WORD/L** loads Word and puts you right back in the last file you were working on.

Although there are more than a dozen switches, Table 13-1 lists the ones you'll most likely use.

Table 13-1	Command Line Switches
Switch	**What Happens**
/L	Puts you in the last document you were working on.
/I	Cursor stops blinking (in graphics).
/P	Installs Word 6.0 function keys.
/T	Installs Word 5.0 function keys.
/Z	Returns preceding switches to defaults.
/Y	Uses Word 4.0-style scrolling. Instead of advancing one line at time at the bottom, Word scrolls half a screen forward.

Automating macros

You can make a macro run automatically when you start Word. For example, if you use multiple windows a lot, you can have a macro that asks you how many files you want and their names and loads them all automatically when you get into Word. Another possibility is to load a certain printer driver or whatever you need.

Using the command line method

To tell Word to run a macro, you need another command line switch. Technically, this should be in Table 13-1, but I cheated. Because it is macro-related, I wanted to talk about it here.

To make a macro run when you invoke Word, type **WORD/M** *macroname* and press Enter.

Using the AUTOEXEC method

The other way to program a macro to run automatically is by naming it AUTOEXEC. When you invoke Word, it finds and carries out the commands in any macro named AUTOEXEC. The only drawback to this method is that it *always* runs.

Much Ado about Spaces — and Hyphens

How can making a space or a hyphen get complicated? Well, leave it to a computer .... This is another one of those forget-about-how-it-worked-on-a typewriter commands.

Ever have a "Mr." on one line and the last name pop down to the next? Ever put in a hyphen, but then when the wording changed, the hyphen was in the middle of a line instead of at the end?

You can have control over each of these situations.

Nonbreaking spaces

Love may not always keep us together, but nonbreaking spaces never fail. Because it's considered very bad form to have a person's title on one line and the name on the next, you can link the two together with a *nonbreaking space*. To keep Ms. Smith together, you type **Ms.**, press Shift+Ctrl+spacebar, and type **Smith**. From that moment forward, Word sees "Ms. Smith" as one unit and treats it as such.

Nonbreaking hyphens

A nonbreaking hyphen — you can see where this is going, can't you? — works like the nonbreaking space. Let's say that the person's name is Ms. Smith-Browne. You create the hyphen by pressing Shift+Ctrl+-. Whatever is on the left and right of the hyphen is treated as one unit.

Creating optional hyphens

You can put a hyphen at the end of the line that is smart enough to know that if things change and it's no longer at the end of the line, that it should become invisible. Pretty clever for a hyphen. To make an *optional* hyphen, press Ctrl+-.

Making an em-dash

With typewriters, you create a dash by typing two hyphens in a row. With a computer, you can still type two hyphens, of course, but if you've got a halfway-decent printer, you'll want to create a real dash (known as an em-dash) by holding down the Alt key and typing 15 on the numeric keypad (make sure that Num Lock is turned on), and then releasing the Alt key. This gives you a classier-looking dash. Doubtless this little maneuver will win you the new account.

Searching for Nonprinting Symbols

In Chapter 7, we discovered that you can search for a page break symbol (the periods across the page). There are other weird items you can Alt+**Edit** ⇨ **S**earch for, should the need arise. And, as you know, you can get some weird needs with a computer.

The caret symbol (^) is on the 6 key on the keyboard (*not* the 6 on the numeric keypad). Shift+6 makes the caret.

Table 13-2 lists various symbols and what to press to search for them.

Table 13-2	Search for Symbols
Symbol	*What To Search For*
Paragraph	^p
Tab	^t
Page or section break	^d
New line	^n
Nonbreaking space	^s
Optional hyphen	^-
Column break	^c
Blank space	^w
Question mark	^?
Caret	^^

An additional note: Although there's no "official command" to do this, if you need to search for nonbreaking hyphens, you can do it. When in the Search dialog box, hold down the Alt key, type **196** (on the numeric keypad to the right — make sure that Num Lock is turned on), and then release the Alt key.

Chapter 14

Learning to Love Labels

. . . .

. . . .

*P*roducing mailing labels is, without a doubt, the Holy Grail of many computer users. Printing out a sheet of labels is the ultimate symbol of being organized and of mastering your computer.

If you survived Chapter 11's "Merging Mania," then you're very close to being able to do labels. So come on, take a chance.

In the past, constructing a label grid was, at best, daunting, requiring much ruler action and at least an afternoon of tedious trial and error.

The good news is that Microsoft has provided a very helpful label macro that actually takes most of the grunt work out of label template construction. You can probably even leave your ruler in your desk drawer.

As you go through the effort of building a label template, keep in mind that after you've gone through this setup, you probably will never have to mess with the template construction again. You can update your database all you want, but you won't have to touch the template — unless you buy different labels.

Erecting Diabolical Databases

Before you can worry about making labels, you first need to have a database — you know, the stuff you're going to print. If you don't have the names and addresses typed up yet, jump back to Chapter 11 and take a look at "Merging Mania." Create a database and then come back here.

To construct the template, you need to know the name and path of your database file. If you don't have it memorized, *write it down* — you'll need it later.

 If your printer doesn't support TrueType fonts, make sure that each of your address elements is no longer than about 23 characters — otherwise, it won't fit on a single line of a label and will wrap to the next line, causing all sorts of mischief.

Purchasing Labels

The decision about label purchasing is, believe it or not, very important. You want to select labels that Microsoft's label macro knows about. If you don't, you're in for some serious grief. My recommendation is that you purchase Avery 5260 labels — or something 5260-compatible — to start with.

These labels allow for up to six lines in the address and print three-across (also known as *three-up*) on the sheet. This can accommodate most needs. Avery 5260 labels are available in office supply stores, software stores, and through catalogs. They are as common as water. However, if the 5260 size labels don't work for you, then just purchase something else from Avery.

Whatever you decide to buy, make sure that you've got them nearby — or at least know the "model number" — because you will construct the template by using that label's specifications. In the instructions that follow, I'll use the Avery 5260 as an example; you can substitute your own purchasing decision.

Constructing the Template

To start out with a clean slate, quit Word and then restart. Follow the steps in the next sections.

Loading the label macro

From the blank Word screen, follow these steps:

1. Press Alt+T**o**ols ⇨ **M**acro.

   This gets you into the Macro dialog box.

2. Press Alt+**O**pen Glossary.

   At this point, one of the names in the Files list box should be LABEL.GLY. If not, quit Word, type **CD\WORD**, and press Enter. Start Word again and follow the first two steps.

3. Type **LABEL.GLY** and press Enter.

   After a few seconds, you should see a screen like that shown in Figure 14-1.

4. Type **LABEL** in the Macro **N**ame box.

5. Press Alt+**R**un.

   After a few seconds, you see the screen shown in Figure 14-2.

6. Press Enter.

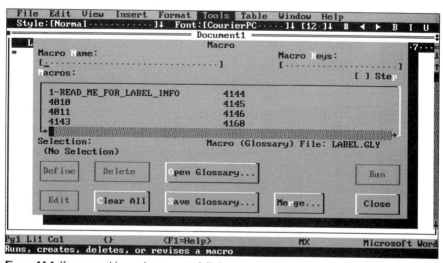

Figure 14-1: If you see this, you've successfully loaded the label-making macro — marvelous!

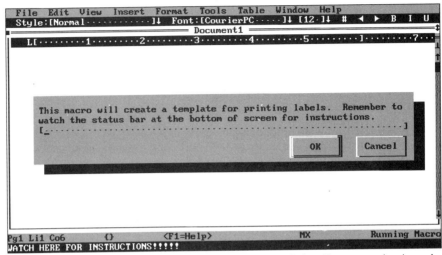

Figure 14-2: This means you're not in Kansas anymore — the label-making process has begun!

Entering the specs

You now have to answer questions about the labels you intend to use.

1. When Word asks for the Maker of Label, press 1 and then Enter for Avery.

2. You then see an informational screen that tells you what's happening next. Just press Enter to move along.

Can't find MSLBL1.DOC!

If Word never tells you Can't find MSLBL1.DOC, then you don't have to worry about reading this warning. However, if you do get the thrill of seeing this dialog box, don't worry, it's not fatal. There are two files that LABEL.GLY needs to work properly: MSLBL1.DOC and MSLBL2.DOC. When you're making the label template, LABEL.GLY assumes that its two companion files are in the current directory. If you are in C:\WORD\INVOICES, for example, but LABEL.GLY is stored in C:\WORD, LABEL.GLY is not smart enough to look for the two helper files back in C:\WORD. What you need to do is copy all three files into the C:\WORD\INVOICES directory — then start again.

3. Highlight the Product Number of the labels you purchased.

   Look at Figure 14-3. Find your model number and highlight it. Don't just point to it, actually highlight it, as in the example.

```
 File  Edit  View  Insert  Format  Tools  Table  Window  Help
 Style:[Normal*··········]↓  Font:[CourierPC·····]↓ [12·]↓  #  ◄  ►  B  I  U
═══════════════════════════ MSLBL1.DOC ═══════════════════════════
  L0[·········1]┬········2·······┬·····3····┬·····4·······┬······5······┬·······6·······┬······7···
      PRODUCT·        PRODUCT·DESCRIPTION◄      LABELS·ACROSS·      LABELS·DOWN·
      NUMBER◄                                   PAGE◄              PAGE◄

      5267◄           Return·Address◄                4◄                20◄
      5160◄           Address◄                       3◄                10◄
      5260◄           Address◄                       3◄                10◄
      5161◄           Address◄                       2◄                10◄
      5261◄           Address◄                       2◄                10◄
      5162◄           Address◄                       2◄                 7◄
      5262◄           Address◄                       2◄                 7◄
      5163◄           Address/Shipping◄              2◄                 5◄
      5164◄           Address/Shipping◄              2◄                 3◄
      5660◄           Clear·Address◄                 3◄                10◄
      5662◄           Clear·Address◄                 2◄                 7◄
      5663◄           Clear·Address◄                 2◄                 5◄
      5266◄           File·Folder◄                   2◄                15◄
      5196◄           3-1/2"·Diskette◄               3◄                 3◄
      5096◄           3-1/2"·Diskette·Red◄           3◄                 3◄

 Pg1 Li? Co5        {}          <F1=Help>                    MX        Running Macro
 Highlight the product number of the label that you are using and press enter.
```

Figure 14-3: The critical moment where you tell Word what labels you have. Did you ever know there were so many kinds of labels? Someone definitely needs to get a life.

4. Press Enter.

   You may see, at the bottom of the screen, the message that Word is `Setting label parameters`. That's a good thing.

5. Eventually, Word wants to know whether you want `a single label, a page of the same label or print merge multiple labels`. At this time, we're doing the print merge multiple labels. Press 3 and Enter.

Attaching your database

You're doing great. By now, the label grid honeycomb is set up. Next comes the part where you tell Word what to print on the labels — the part that requires the most work from you. Look on the bright side: After you complete this section, you're home free.

1. Word now informs you that you need to know the name of your database to negotiate past the next screen. For now, press Enter. You'll end up with Figure 14-4.

2. Type the database file name — the one I told you to write down. Include the path if you have to. In Figure 14-4, my database was given a very original name: DATA.DOC. You type yours and press Enter.

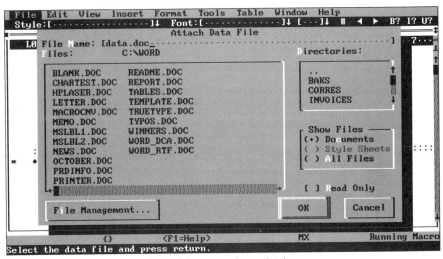

Figure 14-4: This is where you tell Word the name of your database.

What you want to see, at the bottom of the screen, is the message that the database was accepted. If you make a typo or forget the path when you type a database name, Word just says `invalid header record` and gives you another chance.

If you've done everything correctly so far, you'll see Figure 14-5.

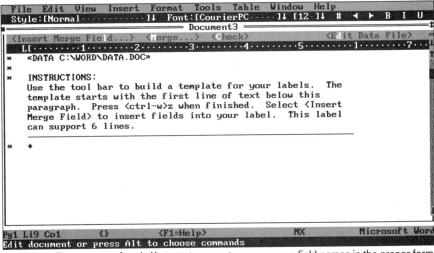

Figure 14-5: The moment of truth. You must now enter your merge field names in the proper format.

The next step is a variation on "Creating the main document," which we did in Chapter 11. Each element of your name and address list is represented by a *field name*. If you want a name and an address to appear on the label, the associated field names must be typed — in the pattern of the mailing address — below the line in Figure 14-5.

In my database in Figure 14-6, I have fields for First and Last name, Company name, Address, City, State, and Zip. I entered them as follows, using the Ctrl+[and Ctrl+] for the « and » (or you can press Ctrl+Insert Merge Field to select from the field names in a dialog box, as in Chapter 11).

On the computer screen, this looks like Figure 14-6.

3. Enter *your* database fields like the following example:

```
«First» «Last»
«If Company»«Company»
«ENDIF
«Address»
«City», «State» «Zip»«IF Company="">
ENDIF
```

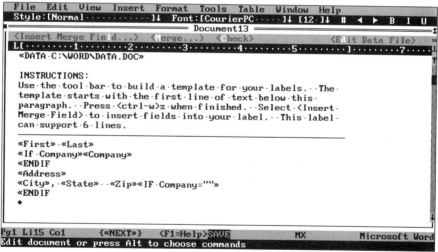

Figure 14-6: The stuff below the line is what you type. Would you believe that this is the simple example?

Making up for blank lines

As mentioned in "Merging Mania," not everyone in your database has all the name and address elements. For example, some people have company names and some don't. Word's normal reaction to "missing" address elements is to leave a hole in the address where the data would have appeared. The magical IF statement cures the missing data blues. In the second line of the example label, we've got an IF statement that says, "If there's a company name, stick it in here. If there isn't, then don't stick it in here and don't leave a blank line in the middle of the address."

That solves one problem, but it's also the beginning of another. The reality now is that some addresses will have four lines and some will have three.

When you're making a letter, if the thing is one line shorter or longer at the bottom of the page, it's not a big deal.

With labels, however, it's a whole other ball game. Whatsoever thou takest away must thou put back. Or everything falls apart.

Therefore, we have the additional IF statement at the end of the label, which says, "IF there was no company name in the address, stick an extra blank line at the end of the this label to even things out."

That's why we need:

```
«IF Company=""»
«ENDIF
```

In essence, what you're typing is, "IF **COMPANY** equal sign, quotation mark, quotation mark."

Missing chevrons (« »)

Did you notice that there are no chevrons on the right of our ENDIFs? No, we didn't make a typo. They are missing on purpose. It's all part of the metaphysics of merging — and it's the way to make sure that there are no unintended blank lines. Make sure that you type the chevrons exactly as shown.

Bringing it on home

After you've got your label data entered:

1. Press Ctrl+WZ.

   If everything is going correctly, the status bar should say Running Macro in the lower right.

   If you get OUT OF MEMORY, as in Figure 14-7, don't panic. It's okay. Just press Enter. Then, when asked whether you want to save the file, say Yes, and when prompted, give it a name — any name. You could even call it TEMPLATE if you want — and then press Enter.

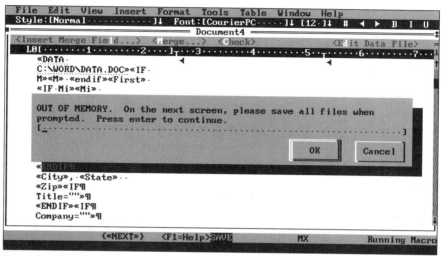

Figure 14-7: Don't let the OUT OF MEMORY message drive you out of your mind. Word needs to regroup its thoughts.

2. When you get Figure 14-8, heave a sigh of relief and celebrate. You've made a label template. Oh, and press Enter.

   ✔ Be sure to save the file, also.

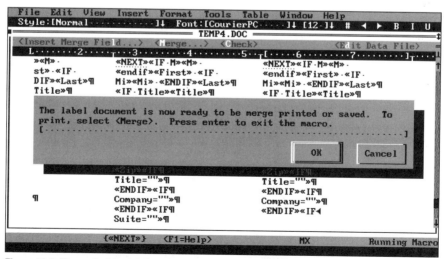

Figure 14-8: The end of the rainbow — you've survived the label-making macro. Press Enter and celebrate.

Using the label template

After you have a label template, as in Figure 14-9, you are ready to print — theoretically. However, the voice of experience suggests the following steps before printing.

Apply a smaller font to the template — Arial 10 pt. is a good choice. This is a very readable size, but allows for more characters in the addresses and helps circumvent the dreaded word-wrap disease. To apply the smaller font:

1. Highlight the document by pressing Shift+F10.

2. Press Ctrl+F to pop up the Ribbon.

3. Press Alt+down arrow to reveal your fonts.

4. Highlight Arial.

5. Press Tab.

6. Type **10**.

7. Press Enter.

Next, do a test print on plain paper before printing on the actual labels. This allows for two things: to see that there are no problems with how the addresses actually print, and to let you compare the printout to the label sheet to make sure that everything lines up properly.

When you're ready to print, all you have to do is what we did in Chapter 11.

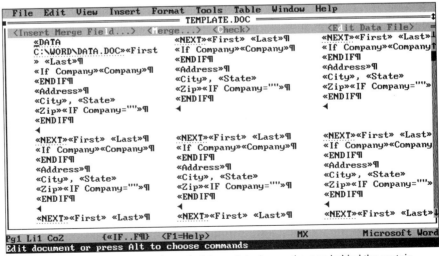

Figure 14-9: Here it is, the great and wonderful template. Ignore the man behind the curtain.

1. Press Alt+**Merge**.

2. Press **Print**.

   Or select certain records (like your first and fifth addresses) to be printed.

3. The Print dialog box pops up — press Enter to actually commence the printing.

   ✔ Do not become alarmed if the last row of labels is not used. That's just the way it works. Be happy for what you got. And, hey, why not use the leftover labels on your floppy disks?

What they don't tell you

The address label template we just created is a basic, workable setup. However, you may want to have a more complete database that includes all conceivable elements of an address: Mr./Ms., First Name, Middle Initial, Last Name, Title, Company Name, Address, Suite, City, State, and Zip.

Just as in the basic example, we have to be prepared for the fact that not everyone will have all those elements in the address. To accommodate all the possibilities, we've got to use loads of IF statements. Here's the setup for the complete situation:

```
«IF M»«M» «endif»«First» «IF Mi»«Mi»«ENDIF»«Last»
«IF Title»«Title
«ENDIF
«IF Company»«Company»
«ENDIF
```

```
«Address»
«IF Suite»«Suite»
«ENDIF
«City», «State» «Zip»«IF Title=""»
«ENDIF
«IF Company=""»
«ENDIF
«IF Suite=""»
«ENDIF
```

See Figure 14-10 to see how this looks on screen.

It's important to note where the spaces are in the first line. If you don't do it *exactly* that way, the people without middle initials will have extra spaces — or no spaces — between their first and last names. Don't forget to put chevrons only where indicated.

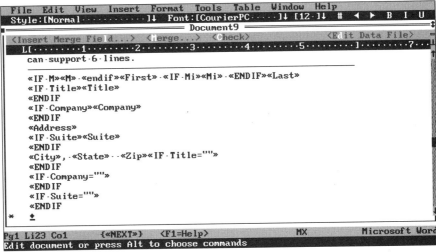

Figure 14-10: Obviously the product of a sick and demented mind, this setup prints labels for every conceivable situation. Or at least, every situation I can conceive.

Troubleshooting

If, heaven forbid, your labels don't line up properly, here are a couple of things to try.

1. Highlight the template (Shift+F10) and use Alt+Forma**t** ⇨ **M**argins to adjust the top or bottom margin.

2. Use the Alt+**T**able ⇨ Select **T**able command and adjust column height and width.

3. Make sure that the labels you bought and the labels you *told* Word you have match.

4. Go to Jamaica for a week.

Chapter 15

Features You've Seen ...
and Ignored

I'm still convinced that Bill Gates (the president of Microsoft) is somehow related to that Ronco guy — you know, the guy who sells that "slicing, dicing, peeling — but wait, that's not all!" thingie — because Word does so much. Here are some goodies that can get forgotten in the shuffle.

Calculating for the 90s

This has got to be the J.R. Ewing command, right?

If you create expense reports, tables, invoices, lists, and so forth — anything with numbers — you need the Calculate command. After you type your numbers, highlight them and press F2. I wouldn't recommend throwing out your pocket calculators yet, but being able to add a column of numbers easily is handier than you might expect. To perform simple addition:

1. Highlight the numbers you want to add up.

   To highlight a vertical *column* of numbers, use Ctrl+Shift+F8 to activate another ignored command: Column Select. If you use normal highlight commands, the highlighting smears across all columns.

2. Press F2.

The result appears at the bottom of the screen and in the Scrap (see Figure 15-1).

3. Move the cursor to where you want the result to appear and press Shift+Ins to insert the result from the Scrap into your document.

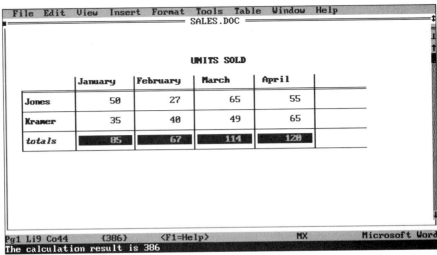

Figure 15-1: To add numbers, highlight and press F2, and faster than you can say, "where's my calculator?" the answer appears at the bottom of the screen and in the Scrap.

Admittedly, addition is the easiest calculation to do. However, if you need it, Word also subtracts, multiplies, divides, and does percentages. See Table 15-1, if you're willing to put some effort into it. (This is where you might as well use your calculator.)

Table 15-1		Mathematics 101	
To	*Use*	*Example*	*Result*
Add	+ or use nothing	100 100 or 100 + 100	200
Subtract	– or ()	100 – 50 or 100 (50)	50
Multiply	*	5 * 100	500
Divide	/	100/5	20
Percentage	%	5%*100	5

Remember sitting around in algebra class wondering when you'd ever, in your life, use that stuff? Well — this is it! With a little parenthetical action — just like you learned in algebra — you can calculate numbers in a small group first, before having another calculation applied. I guess algebra is always going to sound like algebra. Here are some examples:

✔ **(100 200 300) *30%**

The first three numbers are totalled and then multiplied by 30%

✔ **(100 200 300) * (100 – 30)**

The result of the calculations in the first group of numbers is multiplied by the result of the calculations in the second group of numbers.

✔ **(100/2)/10**

The result of the calculation in the parentheses is divided by 10.

When calculating highlighted numbers, Word ignores all text, dollar signs, and anything else other than numbers and the symbols in Table 15-1.

One of the big pains in the pocket protector about Word's Calculate command is typing all those symbols to do the calculations and then having go back and erase them for the printout. Another approach is to format the symbols as hidden text.

First, make sure that you can see hidden text (press Alt+View ➪ Preferences and then press Alt+Hidden Text). Then, as you enter the symbols, format them as hidden (highlight and press Ctrl+H). After you've done all your calculations, hide the symbols before printing (go back and do the Alt+View ➪ Preferences and press Alt+Hidden Text again). That way, the symbols are there if you need to enter new numbers and recalculate — but they won't print. No one will ever know.

Sorting the Sordid

The poor Sort command has been kicked around more than any other command I can think of. In Word 5, it was Library Autosort, in Word 5.5, it was Utilities Sort. Now it's Alt+Tools ➪ Sort.

Other than its location, the command itself has remained the same for many years. And, from what the people I deal with say, it's been ignored for many years as well. Basically, Sort brings order to chaos and whips unruly data into shape.

For example, Figure 15-2 — just a small sample table — shows us some data begging for organization.

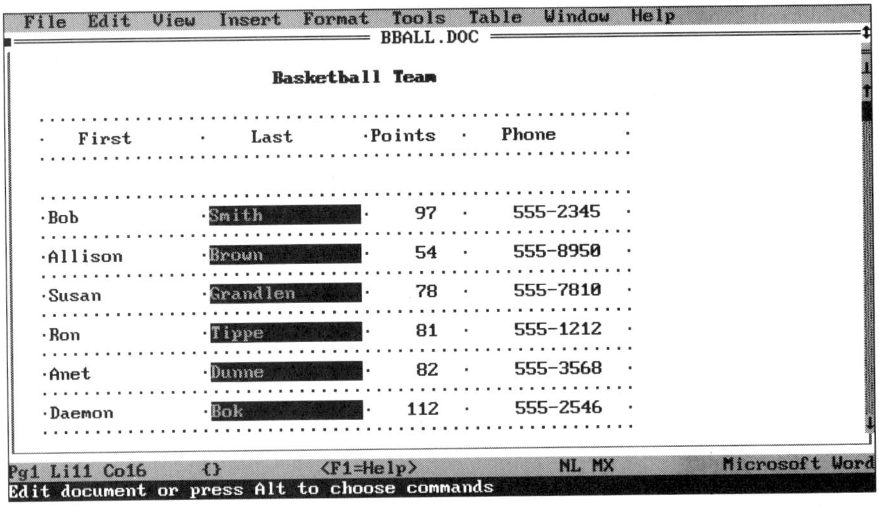

First	Last	Points	Phone
Bob	Smith	97	555-2345
Allison	Brown	54	555-8950
Susan	Grandlen	78	555-7810
Ron	Tippe	81	555-1212
Anet	Dunne	82	555-3568
Daemon	Bok	112	555-2546

Figure 15-2: Sort data by selecting the column to be sorted on and issue the Sort command.

To sort the data:

1. Highlight the column containing the data by which you want to sort.

   You can sort by any of the columns of text you create. If you're not in a Table format, remember that Ctrl+Shift+F8 turns on columnar highlighting.

2. Press Alt+Tools ⇨ Sort.

   You see the Sort dialog box (see Figure 15-3). The default settings are, in virtually all cases, the way to go.

3. Press Enter.

   When Word organizes the column you select, the data to the left and the right of it will "stick" with the sorted text.

   - Do not select Sort Column Only unless you want to reorganize the highlighted column but leave all the other material alone. If we used this feature with Figure 15-3, sorting on last names, Bok would become the last name of Bob.
   - Case Sensitive is another option you should avoid unless you really want it. Computers look at things a lot differently than we do. In this option, numbers go first, uppercase goes before lowercase, and so on.

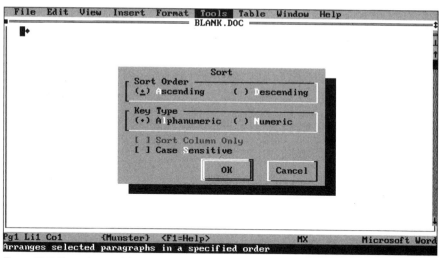

Figure 15-3: Up or down, alpha or numeric — all the questions that plague our times. Avoid Sort Column Only and Case **S**ensitive.

Customizing Word

For finicky types — like myself — there are a couple more items about Word that you may want to modify, using the Customize dialog box (see Figure 15-4). The Customize dialog box isn't news, but you may not have noticed the features on the right that you can modify.

You can get to the Customize dialog box by pressing Alt+**T**ools ⇨ **C**ustomize (or, take the long cut by pressing Alt+**V**iew ⇨ **P**references ⇨ **C**ustomize).

Converting text to a table to calculate

It's especially helpful when the material to be organized or calculated is in a table, because the columns of data are so neatly organized.

Remember that all data that has been entered and separated with Tabs (or commas) is eligible for conversion to a table. You may not want a table, per se, in your document — and that's okay. Just convert the text to a table for the duration of a sort or calculation. After that business has been completed, turn the table back to text.

Just highlight the text to be converted and select Alt+**T**able ⇨ Convert to **T**ext/Table.

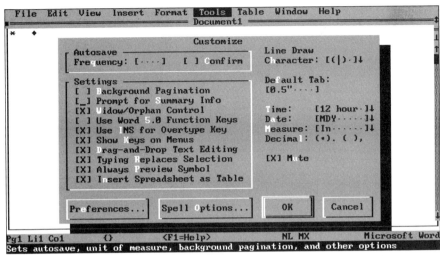

Figure 15-4: Ever want to tell your computer to shut up? Now you can by selecting Mute.

Silencing the computer

My favorite command is **Mute** — which turns off the constant, infernal beeping when you make a mistake. Uh, but of course, because I'm a professional and I've never made a mistake, I wouldn't know from firsthand experience what it's like to get a beep. But I can *imagine* that it may be annoying. However, most people prefer the audio warnings. You decide.

Changing the default Tab width

When you press Tab, the cursor moves forward half an inch. This is the normal Tab setting (normal for Word, that is). You can change it to any measure you want by going to the Default Tab text box and typing a new number.

Speeding up the cursor

Here's a secret ... you can change how fast the cursor zips across the screen when you're using arrow keys and the Backspace key. However, the people at Microsoft decided that the cursor speed wasn't a customization — it was a preference. That means you have to press Alt+View ⇨ **Pr**eferences and select S**p**eed in the Cursor Control box. Nine is as fast as you can go. I recommend it.

Hyphenating Words

In the old days — like when I first entered the workforce — being able to decide where and how to end the typewritten line was a real talent. You'd let a word violate the margin by a character or two or hyphenate the word — whatever it took to make sure that the text didn't look real raggedy. With word wrap, however, the decision about the end of the line has been removed from your consciousness. And, mostly, that's just terrific.

However, every now and then, some big word gets wrapped to the next line, ending the preceding line a little short, as in Figure 15-5. If you've had this happen and it bothered you, then here's how to fix it. If you don't care how it looks as long as it's spelled properly, then that's fine, too — and you can go on to the next section.

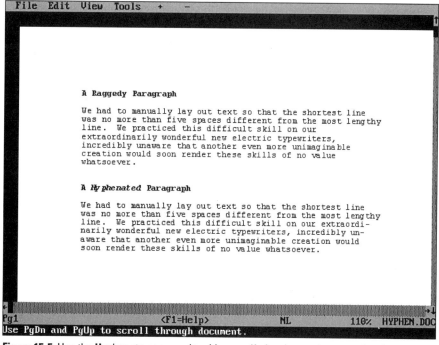

Figure 15-5: Use the **H**yphenate command to rid yourself of embarrassing raggedy edges.

To hyphenate your text:

1. Highlight the text you want to hyphenate.

   You don't have to do the whole document, if you don't want to. Maybe you have one troublesome paragraph.

2. Press Alt+Tools ⇨ **Hyphenate**.

   A small dialog box asks whether you want to Confirm the hyphens (or just let Word go to it) and whether it's okay to hyphenate capitalized words (in case you don't want to).

3. Press Enter.

   Unless you chose to Confirm the hyphens, Word just does the job and hyphenates the words with *optional hyphens*. An optional hyphen is one that appears only if the word lands at the end of the line. If it doesn't, the hyphen becomes invisible.

   If you did want to confirm the hyphens, then you have to say Yes or No — or even reposition the hyphen — one word at a time.

   ✔ Later, if you reword your text — altering which words appear at the end of the line — you have to go through the process again.

Counting Words

If you ever want to know how many words you've written, then your curiosity is about to be satisfied.

1. Highlight the text you want to count.

2. Press Alt+Tools ⇨ **Word Count**.

3. Press Enter.

   The number appears at the bottom of the screen and in the Scrap.

In Word 5, the only way to get a word count is to run the spelling checker. This is much better.

Chapter 16

Sharing with Others

● ●

In This Chapter

▶ Trading files with a fellow Word for DOS user

▶ Giving files to someone using a Microsoft family word processor

▶ Getting files from a Microsoft family word processor

▶ Handling foreign file formats

▶ Forcing file-format friendliness

● ●

*W*hen I started in the computer industry, the "big concept" touted by pundits was the advent of the "paperless office." What a joke. Thanks to computers and desktop publishing, more paper than ever is being used. (I hope everybody out there is recycling their computer paper and toner cartridges.)

However, one of the planks in the paperless office platform — that people should be able to share files and data — is not so pie-in-the-sky.

That was a good thing.

However, the road to sharing and caring is often blocked by two issues: How to physically get the data from point A to point B; and, if by some miracle you get that accomplished, how to get one computer system to use files created on another. And what if one of those systems is a Macintosh?

Version 6 makes all this easier — actually, it makes it possible. However, let's start with the easiest file-sharing scenario and work our way up.

Trading Files with a Fellow Word for DOS User

This is the simplest situation. You copy the file to a floppy disk and then, using the venerable "sneaker net" (that is, you walk over to where the other computer is), you give the disk to your coworker, who copies it onto his or her system. No problem.

1. Press Alt+File ⇨ File Management.

2. Highlight the file you want to copy and press the spacebar.

3. Press Alt+Copy.

4. Type **A:.**

   If you're copying to drive B, substitute that B for A.

   If you're using a style sheet and the recipient of the file doesn't have that style sheet, be sure to press Alt+Copy **S**tyle Sheets.

5. Press Enter.

Now, march the disk over to the other person's computer and stick the disk in drive A (or B). Be ruthless.

1. Press Alt+File ⇨ File Management.

2. Press Alt+**S**earch.

3. Type **A:** and press Enter.

4. Highlight the file to be copied and press the spacebar.

5. Press Alt+Copy.

   The path name that appears should be your friend's current directory. If it isn't, type the current directory. Hope that your friend knows where the files should go.

   If you need the style sheets, be sure to press Alt+Copy **S**tyle Sheets.

6. Press Enter.

   > ✔ Don't assume that just because you use 3.5" high-density disks that your friend does also. Make sure that your disk sizes are compatible. If necessary, get a disk from the other person and check it out on your computer in advance. And vice versa.

✔ When copying the file onto the other computer, proceed with caution if you get an overwrite existing file? message. That means there's a file on the destination hard disk with the same name as the file you're copying and that file will be erased if you proceed. If you're just updating the file or something, that's okay. If not, don't make a mortal enemy of your coworker by erasing his or her files.

✔ You can find more on File Management in Chapter 13.

Giving Files to Someone Using a Microsoft Family Word Processor

If you are working with someone who uses Word for Windows, Word for the Macintosh, or Microsoft Works, then you're in luck. You can now use Save **As** to save your file as... Word for Windows, Word/Mac and, not surprisingly, Microsoft Works (RTF).

1. Press Alt+**File** ➪ Save **As**.

   You end up in the Save As dialog box.

2. Type a new File **Name**.

   Don't overwrite your own file — type a new name.

3. Press Alt+Forma**t**.

4. Select the file format in which you want to save your file.

5. Press Enter.

   Depending on the format, it may take a few seconds to complete the task. Watch for exciting progress reports at the bottom of the screen.

Proceed with the copying process as you did previously.

1. Press Alt+**File** ➪ **F**ile Management.

2. Highlight the file you want to copy (remember to copy the file with the *new name*) and press the spacebar.

3. Press Alt+**C**opy.

4. Type **A:**.

   If you're copying to drive B, substitute that.

Getting along with Macs

Some Macintoshes actually can copy from and to 3.5" high-density IBM-compatible disks. If you're dealing with someone who's so equipped, and you've got a 3.5" high-density drive, you're in business.

If he doesn't know whether his drive can read your disks, it's real easy to find out. Just stick one of your disks in his Macintosh. If the Mac lists your files, you can start your victory dance. If the Mac wants to initialize it — then the Mac can't use the disk.

Don't give up yet. An alternative is to buy software that temporarily transforms your floppy drive into a Mac drive. One such program is called Mac-In-Dos™.

If you have a modem, you can transfer the files over the phone. Unfortunately, it'll take another book to explain how to do that. If you do have a modem, though, you have that option.

Finally, when you get a file back from Word for Mac users, be sure to tell them to save the file they're giving you as Word for DOS! That way, your system will be able to use it.

If you're using a style sheet and the recipient of the file doesn't have that style sheet, be sure to press Alt+Copy **S**tyle Sheets.

5. Press Enter.

6. Now, hope the other person knows how to copy files onto her system. If she doesn't — call someone for help and find out!

> ✔ If Word won't convert the file, you may have to run your Word 6 Setup disks and have the converters installed.

> ✔ Word for Windows and Word for the Mac make use of your style sheets, so be sure to copy them, if applicable.

Getting Files from a Microsoft Family Word Processor

When you receive a file from someone else, make sure that the file is saved in the proper format. Then copy the file onto your computer.

1. Press Alt+File ⇨ **F**ile Management.

2. Press Alt+**S**earch.

3. Type **A:*.*** and press Enter.

4. Highlight the file you want to copy and press the spacebar.

5. Press Alt+**C**opy.

   The Path **N**ame should be for the current directory on your friend's hard disk. If it isn't, type it in.

   If you need the style sheets, be sure to press Alt+Copy **S**tyle Sheets.

6. Press Enter.

So far, so good.

Now you need to open the file.

1. Press Alt+**F**ile ⇨ **O**pen.

2. Type the file name and press Enter.

3. Answer OK when Word asks whether you want to display the file in Word format. This means that Word is translating the file for you.

You then see the file on-screen and you're ready to go. Of course, be sure to save it.

Handling Foreign File Formats

If you're trying to trade files with someone who doesn't have a Microsoft family product, you need to get a *file conversion* program. If you're doing straight letters, not much fancy formatting, these programs will work for you:

✔ Microsoft offers a Convert disk that changes WordStar™, WordPerfect™, and MultiMate™ files into Word files — but not back again (obviously, they want to keep you using Word).

✔ WordPerfect™ comes with a Convert disk that translates Word files into WordPerfect™.

✔ There are commercial programs "out there" that mediate file-incompatibility problems. An excellent program to consider is Software Bridge™.

Forcing File Format Friendliness

There is a universally acceptable file format called ASCII (pronounced ASSKEY). ASCII files contain only alphanumeric characters and Enters. No formatting, no tables, no nothing. Just text.

If you need to give someone a file no matter what, save your file as Text Only (Word's version of ASCII), and the other system will be able to use your file no matter what — as long as the system can read your disk.

And, if someone gives you an ASCII (or Text) file, Word can open it — though it may grumble a bit about "not recognizing the format."

Part IV
Part of Tens

In this part . . .

*F*ast food! Instant gratification! Here today, gone tomorrow! Why not add *sudden knowledge* to the slate? The next six chapters are all lists, covering everything you need to know for Type-A types who are merrily working your way toward your first cardiac arrest. Have fun!

Chapter 17
Ten Most Important Commands

*J*ust to prove how simple and easy to use Word is, we've done the impossible — reduced several hundred pages of text to ten commands. With these commands, you can fetch a file, edit it, format it with any font, save it, print it, back it up, and then leave the program.

Hold on to your hats!

Open File

This is the get-a-file command: Alt+File ⇨ **O**pen. Select your file name, or type a new file name if you want to create a new file, and then press Enter.

Highlight

Press F8 once and then use the cursor keys to highlight the text you travel over. Pressing F8 repeatedly highlights a word, a sentence, a paragraph, and the document.

Cut/Paste

Okay, I cheated by counting Cut and Paste as one command. Anyway, highlight the text and press Shift+Del to delete and then move the cursor to where you want the text to appear. Press Shift+Ins.

Repeat

The repeat-last-action command — F4 — is the handiest thing on the planet. For example, if you format a character or paragraph, you can repeat that formatting process someplace else with F4. If you just typed a Tab and a number, pressing F4 repeats that action. Want to repeat a macro? Try it. It's terrific.

Undo

To cancel the preceding action, press Alt+Backspace. Even if you've just numbered a list or deleted a paragraph, Undo puts it back the way it was.

Ribbon

Ctrl+F pops up the formatting Ribbon at the top of your screen. From there, you can access any font, any size, create a table, indent and outdent, boldface, italicize, and underline. That's a lot for a little Ribbon.

Save

If you get one message in this book — it's not enough. But one of the things you *should* remember is to save often with Alt+**File** ⇨ **S**ave.

Print

It's no good keeping the file in the computer. Print it! Press Alt+**File** ⇨ **Print**.

Copy to a Floppy

Other than saving, backing up is an incredibly important issue. Be a role model for your children and coworkers.

1. Put a blank disk in the floppy drive.
2. Press Alt+**File** ⇨ **File Management**.
3. Highlight the file you want to copy.
4. Press the spacebar to select the highlighted file.
5. Press Alt+**C**opy.
6. Type **A:** and press Enter.

   ✔ After you're returned to the File Management screen, press Esc to get back to your file.

   ✔ If you're not using drive A, substitute the drive letter you are using — like B, for example.

Exit

To leave the program, press Alt+**File** ⇨ **Ex**it Word (or Alt+F4, just like in Windows).

Chapter 18

Ten Ways to Get out of Trouble

*N*obody likes feeling helpless when something goes wrong with the computer. Especially because it's always the computer's fault — or Word's. So it's good to have a few tricks up your sleeve to put your persnickety machine in it's place.

A few of these ways to get out of trouble depend on some advance planning on your part. Read this now — when you're not in trouble — so that you can prepare for the day that it happens.

The day the computer freezes!

Look at the Message Bar

If nothing seems to be working, the first thing to do is to look at the message bar at the bottom of the screen. It may be telling you what's going on — or what you should do.

Try Pressing Esc

Esc means "cancel." Often, it's all you need to get out of a weird situation. Think of it as the "beam me outta here, Scotty" command. Sometimes the simplest thing is overlooked during a panic attack.

Try Both the Mouse and Keyboard

When something isn't working, try the mouse *and* the keyboard command for that operation. Sometimes one works when the other is locked up. Sounds weird, I know, but we're talking about computers here. It's worth a shot.

Try to Save

If you're ready to declare a Mayday, always try saving first — just in case. If you can't save, and there's something on the screen you don't want to lose, write it down. Crude, but effective.

Wait a Minute

Another weird suggestion, but I've seen it work. Sometimes just walking away from the machine for a few minutes gives it the solitude it needs to sort things out. Walking away also may keep you from doing something that you might later regret. If nothing changes in 5 or 10 minutes, though, move on to another option.

Reboot the Computer

If nothing else works, you have to turn the computer off and then turn it back on again. This is not good. But sometimes a man's gotta do what a man's gotta do. (If you have a reset button, this is the time to use it.)

Try Finding Files

If you had to reboot, you may still be able to recover from the situation by finding your BAK or TMP file, as described in detail in Chapter 13 — in the section "Finding Files."

Copy Your MW.INI File

There is one file in Word that keeps track of your color settings, your printer driver, and your preferences and customizations. I bet you can guess its name — MW.INI. It's a good idea to back it up in case you accidentally erase it.

Put a blank disk in drive A and:

1. Press Alt+File ⇨ MS-DOS Commands.

2. Type **COPY C:\WORD\MW.INI A:** and press Enter.

   When DOS finishes copying the file, you are told to press any key to return to Word. Do so.

   ✔ If you want to copy the file to drive B, substitute that drive letter in the command. Also, if your Word program is not installed in C:\WORD, substitute your drive and directory.

If something goes wrong with your color or setup, you'll have this file to fall back on. If you need it, you can copy it back to your system with:

1. Press Alt+File ⇨ MS-DOS Commands.

2. Type **COPY A:MW.INI C:\WORD** and press Enter.

   ✔ Again, substitute your drive and directory as needed.

Keep a Written Record of Your Setup

It's a good idea to have written down, someplace, the correct name of your printer and your home base directory, just in case the name of your printer accidentally gets deleted or you get lost on your hard disk.

To find your printer name, Press Alt+**F**ile ➪ **P**rinter Setup. Make a note of:

1. The **P**rinter File.

2. The Printer **N**ame.

3. The directory name underneath the Printer **N**ame.

To find your home base directory:

1. Press Alt+**F**ile ➪ **O**pen.

2. Do you see your normal file names? If so, you're in your home base directory. Write down the path, which is located to the right of the word `Files`.

If writing down this information seems like an incredible effort, you can do a Print Screen of the two areas in question instead. Turn on your printer and press Print Screen (a button on your keyboard), and the contents of the screen are dumped to the printer. It won't be a pretty sight, but the basic info is there. (If you have a laser printer, you have to press — on the printer — the On Line and then the Form Feed buttons to get the page out.)

Call Microsoft

Don't laugh. If you're truly in a jam, you'll try *anything*. Maybe today will be your lucky day. At least you'll feel like you're doing something. See Chapter 21 for Microsoft's technical support line.

Chapter 19

Ten Ways to Avoid Trouble in the First Place

- -

In This Chapter

▶ Save your files constantly

▶ Never turn off the computer before you quit Word

▶ Back up every day

▶ Quit and restart Word once every four hours

▶ Don't overwrite the existing file

▶ Never play chicken with the SAVE light

▶ Never take a floppy disk out of the drive when the drive light is on

▶ Don't change your hardware in the middle of a big project

▶ If you've got an older system, keep your files under 100 pages long

▶ Don't let a smile be your umbrella

- -

Save Your Files Constantly

Every few minutes, save your file (Alt+File ⇨ Save or Shift+F12). Even if you're leaving the room for "just a sec," or just to answer the door, or just anything, save. Save until your wrists ache. Also, save before running a spelling check or search and replace (so you can Undo if something weird happens).

Never Turn Off the Computer before You Quit Word

Always use Alt+File ➪ Exit Word (or Alt+F4) to exit the program properly. If you don't, you'll eventually scramble your file. Minimally, you collect a bunch of files ending in TMP that take up space on your hard disk and slow things down.

Back Up Every Day

The worst case I ever heard was about a woman who'd been doing research — for years — on her Ph.D. dissertation and had all her notes on her hard disk. Her hard disk took a dive. She lost everything. Remember, your hard disk *will* go down some day. That is, it will be broken permanently and whatever didn't get backed up will be gone. Forever. Get into the habit. Back up every single day. The life you save may be your own.

The easiest way to back up a file is with File Management.

1. Press Alt+File ➪ File Management.

2. Highlight the file you want to back up.

3. Press the spacebar.

4. Put a blank disk in the floppy drive.

5. Press Alt+Copy.

6. Type **A:** and press Enter.

    Substitute **B:** if you're copying to drive B.

7. After the file is copied (you'll be returned to the File Management dialog box), press Esc to return to your document.

Quit and Restart Word Once Every Four Hours

After working with Word continuously for four hours — this does not mean the computer's just sitting there for four hours, this means you are typing and working for four hours straight — save your file and quit Word. Then start it back up (remember, type **WORD/L** and press Enter to put yourself back where you were) and resume working. If you do this, you can avoid an emergency flashing SAVE situation and a frozen computer.

As you work with Word, it's constantly shuffling your text from a temporary file — a buffer — on the hard disk into the computer's memory. If you work for a long time, especially with big files or memory-intensive activities — like search and replace or mail merge — the buffer file eventually becomes backed up. When you've got a backed-up buffer, it's not a job for Roto Rooter. Oh, no. When the buffer backs up, Word thinks it's out of memory and starts flashing SAVE. Even though you save the file, the flashing SAVE immediately returns because saving doesn't clear out the buffer. Only quitting and restarting Word gives the program a chance to reset the buffer.

Don't Overwrite the Existing File

Unless, in fact, you want to erase the file, say No. A corollary is not to ignore Do you want to save changes to your file? That means you're about to exit without saving the file. Even if you think you just saved it, err on the side of caution. If you get both error messages, then use the Alt+File ▷ Save **As** command to give the file a different name.

Never Play Chicken with the SAVE Light

If you ignore the SAVE light, the computer will freeze and you'll lose your stuff.

In our society, we're used to "just one more minute" having no consequences. So, when the SAVE light comes on, you may think that "just one more minute" of typing won't be a problem. Wrong. Do not push the envelope with the SAVE light. The computer isn't kidding. In fact, you're lucky to get a warning at all. When the SAVE light comes on, stop what you're doing. Save your file, quit Word, and then restart.

Never Take a Floppy Disk out of the Drive When the Drive Light Is On

When the drive light is on, the floppy disk is in use. If you yank the disk out while it's being used, you could upset the delicate balance of the universe and we'll all be destroyed. Or at least your files might be.

Don't Change Your Hardware in the Middle of a Big Project

If you start adding memory, scanners, bigger drives, and so on in the middle of a big project, you'll have the inevitable bugs and learning curve to deal with while you're trying to do your best work. Do yourself a favor and, if possible, wait until things are a little quieter. If things never get quiet, then try to do the changeover during the weekend.

If You've Got an Older System, Keep Your Files under 100 Pages Long

If you've got an older computer (a 286 or older computer) and you don't have any memory above 640K, don't create files larger than 100 pages. Eventually, your file will pop like a balloon, leaving bits o' scrambled file all over your hard disk. No physical damage is done to your hard disk ... but the file will be very difficult to put together. Much like Humpty Dumpty.

Don't Let a Smile Be Your Umbrella

In other words, save your charm for people. When it comes to computers, don't try to bluster your way through and ignore the rules. The people who get in the worst trouble are those who think they can somehow get by without saving or backing up and so on. Do the stuff you're told to do and stay out of trouble. Ignore the rules and pay the price down the road. Guaranteed.

Chapter 20

Ten Macros for People Who Hate Macros

. . . .

In This Chapter

▶ Programming macros

▶ Using the macro

▶ Editing a macro

▶ Saving the macros permanently

▶ Presenting — ten macros

. . . .

*I*n Chapter 11, we played with recording macros — you typed it, and Word recorded your keystrokes. Now we're going to extend the joy by *programming* macros — and you don't have to be a propeller head to do this successfully, either. All you have to do is type the macro instructions, highlight the text, and then tell Word that it's a macro.

The advantage of programming a macro, rather than recording the macro, is that sometimes you need Word to do something special that can't be recorded.

For example, when programming a macro, you can write your own dialog boxes, as illustrated in Figure 20-1, or turn off the menus, and much, much more. In fact, if you want to give up any semblance of a personal life, you can spend hours and hours writing incredible little programs with Word's macro language.

Remember, the point here is to get your feet wet. Try something new. The macros here are very, very basic, and — more important — very short. Length is a key issue, considering that the first step is to type the macros and the more stuff you have to type, the more likely a typo will creep in.

Select a macro that interests you from the list at the end of this chapter. Then follow the instructions to program, edit, and save your macro.

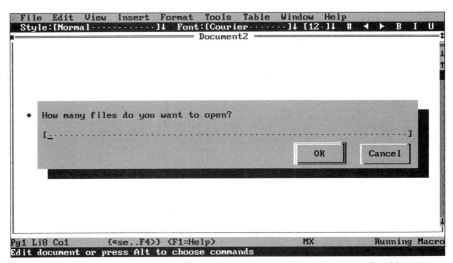

Figure 20-1: Programming macros enables you to roll your own dialog boxes — like this one from the "Open a bunch of files" macro.

Programming Macros

The first step in macro creation — programming. Get into a Word document screen and follow these steps:

1. Type the macro text from the list, *exactly* as shown.

   Use Ctrl+[and Ctrl+] to create the « and », respectively.

2. Highlight the macro text.

3. Press Alt+T**o**ols ⇨ **M**acro.

   This takes you to the Macro dialog box.

4. Type a macro name.

   An example is **SUPER_EXIT** — the first macro in the list.

5. Press Tab.

6. Enter a *hotkey*.

   The hotkey is the key combination you want to press to make the macro happen. This is like Word's speed-formatting keys. For example, you may want to use Ctrl+S for the Super Exit macro. When entering the hotkey in this dialog box, you press the keys, and Word types what you're pressing.

7. Press Alt+**D**efine.

Congratulations, you have just programmed a macro!

Using the Macro

After you've programmed the macro, use the hotkey to make it "go" — or *run*. If you programmed the Super Exit macro with the Ctrl+S hotkey, just pressing Ctrl+S saves all open files and exits Word.

> ✔ If you get an error message when you run the macro, make a note of Word's complaint (see Figure 20-2). You probably made a typo. Use the editing instructions that follow to correct the macro — you don't have to start from scratch if you make one little mistake.

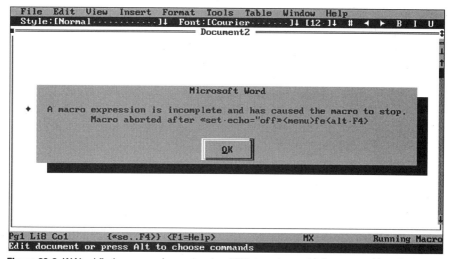

Figure 20-2: If Word finds an error in your syntax, it'll let you know. Make a note of it and edit the macro. In case you're curious, the error here is a missing second quote mark from the word *off*.

Editing a Macro

You've typed a macro and now you need to change it. Perhaps, and this probably isn't the case, you made a typo when you entered the macro in the first place. This is how to correct an already-typed-in macro.

1. Type the name of the macro (such as **SUPER_EXIT**).

2. Type a ^.

   That's a caret — hold down Shift and type the number 6 — but not the number 6 on the numeric keypad to the right.

3. Press F3.

   This causes the macro text to appear on-screen.

4. Make your edits.

   If you can't see what's wrong with it compared to the macro in the book, try getting someone to look at the book while you read the keystrokes out loud — that'll usually do the trick. Think of it as a quiet, sharing moment.

   After you've made your corrections, continue with Step 5.

5. Highlight the macro text.

6. Press Alt+Tools ⇨ **Macro**.

   This takes you to the Macro dialog box.

7. Type the macro name again.

   Use the same name you used before — for example, **SUPER_EXIT**. At this point, the hotkey may automatically appear to the right. If it doesn't, Tab to the right and press the desired hotkey.

8. Press Alt+**Define**.

9. Word asks whether you want to replace the existing macro.

   Yes!

After you've done this, try running the macro again.

✔ If, in Step 6, you get a message telling you that the `Key code has already been assigned`, it means that the hotkey is already being used by another macro with a different name. You have two choices: Select another hotkey, or delete the other macro that ripped off your hotkey and then give it to the new macro.

Saving the Macros Permanently

If you like the macros you create, be sure to save the Glossary so that you'll have them next time, as follows:

1. Press Alt+Tools ⇨ **Macro**.

2. Press Alt+**Save Glossary**.

3. Press Enter.

Presenting — Ten Macros

Here are ten macros. At least one of them should appeal to you. However, the purpose of a macro is to simplify your life — and you're really the only one who knows what you need.

Super exit

This macro saves all open files and exits:

```
«SET Echo="Off"»<menu>fe<Alt F4>
```

Transpose

This macro lets you flip the current letter or word with the letter (or word) on the left.

Transpose letters

The letter the cursor is on switches places with the letter on the left:

```
<Shift right><Shift Del><left><Shift Ins>
```

Transpose words

The word the cursor is on switches places with the word on the left:

```
<F8><F8><Shift Del><Ctrl left><Shift Ins>
```

Copy a file from drive A

Word asks you the name of a file to copy and then copies it for you. Substitute **B** for **A**, if you want to copy from drive B:

```
«ASK filename = ? Name of document file to copy?»
<menu>fdcopy a:\«filename».doc<Enter>
```

Just say print

This prints one copy of your document, no questions asked — just like Word 5's print command:

```
«SET Echo="off"»<Shift F9>1<Alt A>a<Enter>
```

Show all/show none

Turns on (or off) the Show All command:

```
«SET Echo="Off"»<menu>ve«IF Field="No"»a<enter>«ENDIF»
«IF Field="Yes"»<Alt A><Alt T><Alt O><Alt P><Alt S>
<Enter>«ENDIF»
```

Cut and paste step-by-step

This takes you through cut and paste, with prompts in the message bar. This assumes that you're using the default Insert and Overtype configuration:

```
«pause Go to beginning of text to be moved and press
Enter»<F8>«pause Cursor to end of text to be moved and
press Enter»<Shift Del>«pause Cursor to new text location
and press Enter»<Shift Ins>
```

If you're not using the default Insert setting, use this instead:

```
«pause Go to beginning of text to be moved and press
Enter»<F8>«pause Cursor to end of text to be moved and
press Enter»<Del>«pause Cursor to new text location and
press Enter»<Ins>
```

Opens a bunch of files

You tell Word how many files to open and what their names are. Word gets them:

```
«SET Echo ="Off"»«ASK files = ? How many files do you want
to open?»«REPEAT files»«ASK filename = ? Name of file to
open?»<menu>FO«filename»<Enter>«ENDREPEAT»<menu>WA
```

Prints a list of files in a directory or on a floppy

Word asks the name of the drive or directory to print. You can give any DOS drive/directory/file combination:

```
«ASK object = ? Enter name of drive or directory and press
Enter. Wildcards okay (e.g. A: or C:\word\*.DOC)»«SET
Echo="Off"»<menu>FD<space>dir<space>«object»<space><space>
PRN <Enter>
```

Prints a list of document files in the home base directory that need to be backed up

This prints a list of DOC files that haven't been backed up. The files are the ones in your home base directory:

```
<menu>fddir/a:a<space>«startupdir»\*.doc<space><space>
PRN<Enter>
```

Use file management to find files containing certain text

Word asks what text you want to search for. After the job is finished, Word leaves you in the File Management dialog box with the files that contain the search text:

```
«ASK textsearch = ? Text to find?»«SET
Echo="Off"»<menu>FF<Alt S><Alt T>«textsearch»<Enter>
```

After a text search, the File Management dialog box stays in that search format until you exit Word. If you want to have it return to a show all files mode, make a second macro that returns the File Management setup to normal after a text search:

```
<menu>FF<Alt S><Alt T><Del><Enter><Esc>
```

Chapter 21
Ten Ways to Get More Help with Word

. . . .

In This Chapter

▶ Press F1

▶ Use Alt+Help

▶ Do the lessons that came with the program

▶ Get FastTips

▶ Call Microsoft

▶ Look in the manual

▶ Join a users' group

▶ Call a nerd friend

▶ Use CompuServe

▶ Use Microsoft's Download Service

. . . .

I heard this story about how they train elephants so that they won't run away. (I think the "they" in this case is circus people.) Anyway, when they get a new baby elephant, they put a ring around its ankle and then chain it to a stake. The baby tries, but can't break free. Eventually, the baby gives up and stops trying to get away. Even after the elephant grows up and becomes very strong, the same baby-sized stake holds it, because the elephant "knows" it can't get away and doesn't try.

How does all this apply to you?

Well, you may have felt totally out of your element when you started with computers. But by now you've advanced. You may think you still don't know anything, but be honest — there are things you now do routinely that you once thought were beyond your capacity. You *have* advanced. Remember to keep testing the stake.

Let go of the "hopeless" mind set and take advantage of all the helpful resources right at your fingertips.

Press F1

Have you tried pressing F1 lately? Maybe, during the first week you used a computer, you pressed F1 to get help and found the "help" fairly useless. Have you tried it again lately? You now may find — especially after going through this book — that it makes some sense.

You also can invoke Help by clicking the <F1=Help> command button at the bottom of the screen, if your status bar is turned on.

Use Alt+Help

The last menu in Word is Help. Alt+**H**elp gets you Figure 21-1. From this menu, you can look up any topic with the **I**ndex, find out the precise keystrokes with **K**eyboard, and even start the **L**earning Word program. Plus, of course, even more. Don't forget this menu is here. And use it.

> ✔ Buried away in the Help menu are the 20 most commonly asked questions. Press Alt+**H**elp ➪ Product **S**upport. Then highlight <Answers to Common Questions> and press Enter.

Did you notice in Figure 21-1 that there's a Word 5.0 to 6.0 help feature? It's a quick way to look up what it was and find out what it is.

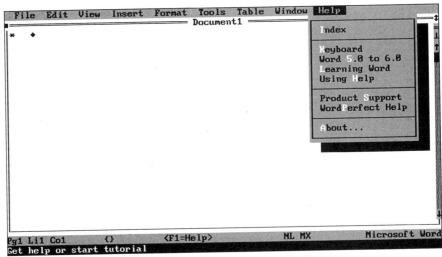

Figure 21-1: The Help menu. Remember, a Help menu is a terrible thing to waste.

Do the Lessons That Came with the Program

Take the time to go through the Learning Word program. It's not difficult. Each lesson is broken down into tiny segments that usually don't take longer than 10 minutes to do. In fact, before you start the lesson, a notice pops up to inform you of how long the lesson will take. Then, when you're in the lesson, you don't have to take notes, because you can print anything that appears on-screen if you press the Print Screen key on your keyboard.

One way to start the lessons is to Press Alt+**Help** ⇨ Learning Word. You wind up in the Learning Word opening screen (see Figure 21-2).

Get FastTips

Microsoft has a service — called FastTips — that provides recorded answers, in English only, to the 50 most common Word questions. When it comes to computers, you should hope and pray that all your problems are "common." FastTips is available 24 hours a day, seven days a week. You also can have these helpful tips sent to your fax machine.

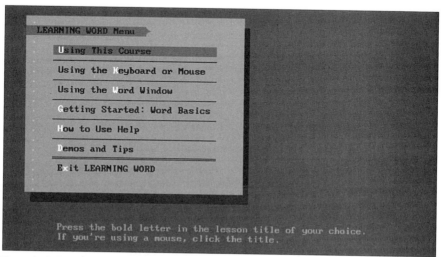

Figure 21-2: The Learning Word system provides a kinder and gentler way to try out many great features.

Get a paper and pencil ready and call FastTips with your touch-tone phone at (206) 635-7211. Recorded voices guide you through the process.

The first option you are offered is to receive, over your fax machine, a map — or a flow chart — of the help voice menu. Get it. Otherwise, you'll be on the phone forever as the voice goes through all the topics verbally.

After you've perused your options on the FaxMap, call again and go directly to the question you have in mind.

Call Microsoft

Sometimes you need to talk to a human being. I understand they have some at Microsoft Corporation.

Microsoft Product Support Services (PSS) is open for business from 6 a.m. to 6 p.m. (Pacific Time), Monday through Friday, at 206-635-7210. If you're looking for help outside the United States, the Microsoft International Customer Service number is 206-936-8661. Microsoft also provides help for the deaf using a special TDD/TT modem at 206-635-4948 (same hours).

Before you call Microsoft, make sure that you've got Word running on the computer — and a good book in your hand; you may have to wait on hold for a few minutes.

When talking to a tech support person:

- **Be pleasant.**

  As frustrated as you feel, remember that the person answering the phone didn't invent the program or decide how many technical support personnel to hire. If you're angry, write Microsoft a letter or ask to speak to someone in charge. The techies are there to help.

- **Tell them the version of Word you're using.**

- **Provide a concise description of what's going wrong.**

  If you have to, write it down — it'll give you something to do while you're on hold.

- **Describe any changes made to your system lately.**

  Did you just install a new game, more memory, or the like? Did your system function properly before, but now it doesn't? This is key information.

TIP

Talking tech with the big boys

When you call for technical support, the people on the other end of the line may start asking you questions for which you have no answers.

Fortunately, Microsoft has finally come to realize that average people will answer "hammer and wrench" when asked what kind of hardware they have. To accommodate this, Microsoft has provided a program called Microsoft Diagnostics free with every copy of Word. In fact, it's on your hard disk right now!

To find out all the technical junk about your computer:

1. Press Alt+File ⇨ MS-**DOS** Commands.

    You should see the MS-DOS Commands dialog box.

2. Type **MSD** and press Enter.

This puts you in the Microsoft Diagnostics program. You don't have to understand anything that you see.

3. Turn on your printer.

4. Press Alt+**R**.

    A several page report prints out. This report specifies your computer's capacity and how it is all set up.

5. When the printing is finished, press Alt+**X**.

6. When told to do so, press any key.

This puts you back into Word, where you were before you made this wild excursion.

Now, when the Microsoft tech finally picks up the phone and asks you what kind of system you have, you can read the "computer name" right off your report.

Look in the Manual

Radical thought, I know, but I'm just putting the idea out there.

Join a Users' Group

It's like therapy for your software. Everyone stands up and shares his or her problems with the group and then group members give suggestions and validate your feelings. You can find users' groups in local community newspapers. Or you can start your own. Tell everyone else to bring cookies and soft drinks and you'll at least get a bunch of free junk food.

Call a Nerd Friend

It's important to have nerd friends. Your nerds can help you with your computer interface, and you can help them with their social interface. Invite them to dinner; introduce them to food groups that don't contain sugar or caffeine.

One hint for successful nerd interfacing: Don't call and say, "I have a quick question." Nerds know the questions are quick — it's the *answers* that take a long time. (It's like calling up the President with one quick question, "When are we going to have world peace?" You see that a quick question doesn't necessarily generate a quick reply.) Instead, when you call your nerd, say, "I'm in trouble, do you have a few minutes or should I call back later?"

Use CompuServe

If you've got a modem — or you've got a friend who has a modem — you also can contact Microsoft Product Support Services on CompuServe. However, a word of caution: If you decide to become involved with CompuServe, you have definitely taken a giant step toward nerdiness.

- ✔ If you're already a member of CompuServe, type GO MICROSOFT at any ! prompt.
- ✔ If you want to join CompuServe, call 800-848-8199 (operator 230) and ask for the introductory kit for users of Microsoft software.

Use Microsoft's Download Service

Another modems-only opportunity is the Microsoft Download Service. Microsoft maintains a free bulletin board system so that you can download updated printer drivers and technical aid. The number is 206-936-6735, and the settings are the usual (8-N-1). However, you still can get printer drivers by calling Product Support Services and asking.

Chapter 22
Ten Most Commonly Asked Questions

M icrosoft may have its 20 and 50 most commonly asked Word questions, but I have another set of questions I've been asked repeatedly.

It Won't Stop Underlining

You used the underline command — and now it won't stop underlining. To make it stop, highlight the stubborn text that's not supposed to be underlined and press Ctrl+spacebar. If it keeps on underlining anyway, highlight a paragraph above and below the offending underline and press Ctrl+spacebar again. That should do it.

Another similar question is why the text won't stop centering. Just highlight the text you don't want to be centered and press Ctrl+X.

The Screen Flashes

If the screen flashes, text moves around, and everything is sluggish, look at the status bar — do you see LY to the left of Microsoft Word? If so, you're in Layout mode. To get out of Layout mode, press Alt+View ⇨ Layout.

My Formatting Suddenly Disappeared

You've probably deleted a paragraph symbol. Try Alt+Backspace to Undo. Review Chapter 2 and Chapter 7.

I Can't Find My Files

You probably started Word from the wrong place on your hard disk. Quit and start over again. More on finding lost stuff in Chapter 13.

The Words on the Left Have Disappeared

Don't worry, nothing bad has happened to your text. Just press Ctrl+Home to recenter the screen.

The Words Run Off the Right Side of the Screen

This could be either of two things. First, check the status bar. Does it say LY to the left of Microsoft Word? If so, you're in Layout mode. To get out of Layout mode, press Alt+View ⇨ Layout. Alternatively, press Alt+F7 — which turns off Show Line Breaks mode. (If you want to know what that means, see Chapter 7.)

I Gave the Print Command, but All I Get Is a Blank Page

Check your Print dialog box (press Alt+**File** ➪ **P**rint). The **P**age Range is probably set on Selection — and you have nothing selected. Change P**a**ge Range to All, and then press Enter to print.

The Speed-Formatting Keys Don't Work

Remember that any macros *you* create supersede Word's own speed-formatting keys. The speed formatters also take a back seat to the macros in the Glossaries. To get "back" to the speed-formatting function, press Ctrl+A, and *then* Ctrl+speed-formatting key. So, to underline, you'd press Ctrl+A and then Ctrl+U. Some shortcut.

When I Type, the New Text Wipes Out the Old Text

You're in Overtype mode (see the OT at the bottom of the screen to the left of Microsoft). To get out of Overtype mode, press Ins.

I Can't Type Any Letters or Press Any Function Keys — Nothing Works

Look in the lower right-hand corner of the screen. Does it say MOVE? Sounds like you're stuck in a window-moving maneuver. You probably meant to press Shift+F7 for the Thesaurus, but pressed Ctrl+F7 — the **M**ove command — instead. Just press Esc. When things get weird, always try pressing Esc. More ideas for handling the frozen computer are in Chapter 18, "Ten Ways to Get Out of Trouble."

Part V

Appendixes

The 5th Wave — By Rich Tennant

"WOW! I DIDN'T EVEN THINK THEY _MADE_ A 2000 DOT PER INCH FONT!"

In this part . . .

The Appendix usually is used by the book industry to fatten up the book a bit so that you feel you're getting your money's worth. Well, we've fooled them this time because we've actually put useful things in our Appendices. Or is it Appendicii. Or Appendicitis?

Anyway, this is where we've got a resource guide for the products mentioned elsewhere in the book and the survival guide for those going from Word 5.0 to Word 6.0.

Appendix A
Adding on to Word

*O*ne of the signs that the line separating reluctant user from rabid hobbyist has been crossed is the emergence of the desire to buy more things "for the computer." In my continuing effort to be a bad influence, here is a list of items mentioned in previous chapters — and a few additional items — along with names and numbers for purchasing or for further inquiry.

In case your mate has heard the "business expense" excuse too many times, drop a reminder that Christmas is always around the corner.

Thesaurus, Foreign Language Dictionaries

Alki Software has produced an expanded thesaurus that replaces the one that comes with Word. Although it is still a "business English" thesaurus, it is an improvement over the original. Alki also offers foreign language replacements to Word's spelling checker so that you can check the spelling of your document in French, Dutch, German, Italian, Swedish, Spanish, or even British English!

Alki Software
219 First Avenue North, Suite 410
Seattle, WA 98109
800-NOW-WORD (669-9673)

TrueType for DOS

Although Word uses TrueType fonts whether they are "for Windows" or "for DOS," this package lets you get crazy and make your own special effects with the provided fonts. Also, it automatically updates your printer driver, with no intervention required on your part.

MicroLogic Software
1351 Ocean Avenue
Emeryville, CA 94608
800-888-9078

Printer Buffer

The printer buffer also requires the purchase of a cable — which, of course, they'll sell you. You can buy the buffer in a number of configurations. Chances are, you'll need a parallel buffer with 1M of memory.

Central Computer Products
330 Central Avenue
Fillmore, CA 93015
800-456-4123

Mac-In-Dos

This is software that enables a PC to format and copy (to and from) a Macintosh disk.

Pacific Micro
201 San Antonio Circle, C250
Mountain View, CA 94040
415-948-6200

MacSEE 2.0

A watered down, though free, program that enables you to copy files to and from Mac disks, but does *not* format them. The catch is that you have to get it from CompuServe. If you don't know what CompuServe is, you don't have it. If you do know, then GO ZENITH and find MACSEE.ZIP in the DOS Utilities Library (5).

Norton Utilities

A "must" for every computer system — the safety net for your computer system.

Symantec Corp.
10201 Torre Avenue
Cupertino, CA 95014-9854
800-441-7234

Direct Access

Not a product — it's a catalog of products that enhance your Word usage. Typical items include clip art, label printers, scanners, fonts, and so on.

Affinity Publishing, Inc.
190 Queen Anne Ave. North, Suite 220
Seattle, WA 98109
206-281-0089

Keyboard Templates

If you're interested in a totally complete keyboard template — rather than the all-you-need-to-know template provided with this book — call the following catalog company, because they carry two such keyboard templates.

Global Computer Supplies
2318 E. Del Amo Blvd, Dept. 42
Compton, CA 90220
800-845-6225

Power Up!

Another catalog. Although not geared specifically to Word users, it includes helpful add-ons. My favorite is Address Book Plus — not only a great address book program, but the names and addresses entered in it can be exported for use by Word for mail merging. And vice versa.

Power Up Software Corporation
P.O. Box 7600
San Mateo, CA 94403
800-851-2917

Paper Direct

It's a catalog of paper products. Especially wonderful if you have a laser printer.

Paper Direct, Inc.
P.O. Box 677
Lyndhurst, NJ 07071-0677
800-A-PAPERS

Microsoft File Conversion Program

Microsoft offers software ($15 plus shipping) that converts files created with other word processors — like WordPerfect, WordStar, and MultiMate — *into* Word files.

800-426-9400

Software Bridge

This program supports loads of file formats and can convert them into Word files and back again.

Systems Compatibility Corp.
401 N. Wabash, #600
Chicago, IL 60611
800-333-1395

Ultravision

Ultravision works with any computer using an EGA or better graphics card to add clarity and brightness to the letters on screen. You also can change the size and font of your on-screen characters. Plus, on laptops, the Word screen is enlarged and the blank space around the display is reduced.

Personics
234 Ballardvale St.
Wilmington, MA 01887
508-658-0040

XTreeGold

A hard-disk management system that works something like Word's File Management (you tag files to be copied, deleted, and so on). If you're queasy about "hard disk management," buy the "easy" version.

XTree Company
4115 Broad St., Building 1
San Luis Obispo, CA 93401-7993
800-964-2490

Appendix B

Surviving the Transition from Word 5.0

*W*hy change from Version 5 to 6 when Word 5 does the job? Well, your typewriter probably "did the job," too. But when you saw what word processing was all about, you dumped that typewriter in a New York second. The reason you took that leap of faith from typewriter to word processor in the first place was because you saw how it could help you make things easier.

On the other hand, you may now be struggling with the "Word 6 Learning Curve versus Benefits equation" — trying to decide whether it's all worth it. If everything goes right, this chapter can help ease that learning curve. And, if you haven't yet, flip through the Table of Contents; you'll see some new and exciting changes to Word 6 — which should prove that the benefits are worth it.

Top Ten Reasons to Use Version 6

These aren't just the Top Ten New Features. These are the top ten ways your life will be made simpler:

1. The Ribbon makes font formatting available at all times.

2. Commands are now in English.

   For example, "Transfer/Load" has been replaced by File/**O**pen; "Library/Document-retrieval" has been replaced by File/File Management; and "Transfer/Clear" has been replaced by File/**C**lose. Okay, not exactly English — but a lot closer. And, as an extra added attraction, you never need to "hit F1 to get a list."

3. Drag-and-drop "one-step" editing eliminates tedious cut and paste.

4. The blow-you-away Table feature lets you create (and import) spreadsheets, side-by-side text, and more — *easily*.

5. Get a buzz from using nine full-screen active windows, letting you have direct access to many files at once.

6. Merge Helper — not to be confused with Hamburger Helper — makes merge printing a lot easier. There's also help with creating macros (no more "^").

7. If grammar ain't your bestest subject, you'll love Word 6's grammar checker. (And improved thesaurus and spelling checker, too.)

8. TrueType fonts are included to help you make your documents look like a million dollars — for free!

9. Word 6 comes with an envelope macro that *really* works!

10. Word 6's commands are like Windows, Word for Windows, and Macintosh.

Top Ten Reasons Not to Change

1. Word 6's commands are like Windows, Word for Windows, and Macintosh.

2. You don't like any of the new features.

3. You're in the middle of a big project.

4. You don't want to give Bill Gates any more money.

5. The person who set up your system also created a complex set of macros that do everything for you and that person has either disappeared from your life or is unwilling to update the macros.

6. Using arcane terminology like Gallery and Thumb instead of Style Sheet Window and Scroll Box makes you feel superior.

7. Any change makes you nervous — you're still in therapy from the loss of the ALPHA command from Version 4!

8. You never want to use a mouse.

9. You'd rather take a nap.

10. You're Andy Rooney and you just like things the way they used to be.

Meeting Word 6 — Looks Aren't Everything

My first word processing program was called Perfect Writer. For a while there, it was the number one best-selling word processing program. I would have bet the house that I would never learn another one. Time, however, has a way of chipping away at words like "never." Over the years, I've learned two versions of WordStar and every version of Microsoft Word except the first.

"Sure," you say, "but you're a computer person, Beth. I'm not. This new version of Word looks really different ...."

Exactly — and that's the key thing to realize: It only *looks* really different, but the basics are still there. Yes, there are new features and changes, but you aren't starting from scratch. Everything you've learned over the years will still be useful.

Let's try an experiment. In Word 5.0, pressing Esc Format gets you Figure B-1.

In Word 6.0, pressing Alt (which basically replaces Esc) and Format gives you Figure B-2.

Word 5.0's Format menu has Character, Paragraph, and so forth, and the Word 6.0 Format menu isn't all that different. Version 5.0's menus are horizontal. Version 6 is vertical. Of course, some things have been renamed and reorganized, but, be honest now, doesn't it seem more familiar than different?

Okay, Division is gone, but doesn't Margins and Sections make more sense? Isn't Header/Footer more logical than Running Head? And Search and Replace formats is now an option when you invoke the Search command. Seems reasonable.

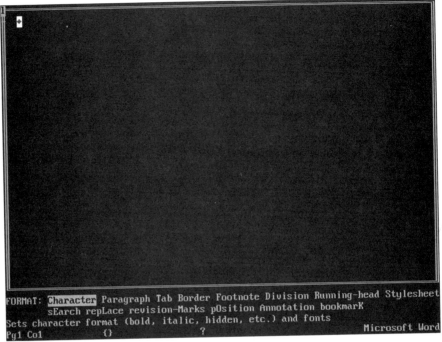

Figure B-1: The friendly FORMAT menu in Word 5.0.

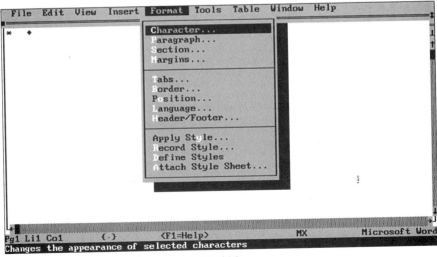

Figure B-2: The Format drop-down menu in Word 6.0.

If you look at the new screen display and find it filled with more stuff than you'd care to deal with, don't worry. You can customize the screen as you please — though you're stuck with the drop-down menus.

The reason Microsoft switched over to this new interface is so that it more closely matches its Windows and Macintosh products.

What that means is that after you know how to print in Word 6 — Alt+File ⇨ **P**rint — you now also know how to print in *any* Windows program. Plus, there are many other non-Windows programs (like Norton Utilities and so on) that use the same sort of interface. What you learn here about Word 6 will stand you in good stead as you move out into the world — which you'll have to do eventually.

Installing Word 6

When you install Word 6, don't allow it to overwrite your existing Word 5 program. This will ease your fears about plunging into the new program without a safety net. With your old Word still available, you can always "go back" if you want to. For the most part, Word 6 files work with Word 5. After you're comfortable with Word 6, you can delete the old Word program.

Getting rid of Word 5

After you make the decision to get rid of Word 5, you may be surprised to get the unsettling Access Denied error message from your computer when you try to delete your files. That's because Microsoft made some of the files undeletable for reasons they have never shared with me.

So, to delete all the files in your old Word directory, follow this plan:

1. What we're about to do will delete all files in the directory. If you have any files you want to keep, either move them to the new Word directory or back them up.

2. Go to the directory containing your Word 5 program that you want to delete.

3. Type **ATTRIB –R *.*** and press Enter.

   This makes the undeletable files deletable.

4. Type **DEL *.*** and press Enter.

   This command deletes all files in the current directory.

5. The computer asks whether you're sure you want to do this. Press Y and then Enter to delete all files in the current directory.

   ✔ After a few seconds, the files will be gone and the space on your hard disk will be available for your new version of Word.

   ✔ You can use the same directory for the new version.

Also, when you install Word 6, you have the option to use Word 5.0 function keys. Please try using the Word 6 function keys. No matter what you choose, however, you can always change it (with Alt+T**o**ols ⇨ C**u**stomize).

Taking the First Step

After Word 6 is installed, go through the Learning Word practice lessons. It's a good way to jump into the program without worrying about making mistakes. It provides everything from "Word Basics" to "Demos and Tips."

Changing Keystrokes

There are two big keystroke changes that'll take a few days to adjust to. You may feel clumsy for a while, but you'll get over it faster than you think.

Using Alt to get the menu

In Word 6, Esc has only one purpose — to cancel the current operation. To get to the menu, you now use Alt. However, if you accidentally try to use Esc, you won't set the house on fire. In fact, pressing Esc while in edit mode makes *nothing* happen. So don't worry if you screw up.

Using Ctrl instead of Alt

In Word 5, you used Alt+B for bold and Alt+C for centering. Well, now, because you use Alt to access the menu, you can't use Alt in your speed-formatting keys anymore. You need to learn to use *Ctrl*+B and *Ctrl*+C instead.

But, again, if you accidentally use Alt+B, nothing bad happens. You won't go careening off into some weird place. All that occurs is that the menu bar flickers on and off. No harm done.

Using Ctrl+Shift to apply styles

Your style sheets from previous versions of Word will work, but you have to use Ctrl+Shift+key code instead of Alt+key code to apply them. I'll be the first to admit that this is not an improvement. But one can learn to live with it if one remains flexible in one's outlook.

Undoing what you just did

If you make a mistake, don't worry. Just press Alt+Backspace and all is forgiven.

Spacing changes

In Version 5, the default line spacing was 1. In Version 6, it's "Auto." This means you won't have big fonts printing on top of each other anymore. Word automatically adjusts the line spacing to accommodate the fonts.

Learning Where They Put Things

For the first few days, your best friend is going to be the Help menu. By pressing Alt+**Help** ⇨ Word **5**.0 to 6.0, you can see a complete list of the Word 6 command equivalent to your Word 5 command (see Figure B-3). Microsoft did a good thing with this, because it's all on-line, where you can quickly get to it.

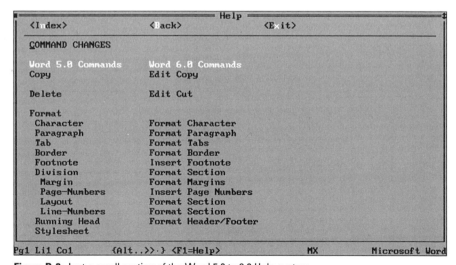

Figure B-3: Just a small portion of the Word 5.0 to 6.0 Help system.

Also, take advantage of F1 to get context-sensitive help whenever you need to know what to do next.

However, because the help is so complete, it can take a long time to find a single command. So, to get you going, here is the "bikini of help" — not very big, but it covers the subject.

If I've missed your favorite keyboard command, then add it to the chart so that you won't be wasting time hunting for commands.

Table B-1	Word 5 to 6 Bikini Survival Guide	
To	*Was*	*Now Press*
Get a file	Transfer, Load	Alt+**File** ➪ **O**pen
Save a file	Transfer, Save	Alt+**File** ➪ **S**ave
Repaginate	Print Repaginate	Alt+**Tools** ➪ Re**p**aginate Now
Print a file	Print Printer	Alt+**File** ➪ **P**rint
Preview	Print Preview	Alt+**File** ➪ Print Preview
Exit Word	Esc, Quit	Alt+**File** ➪ E**x**it
Extend	F6	F8
Spelling check	Alt+F6	F7
Thesaurus	Ctrl+F6	Shift+F7
Cut	Delete	Shift+Del
Paste	Insert	Shift+Ins
Top of Document	Ctrl+PgUp	Ctrl+Home
End of Document	Ctrl+PgDn	Ctrl+End

Note: The Shift and arrow keys still select text.

Appendix C
Krazy Keyboard Kut-Ups

This is not, by any stretch of the imagination, a complete list of keyboard commands, because you don't need a complete list of commands to get by. Basically, this is a more complete Cheat Sheet of most-often-used keyboard commands.

Selecting Text

Anything	Hold down Shift key and move cursor
Current paragraph	Alt+F10
Current sentence	Alt+F8
Current word	Alt+F6
Document	Shift+F10
Column select	Ctrl+Shift+F8
End of sentence	F8, F8, period (.)
Shrink selection	Shift+F8
Turn off selection	Esc
Extend highlight	F8
Word/sentence/paragraph	F8 (repeatedly)

Character Formatting

Bold	Ctrl+B
Underline	Ctrl+U
Toggle text case	Shift+F3
Double underline	Ctrl+D
Font name	Ctrl+F
Font size	Ctrl+P
Hidden	Ctrl+H
Italic	Ctrl+I
Remove character formatting	Ctrl+spacebar

Paragraph Formatting

Center	Ctrl+C
Double-space	Ctrl+2
Single-space	Ctrl+1
Hanging indent	Ctrl+T
Indent text on right and left	Ctrl+Q
Indent text to next Tab	Ctrl+N
Unindent text to preceding Tab	Ctrl+M
Justified	Ctrl+J
Left alignment	Ctrl+L
Right alignment	Ctrl+R
Remove paragraph formatting	Ctrl+X
Style	Ctrl+Shift+key code

Moving Around

End of document	Ctrl+End
Start of document	Ctrl+Home
Line, beginning	Home
Line, end	End
Next window	Ctrl+F6
Paragraph, preceding	Ctrl+up arrow
Paragraph, next	Ctrl+down arrow
Word, backward	Ctrl+left arrow
Word, forward	Ctrl+right arrow
Inside dialog box	Alt+bold letter

Action Keys

Calculate	F2
Cancel	Esc
Delete	Shift+Del
Exit	Alt+F4
Expand Glossary	F3
File open	Ctrl+F1
Help	F1
Insert	Shift+Ins
Menu on/off	Alt
Page break	Ctrl+Enter

Print	Shift+F9
Record a macro	Ctrl+F3
Repeat	F4
Ruler on	Ctrl+Shift+F10
Save	Shift+F12
Search again	Shift+F4
Spell	F7
Thesaurus	Shift+F7
Undo	Alt+Backspace

Appendix D
Rodent Roustabouts

● ●

*T*he mouse certainly gets a workout in Word 6.0. Most of the mouse commands are click-and-drag versions of the keyboard commands and there is no need to rehash them here.

Also, if you're a mouser, you're very familiar with scroll bar maneuvering and Ribbon selecting and the rest, so we won't bother listing those items either. However, there are a few useful, sometimes arcane, commands that are uniquely mouse that you may want to remind yourself to start using more often.

Selecting Text

Word	Double-click
Sentence	Ctrl+left mouse ear
Line	At left margin to left of text, left-click
Paragraph	At left margin to left of text, double-left-click
Document	At left margin, Ctrl+left mouse ear

Moving Text

Move text	Highlight the words to be moved, left-click the selected text, drag to the new location, and release the mouse ear
Copy text	Highlight the words to be copied, Ctrl+left-click the selected text, drag to the new location, and release the mouse ear

Formatting Text

Copy character format	Highlight text to be formatted, then point to character with preferred format and Ctrl+Shift+left mouse ear
Copy paragraph format	Highlight text to be formatted, then point to margin to the left of paragraph containing preferred format and Ctrl+Shift+left mouse ear

Dialog Box Pop-Ups

Double-click	*To get*
Style in Ribbon	Apply Style dialog box
Font in Ribbon	Character dialog box
Section mark	Section dialog box
`<F1=Help>`	Help dialog box
Status bar	Go To dialog box

Index

Macworld Authorized Editions

Designed specifically for the Macintosh user, Macworld Books are written by leading *Macworld* magazine columnists, technology champions, and Mac gurus who provide expert advice and insightful tips and techniques not found anywhere else. Macworld Books are the only Macintosh books authorized by *Macworld*, the world's leading Macintosh magazine.

Macworld Guide To Microsoft System 7.1, 2nd Edition
by Lon Poole, Macworld magazine's "Quick Tips" columnist

The most recommended guide to System 7, updated and expanded!

$24.95 USA/$33.95 Canada/£22.92 UK & EIRE, ISBN: 1-878058-65-7

Macworld Guide To Microsoft Word 5
by Jim Heid, Macworld magazine's "Getting Started" columnist

Learn Word the easy way with this *Macworld* Authorized Edition. Now updated for Word 5.1.

$22.95 USA/$29.95 Canada/£20.95 UK & EIRE, ISBN: 1-878058-39-8

Macworld Guide To Microsoft Works 3
by Barrie A. Sosinsky

Get inside the new Works so you can work more productively—the perfect blend of reference and tutorial.

$22.95 USA/$29.95 Canada/£20.95 UK & EIRE, ISBN: 1-878058-42-8

Macworld Complete Mac Handbook
by Jim Heid

The most complete guide to getting started, mastering, and expanding your Mac.

$26.95 USA/$35.95 Canada/£24.95 UK & EIRE, ISBN: 1-878058-17-7

Macworld PageMaker Bible
by Jo Ann Villalobos

The ultimate insiders' guide to PageMaker 5, combining an authoritative and easy-to-use reference with tips and techniques. Includes 3 1/2" disk of templates.

$39.95 USA/$52.95 Canada/£37.60 UK & EIRE, ISBN: 1-878058-84-3 — Available July 1993

Macworld Networking Handbook
by David Kosiur, Ph.D.

The ultimate insider's guide to Mac network management.

$29.95 USA/$39.95 Canada/£27.45 UK & EIRE, ISBN: 1-878058-31-2

Macworld Guide To Microsoft Excel 4
by David Maguiness

Build powerful spreadsheets quickly with this *Macworld* Authorized Edition to Excel 4.

$22.95 USA/$29.95 Canada/£20.95 UK & EIRE, ISBN: 1-878058-40-1

Macworld Music & Sound Bible
by Christopher Yavelow

Finally, the definitive guide to music, sound, and multimedia on the Mac.

$37.95 USA/$47.95 Canada/£34.95 UK & EIRE, ISBN: 1-878058-18-5

Macworld QuarkXPress Designer Handbook
by Barbara Assadi and Galen Gruman

Macworld magazine's DTP experts help you master advanced features fast with this definitive tutorial, reference and designer tips resource on QuarkXPress.

$29.95 USA/$39.95 Canada/£27.45 UK & EIRE, ISBN: 1-878058-85-1 — Available July 1993

For More Information Call 1-800-762-2974

PC World Handbook

Expert information at your fingertips. Perfect for readers who need a complete tutorial of features as well as a reference to software applications and operating systems. All PC World Handbooks include bonus disks with software featuring useful templates, examples, and utilities that provide real value to the reader.

PC World DOS 6 Handbook, 2nd Edition
by John Socha, Clint Hicks, and Devra Hall

Completely revised and updated! Includes extended features of DOS and the 250 page command reference that Microsoft excludes. A complete tutorial and reference PLUS Special Edition of Norton Commander software.

$34.95 USA/$44.95 Canada/£32.95 UK & EIRE, ISBN: 1-878058-79-7

PC World Microsoft Access Bible
by Cary Prague and Michael Irwin

This authoritative tutorial and reference on Microsoft's new Windows database is the perfect companion for every Microsoft Access user.

$39.95 USA/$52.95 Canada/£37.60 UK & EIRE, ISBN: 1-878058-81-9

Official XTree MS-DOS, Windows, and Hard Disk Management Companion, 3rd Edition
by Beth Slick

The only authorized guide to all versions of XTree, the most popular PC hard disk utility.

$19.95 USA/$26.95 Canada/£18.45 UK & EIRE, ISBN: 1-878058-57-6

QuarkXPress for Windows Designer Handbook
by Barbara Assadi and Galen Gruman

Make the move to QuarkXPress for Windows, the new professional desktop publishing powerhouse, with this expert reference and tutorial.

$29.95 USA/$39.95 Canada/£27.45 UK & EIRE, ISBN: 1-878058-45-2

PC World You Can Do It With Windows
by Christopher Van Buren

The best way to learn Window 3.1!

$19.95 USA/$26.95 Canada/£18.45 VAT UK EIRE, ISBN: 1-878058-37-1

PC World Excel 4 for Windows Handbook
by John Walkenbach and David Maguiness

Complete tutorial and reference by PC World's spreadsheet experts, with a FREE 32-page Function Reference booklet.

$29.95 USA/$39.95 Canada/£27.45 UK & EIRE, ISBN: 1-878058-46-0

PC World WordPerfect 6 Handbook
by Greg Harvey

Bestselling author and WordPerfect guru Greg Harvey brings you the ultimate tutorial and reference – complete with valuable software containing document templates, macros, and other handy WordPerfect tools.

$34.95 USA/$44.95 Canada/£32.95 UK & EIRE, ISBN: 1-878058-80-0 — Available July 1993

PC World Q&A Bible, Version 4
by Thomas J. Marcellus, Technical Editor of The Quick Answer

The only thorough guide with a disk of databases for mastering Q&A Version 4.

$39.95 USA/$52.95 Canada/£37.60 UK & EIRE, ISBN: 1-878058-03-7

PC World You Can Do It With DOS
by Christopher Van Buren

The best way to learn DOS quickly and easily.

$19.95 USA/$26.95 Canada/£18.45 VAT UK EIRE, ISBN: 1-878058-38-X

For More Information Call 1-800-762-2974

Order Form

Order Center: (800) 762-2974 (8 a.m.-5 p.m., PST, weekdays) or **(415) 312-0600**

For Fastest Service: Photocopy This Order Form and FAX it to : (415) 358-1260

Quantity	ISBN	Title	Price	Total

Shipping & Handling Charges

Subtotal	U.S.	Canada & International	International Air Mail
Up to $20.00	Add $3.00	Add $4.00	Add $10.00
$20.01-40.00	$4.00	$5.00	$20.00
$40.01-60.00	$5.00	$6.00	$25.00
$60.01-80.00	$6.00	$8.00	$35.00
Over $80.00	$7.00	$10.00	$50.00

In U.S. and Canada, shipping is UPS ground or equivalent.
For Rush shipping call (800) 762-2974.

Subtotal _____

CA residents add applicable sales tax _____

IN residents add 5% sales tax _____

Canadian residents add 7% GST tax _____

Shipping _____

TOTAL _____

Ship to:

Name_____

Company _____

Address _____

City/State/Zip _____

Daytime Phone _____

Payment: ❏ Check to IDG Books (US Funds Only)   ❏ Visa   ❏ MasterCard   ❏ American Express

Card # _____ Exp._____ Signature _____

Please send this order form to: IDG Books, 155 Bovet Road, San Mateo, CA 94402.
Allow up to 3 weeks for delivery. Thank you!

BOB4D

IDG BOOKS WORLDWIDE REGISTRATION CARD

IDG BOOKS

THE WORLD OF
COMPUTER
KNOWLEDGE

Title of this book: Word 6 For Dos For Dummies

My overall rating of this book: ❑ Very good [1] ❑ Good [2] ❑ Satisfactory [3] ❑ Fair [4] ❑ Poor [5]

How I first heard about this book:

❑ Found in bookstore; name: [6]

❑ Advertisement: [8]

❑ Word of mouth; heard about book from friend, co-worker, etc.: [10]

❑ Book review: [7]

❑ Catalog: [9]

❑ Other: [11]

What I liked most about this book:

What I would change, add, delete, etc., in future editions of this book:

Other comments:

Number of computer books I purchase in a year: ❑ 1 [12] ❑ 2-5 [13] ❑ 6-10 [14] ❑ More than 10 [15]

I would characterize my computer skills as: ❑ Beginner [16] ❑ Intermediate [17] ❑ Advanced [18] ❑ Professional [19]

I use ❑ DOS [20] ❑ Windows [21] ❑ OS/2 [22] ❑ Unix [23] ❑ Macintosh [24] ❑ Other: [25]_____
(please specify)

I would be interested in new books on the following subjects:
(please check all that apply, and use the spaces provided to identify specific software)

❑ Word processing: [26]

❑ Data bases: [28]

❑ File Utilities: [30]

❑ Networking: [32]

❑ Other: [34]

❑ Spreadsheets: [27]

❑ Desktop publishing: [29]

❑ Money management: [31]

❑ Programming languages: [33]

I use a PC at (please check all that apply): ❑ home [35] ❑ work [36] ❑ school [37] ❑ other: [38] _____

The disks I prefer to use are ❑ 5.25 [39] ❑ 3.5 [40] ❑ other: [41]_____

I have a CD ROM: ❑ yes [42] ❑ no [43]

I plan to buy or upgrade computer hardware this year: ❑ yes [44] ❑ no [45]

I plan to buy or upgrade computer software this year: ❑ yes [46] ❑ no [47]

Name: _____ Business title: [48] _____ Type of Business: [49]

Address (❑ home [50] ❑ work [51]/Company name: _____)

Street/Suite# _____

City [52]/State [53]/Zipcode [54]: _____ Country [55] _____

❑ **I liked this book!** You may quote me by name in future
IDG Books Worldwide promotional materials.

My daytime phone number is _____

RETURN THIS
REGISTRATION CARD
FOR FREE CATALOG

❏ YES!

Please keep me informed about IDG's World of Computer Knowledge.
Send me the latest IDG Books catalog.